NOBEL LECTURES IN ECONOMIC SCIENCES 1991–1995

NOBEL LECTURES

INCLUDING PRESENTATION SPEECHES
AND LAUREATES' BIOGRAPHIES

PHYSICS

CHEMISTRY

PHYSIOLOGY OR MEDICINE

LITERATURE

PEACE

ECONOMIC SCIENCES

NOBEL LECTURES

INCLUDING PRESENTATION SPEECHES
AND LAUREATES' BIOGRAPHIES

ECONOMIC SCIENCES

1991–1995

EDITOR

Torsten Persson

Institute for International Economic Studies
Stockholm University

World Scientific
Singapore • New Jersey • London • Hong Kong

Published for the Nobel Foundation in 1997 by

World Scientific Publishing Co. Pte. Ltd.

P O Box 128, Farrer Road, Singapore 912805

USA office: Suite 1B, 1060 Main Street, River Edge, NJ 07661

UK office: 57 Shelton Street, Covent Garden, London WC2H 9HE

NOBEL LECTURES IN ECONOMIC SCIENCES (1991–1995)

ISBN 981-02-3059-1
ISBN 981-02-3060-5 (pbk)

Printed in Singapore by Uto-Print

PRIZE IN ECONOMIC SCIENCES IN MEMORY OF ALFRED NOBEL

Sveriges Riksbank (Bank of Sweden) at their tercentenary in 1968 instituted an Alfred Nobel Memorial Prize in Economic Sciences and placed an annual amount at the disposal of the Nobel Foundation as basis for a prize to be awarded by the Royal Swedish Academy of Sciences. Nobel Prize rules will, mutatis mutandis, be followed regarding nomination of candidates, prize adjudication, prize award and prize presentation. The latter takes place on Nobel Day, December 10, each year. The prize amount will equal that of a Nobel Prize for the same year. Special Statutes and Regulations (valid from January 1, 1969) have been issued for this Alfred Nobel Memorial Prize in Economic Sciences.

FOREWORD

Since 1901 the Nobel Foundation has published annually "Les Prix Nobel" with reports from the Nobel award ceremonies in Stockholm and Oslo as well as the biographies and Nobel lectures of the laureates. In order to make the lectures available for people with special interests in the different prize fields the Foundation gave Elsevier Publishing Company the right to publish in English the lectures for 1901–1970, which were published in 1964–1972 through the following volumes:

Physics 1901–1970	4 vols.
Chemistry 1901–1970	4 vols.
Physiology or Medicine 1901–1970	4 vols.
Literature 1901–1967	1 vol.
Peace 1901–1970	3 vols.

Thereafter, and onwards the Nobel Foundation has given World Scientific Publishing Company the right to bring the series up to date and also publish the Prize lectures in Economics from the year 1969. The Nobel Foundation is very pleased that the intellectual and spiritual message to the world laid down in the laureates' lectures, thanks to the efforts of World Scientific, will reach new readers all over the world.

Bengt Samuelsson
Chairman of the Board

Michael Sohlman
Executive Director

Stockholm, October 1996

PREFACE

At its tercentenary celebration in 1968, Sveriges Riksbank instituted a new award, "The Central Bank of Sweden Prize in Economic Sciences in Memory of Alfred Nobel", and committed itself to supporting the Prize in perpetuity. According to the statutes, the award is given according to the same principles as the original Nobel Prizes in Physics and Chemistry. Thus, the Royal Swedish Academy of Sciences is responsible for the selection of candidates and for the choice of the laureates.

In connection with the Prize Awarding ceremony, which is held in Stockholm each December, the laureates give special Nobel Lectures, in which they present and reflect on their contributions. At the ceremony itself, a member of the Academy gives a brief speech with an elementary summary of the Prize winning contribution. These Nobel lectures and presentation speeches, together with the biographies of the Economics laureates, have been collected in three volumes. Two previous volumes covered the years 1969 to 1980, and 1981 to 1990, whereas the present volume honors the 1991 through 1995 Prizes.[a]

Ronald Coase, who was awarded the 1991 Prize for his pioneering analysis of how transactions costs and property rights shape economic activity, has laid new foundations for managerial economics, given new impulses to economic history, and unsettled the conventional thinking in traditional jurisprudence. Gary Becker, the 1992 laureate, has shown how to apply microeconomic methods to the study of a range of social issues — including education and on the job training, crime and punishment, discrimination, and the role of the family — in a provocative research agenda that has deeply influenced economists, as well as sociologists. By showing how the application of economic theory and statistical method can shed new light on many aspects of economic and institutional change, 1993 laureates Robert Fogel and Douglas North have spearheaded a "new economic history", the methodology of which, by now, has completely transformed the field of economic history. John Nash, John Harsanyi, and Reinhard Selten, who shared the Prize in 1994, have laid a solid foundation for modern non-cooperative game theory by introducing fundamental equilibrium concepts which have become essential tools of the many scholars that formally analyze strategic interactions in economics, political science and biology, The work by 1995 Prize winner Robert Lucas have radically changed macroeconomic thinking and research, by showing how rational expectations formation on the part of economic agents fundamentally alters the conclusions regarding the scope for stabilization

[a] In 1994, John Nash did not give a conventional Nobel Lecture. Instead, the volume includes an edited version of a Nobel seminar that was devoted to his contributions on Game Theory.

policy and creates important pitfalls in policy analysis that relies on statistical relations estimated from historical data.

In summary, the five Prize winning contributions covered in this book have fundamentally transformed subsequent research not only in economics, but also in several related fields.

January 1997 *Torsten Persson*

CONTENTS

ECONOMIC SCIENCES 1991

RONALD H. COASE

for his discovery and clarification of the significance of transaction costs and property rights for the institutional structure and functioning of the economy

THE SVERIGES RIKSBANK (BANK OF SWEDEN) PRIZE IN ECONOMIC SCIENCES IN MEMORY OF ALFRED NOBEL

Speech by Professor Lars Werin of the Royal Swedish Academy of Sciences. Translation from the Swedish text.

Your Majesties, Your Royal Highnesses, Ladies and Gentlemen,

The economic system has an institutional structure, which we often regard as self-evident because we observe it around us every day. But it is actually peculiar and intricate. For instance, people make agreements among themselves in many different ways, ranging from simple purchases to complex contracts; what determines the pattern? Economic activity takes place within a framework of legal rules: contract law, tort law, etc; why are these laws formulated as they are? And why do we have firms at all?

These and other components of the institutional structure must certainly be essential elements in the functioning of the economic system. Nevertheless, economic theory could not answer these questions. This state of affairs annoyed a young economist who had just received his first degree in London in the 1930s. He wrote an essay with the perhaps untactically pretentious title *The Nature of the Firm.* He provided a strong and productive answer to the last question, why firms exist, although hardly anyone bothered to listen. He gradually added building blocks to his theoretical construction, and had eventually—in the early 1960s—set forth the principles for answering *all* of the questions. It was not until the 1970s and 1980s that the breakthrough for his ideas occurred. Astonishingly, basic economics had to be revised, managerial economics received a new foundation and research in economic history new impulses, a new discipline, law and economics, was established on the borderline between economics and legal science, and traditional jurisprudence itself became unsettled. It is for this achievement that the originator, Ronald Coase, is rewarded; no longer an angry young man, but still a most active researcher.

Coase pointed out that a large proportion of the total use of resources takes place *within* firms. Thus, it has deliberately been withheld from the price mechanism—the market system—in order to be coordinated administratively instead. A general theory has to be able to explain this phenomenon; traditional theory could not.

Someone has aptly described Coase's problems as follows. A firm may be regarded as an island of administration in a sea of contracting, in "the sea of markets". If we look out across the economy, we find that it is an archipelago. But why is it an archipelago? Why is it not an open sea of simple contracts between separate individuals? And why are there so many small islands, that is, why are they islets rather than a few large continents?

Coase's answer was that traditional theory disregarded what he called transaction costs, i.e., the time, work and other resources used in order to enter into contracts and manage firms and similar institutions. His relatively simple—but, as it turned out, highly viable—thesis was that a firm arises if the costs of achieving a certain use of resources are lower when carried out administratively as compared to purchases and sales on the market. If it did not cost anything to enter into contracts, then there would be no need for firms.

This was not only a new view of the firm; from now on a searchlight would be aimed at the abundance of variation inherent in the patterns of contracts which comprise what we usually call "markets".

As a next step, Coase showed that whatever is bought and sold or otherwise becomes the object of a contract does not actually consist of goods and other resources, but of rights to the disposal of goods and resources. Rights such as ownership rights, usership rights, etc. are fundamental components of the economy. Of course, rights are also a basic component of the legal system.

In an influential study, Coase began with a now famous hypothetical experiment. He examined a court which has to determine whether a certain right should be awarded to one or the other of two subjects, each of whom is engaged in a particular type of activity. This, in fact, is a very common decision situation in the legal system. If no resources whatsoever would be consumed in contracting, as economists and perhaps even lawyers carelessly used to presuppose, then—according to Coase—it does not really matter how the court decides. The right will still end up with the party who can achieve the largest output. If she does not receive the right directly from the legal or judicial authority, then she will buy it from the other party, who stands to gain by selling it.

The conclusion of the experiment is that if, in reality, transaction costs were zero, then a great deal of legislation would obviously be pointless and unnecessary. Earlier, Coase had found that firms do not serve any purpose if transaction costs are zero. Supported by empirical studies, such as legal cases, he could now draw his fundamental conclusion: that not only firms and large bodies of the law, but the entire institutional structure of the economy can be explained by transaction costs. Transaction costs and a formulation in terms of rights: two relatively simple ideas—but with the power to propel all the economic sciences, and legal science as well, in new directions.

Professor Coase,

By your refusal to take anything for granted, and your skepticism toward conventional wisdom, you have succeeded in explaining the principles behind the institutional structure of the economy. You have remarkably improved our understanding of the way the economic system functions—although it took some time for the rest of us to realize it. On behalf of the

Royal Swedish Academy of Sciences, I congratulate you warmly and sincerely. May I ask you to receive, from the hands of His Majesty the King, this year's Prize in Economic Sciences in Memory of Alfred Nobel.

Ronald Harry Coase

RONALD H. COASE

My father, a methodical man, recorded in his diary that I was born at 3:25 p.m. on December 29th, 1910. The place was a house, containing two flats of which my parents occupied the lower, in a suburb of London, Willesden. My father was a telegraphist in the Post Office. My mother had been employed in the Post Office but ceased to work on being married. Both my parents had left school at the age of 12 but were completely literate. However, they had no interest in academic scholarship. Their interest was in sport. My mother played tennis until an advanced age. My father, who played football, cricket and tennis while young, played (lawn) bowls until his death. He was a good player, played for his county and won a number of competitions. He wrote articles on bowls for the local newspaper and for *Bowls News*.

I had the usual boy's interest in sport but my main interest was always academic. I was an only child but although often alone, I was never lonely. When I learnt chess, I was happy to play the role of each player in turn. Lacking guidance, my reading (in books borrowed from the local public library) was undiscriminating and, as I now realize, I was unable to distinguish the charlatan from the serious scholar. My mother taught me to be honest and truthful and although it is impossible to escape some degree of self-deception, my endeavours to follow her precepts have, I believe, lent some strength to my writing. My mother's hero was Captain Oates, who, returning with Scott from the South Pole and finding that his illness was hampering the others, told his companions that he was going for a stroll, went out into a blizzard and was never heard of again. I have always felt that I should not be a bother to others but in this I have not always succeeded.

Aged 11, I was taken by my father to a phrenologist. What the phrenologist said about my character was, I feel sure, determined less by the shape of my skull than by the impressions he derived from my behaviour. Out of the various printed summaries of character in his booklet, that chosen for "Master Ronald Coase" started: "You are in possession of much intelligence, and you know it, though you may be inclined to underrate your abilities." This printed summary also included the following remarks: "You will not float down, like a sickly fish, with the tide... you enjoy considerable mental vigour and are not a passive instrument in the hands of others. Though you can work with others and for others, where you see it to your advantage, you are more inclined to think and work for yourself. A little more determination would be to your advantage, however." In the written comments, the pursuits recommended were: "Scientific and Commercial. Banking. Accountancy. Also horticulture and poultry rearing as hobbies." Added were some comments about my character: "More hope, confidence and concentration required – not suited for the aggressive competitive side of business life. More active ambition would be beneficial." It was also noted that I was too cautious. It was hardly to be expected that this timid little boy would one day be the recipient of a Nobel Prize. That this happened was the result of a series of accidents.

As a young boy I suffered from a weakness in my legs, which necessitated, or was thought to necessitate, the wearing of irons on my legs. As a result I went to the school for physical defectives run by the local council. For reasons that I do not remember I missed taking the entrance examinations for the local secondary school at the usual age of 11. However, as the result of the efforts of my parents I was allowed to take the secondary school scholarship examination at the age of 12. The only thing I now remember is that at the oral examination I caused some amusement by referring to a character in Shakespeare's "Twelfth Night" as Macvolio. However, this lapse was not fatal and I was awarded a scholarship to go to the Kilburn Grammar School. The teaching there was good and I received a solid education. I particularly remember our geography teacher, Charles Thurston, who introduced us to Wegener's hypothesis on the movements of the continents long before it was generally accepted and who also took us to lectures at the Royal Geographical Society, one of which, on river meanders, discussed the effect of the earth's rotation on the course of rivers. I took the matriculation examination in 1927, which I passed, with distinction in history and chemistry.

It was then possible to spend the two years after matriculation at the Kilburn Grammar School studying for the intermediate examination of the University of London as an external student, which covered the work which would have been taken during the first year at the University as an internal student. I then had to decide what degree to take. The answer was in fact determined by one of those accidental factors which seem to have shaped my life. My inclination was to take a degree in history, but I found that to do this I would have to know Latin and having arrived at the Kilburn Grammar School at 12 instead of 11, there had been no possibility of my studying Latin. So I turned to the other subject in which I had secured distinction and started to study for a science degree, specialising in chemistry. However, I soon found that mathematics, a requirement for a science degree, was not to my taste and I switched to the only other degree for which it was possible to study at the Kilburn Grammar School, one in commerce. Although my knowledge of the subjects on which I was examined was rudimentary, I managed to pass the intermediate examinations and went to the London School of Economics in October, 1929 to continue my studies for a Bachelor of Commerce degree. I took a hodgepodge of courses for Part I of the final examination, which I passed in 1930.

For Part II, I specialised in the Industry Group. I then had an extraordinary stroke of luck, another accidental factor which would affect everything I was to do subsequently. Arnold Plant, who had previously held a chair at the University of Cape Town, South Africa, was appointed Professor of

Commerce (with special reference to Business Administration) at the London School of Economics in 1930. I attended his lectures on business administration but it was what he said in his seminar, which I started to attend only five months before the final examinations, that was to change my view of the working of the economic system, or perhaps more accurately was to give me one. What Plant did was to introduce me to Adam Smith's "invisible hand". He made me aware of how a competitive economic system could be co-ordinated by the pricing system. But he did not merely influence my ideas. My encountering him changed my life. I passed the B. Com, Part II final examination in 1931, but having taken the first year of University work while still at school and three years residence at the London School of Economics being required before a degree could be awarded, I had to decide what to do in this third year. Among the subjects studied for Part II, the one I had found most interesting was Industrial Law and what I had decided to do was to study in this third year for the degree of B.Sc (Econ), with Industrial Law as my special subject. Had I done so I would undoubtedly have gone on to become a lawyer. But that was not to be. No doubt as a result of Plant's influence, the University of London awarded me a Sir Ernest Cassel Travelling Scholarship and although I did not know it, I was on the road to becoming an economist.

I spent the academic year 1931-32 on my Cassel Travelling Scholarship in the United States studying the structure of American industries, with the aim of discovering why industries were organized in different ways. I carried out this project mainly by visiting factories and businesses. What came out of my enquiries was not a complete theory answering the questions with which I started but the introduction of a new concept into economic analysis, transaction costs, and an explanation of why there are firms. All this was achieved by the Summer of 1932, as the contents of a lecture delivered in Dundee in October 1932, make clear. These ideas became the basis for my article "The Nature of the Firm", published in 1937, cited by the Royal Swedish Academy of Sciences in awarding me the 1991 Alfred Nobel Memorial Prize in Economic Sciences. The delay in publishing my ideas was partly due to a reluctance to rush into print and partly to the fact that I was heavily engaged in teaching and research on other projects. I held a teaching position at the Dundee School of Economics and Commerce from 1932 to 1934, at the University of Liverpool from 1934 to 1935 and at the London School of Economics from 1935 on. At the London School of Economics I was assigned a course on the economics of public utilities and finding that we knew next to nothing about the facts relating to these industries, I began a series of historical studies of public utilities in Britain. In 1939, the Second World War broke out and in 1940 I entered government service doing statistical work, first at the Forestry Commission and then at the Central Statistical Office, Offices of the War Cabinet. I returned to the London School of Economics in 1946. I then became responsible for the main economics course, "The Principles of Economics", and also continued with my research on public utilities, particularly the Post Office and broadcasting. I spent nine months in 1948 in the United States on a Rockefeller Fellowship studying the American broadcasting industry. My book, *British Broadcasting: A Study in Monopoly*, was published in 1950.

In 1951, I migrated to the United States. I went first to the University of Buffalo and in 1959, after a year at the Center for Advanced Study in the Behavioral Sciences, I joined the economics department of the University of Virginia. I maintained my interest in public utilities and particularly in broadcasting and during my year at the Center for Advanced Study in the Behavioral Sciences, I made a study of the Federal Communications Commission which regulated the broadcasting industry in the United States, including the allocation of the radio frequency spectrum. I wrote an article, published in 1959, which discussed the procedures followed by the Commission and suggested that it would be better if use of the spectrum was determined by the pricing system and was awarded to the highest bidder. This raised the question of what rights would be acquired by the successful bidder and I went on to discuss the rationale of a property rights system. Part of my argument was considered to be erroneous by a number of economists at the University of Chicago and it was arranged that I should meet with them one evening at Aaron Director's home. What ensued has been described by Stigler and others. I persuaded these economists that I was right and I was asked to write up my argument for publication in the *Journal of Law and Economics.* Although the main points were already to be found in *The Federal Communications Commission,* I wrote another article, *The Problem of Social Cost,* in which I expounded my views at greater length, more precisely and without reference to my previous article. This article, which appeared early in 1961, unlike my earlier article on "The Nature of the Firm", was an instant success. It was, and continues to be, much discussed. Indeed it is probably the most widely cited article in the whole of the modern economic literature. It, and *The Nature of the Firm* were the two articles cited by the Royal Swedish Academy of Sciences as justification for awarding me the Alfred Nobel Memorial Prize. Had it not been for the fact that these economists at the University of Chicago thought that I had made an error in my article on *The Federal Communications Commission,* it is probable that *The Problem of Social Cost* would never have been written.

In 1964, I moved to the University of Chicago and became editor of the *Journal of Law and Economics.* I continued as editor until 1982. Editorship of the *Journal* was a source of great satisfaction. I encouraged economists and lawyers to write about the way in which actual markets operated and about how governments actually perform in regulating or undertaking economic activities. The *Journal* was a major factor in creating the new subject, "law and economics". My life has been interesting, concerned with academic affairs and on the whole successful. But, on almost all occasions, what I have done has been determined by factors which were no part of my choosing. I have had "greatness thrust upon me".

THE INSTITUTIONAL STRUCTURE OF PRODUCTION

Nobel Lecture, December 9, 1991

by

RONALD. H. COASE

University of Chicago, Chicago, USA

In my long life I have known some great economists but I have never counted myself among their number nor walked in their company. I have made no innovations in high theory. My contribution to economics has been to urge the inclusion in our analysis of features of the economic system so obvious that, like the postman in G. K. Chesterton's Father Brown tale, *The Invisible Man,* they have tended to be overlooked. Nonetheless, once included in the analysis, they will, as I believe, bring about a complete change in the structure of economic theory, at least in what is called price theory or microeconomics. What I have done is to show the importance for the working of the economic system of what may be termed the institutional structure of production. In this lecture I shall explain why, in my view, these features of the economic system were ignored and why their recognition will lead to a change in the way we analyse the working of the economic system and in the way we think about economic policy, changes which are already beginning to occur. I will also speak about the empirical work that needs to be done if this transformation in our approach is to increase our understanding. In speaking about this transformation, I do not wish to suggest that it is the result of my work alone. Oliver Williamson, Harold Demsetz, Steven Cheung, among others, have made outstanding contributions to the subject and without their work and that of many others, I doubt whether the significance of my writings would have been recognized. While it has been a great advantage of the creation of the Prize in Economic Sciences in Memory of Alfred Nobel that, by drawing attention to the significance of particular fields of economics, it encourages further research in them, the highlighting of the work of a few scholars, or, in my case, one scholar, tends to obscure the importance of the contributions of other able scholars whose researches have been crucial to the development of the field.

I will be speaking of that part of economics which has come to be called industrial organization, but to understand its present state it is necessary to say something about the development of economics in general. During the two centuries since the publication of *The Wealth of Nations* the main activity of economists, it seems to me, has been to fill the gaps in Adam Smith's system, to correct his errors and to make his analysis vastly more exact. A principal theme of *The Wealth of Nations* was that government regulation or centralised planning were not necessary to make an economic system function in an orderly way. The economy could be co-ordinated by a system of prices (the "invisible hand") and, furthermore, with beneficial results. A major task of economists since the publication of *The Wealth of Nations*, as Harold Demsetz has explained[1], has been to formalize this proposition of Adam Smith. The given factors are technology and the tastes of consumers, and individuals, who follow their own interest, are governed in their choices by a system of prices. Economists have uncovered the conditions necessary if Adam Smith's results are to be achieved and where, in the real world, such conditions do not appear to be found, they have proposed changes which are designed to bring them about. It is what one finds in the textbooks. Harold Demsetz has said rightly that what this theory analyses is a system of extreme decentralization. It has been a great intellectual achievement and it throws light on many aspects of the economic system. But it has not been by any means all gain. The concentration on the determination of prices has led to a narrowing of focus which has had as a result the neglect of other aspects of the economic system. Sometimes, indeed, it seems as though economists conceive of their subject as being concerned only with the pricing system and that anything outside this is considered as no part of their business. Thus, my old chief and wonderful human being, Lionel Robbins, wrote, in *The Nature and Significance of Economic Science*, about the "glaring deficiencies" of the old treatment of the theory of production with its discussion of peasant proprietorships and industrial forms: "It suggests that from the point of view of the economist 'organisation' is a matter of internal industrial (or agricultural) arrangement—if not internal to the firm, at any rate internal to 'the' industry. At the same time it tends to leave out completely the governing factor of all productive organisation—the relationship of prices and cost..."[2]. What this comes down to is that, in Robbins' view, an economist does not interest himself in the internal arrangements within organisations but only in what happens on the market, the purchase of factors of production and the sale of the goods that these factors produce. What happens in between the purchase of the factors of production and the sale of the goods that are produced by these factors is largely ignored. I do not know how far economists today share Robbins' attitude but it is undeniable that microeconomics is largely a study of the determination of prices and output, indeed this part of economics is often called price theory.

This neglect of other aspects of the system has been made easier by another feature of modern economic theory—the growing abstraction of the analysis, which does not seem to call for a detailed knowledge of the actual economic system or, at any rate, has managed to proceed without it.

[1] Harold Demsetz, *Ownership, Control and the Firm* Volume I, page 145.

[2] Lionel Robbins, *The Nature and Significance of Economic Science* (1932), page 70.

Holmstrom and Tirole, writing on *The Theory of the Firm* in the recently published *Handbook of Industrial Organization,* conclude at the end of their article of 63 pages that "the evidence/theory ratio... is currently very low in this field"[3]. Peltzman has written a scathing review of the *Handbook* in which he points out how much of the discussion in it is theory without any empirical basis[4]. What is studied is a system which lives in the minds of economists but not on earth. I have called the result "blackboard economics". The firm and the market appear by name but they lack any substance. The firm in mainstream economic theory has often been described as a "black box". And so it is. This is very extraordinary given that most resources in a modern economic system are employed within firms, with how these resources are used dependent on administrative decisions and not directly on the operation of a market. Consequently, the efficiency of the economic system depends to a very considerable extent on how these organisations conduct their affairs, particularly, of course, the modern corporation. Even more surprising, given their interest in the pricing system, is the neglect of the market or more specifically the institutional arrangements which govern the process of exchange. As these institutional arrangements determine to a large extent what is produced, what we have is a very incomplete theory. All this is beginning to change and in this process I am glad to have played my part. The value of including such institutional factors in the corpus of mainstream economics is made clear by recent events in Eastern Europe. These ex-communist countries are advised to move to a market economy, and their leaders wish to do so, but without the appropriate institutions no market economy of any significance is possible. If we knew more about our own economy we would be in a better position to advise them.

What I endeavoured to do in the two articles cited by the Royal Swedish Academy of Sciences was to attempt to fill these gaps or more exactly to indicate the direction in which we should move if they are ultimately to be filled. Let me start with *The Nature of the Firm.* I went as a student to the London School of Economics in 1929 to study for a Bachelor of Commerce degree, specialising in the Industry group, supposedly designed for people who wished to become works managers, a choice of occupation for which I was singularly ill-suited. However, in 1931, I had a great stroke of luck. Arnold Plant was appointed Professor of Commerce in 1930. He was a wonderful teacher. I began to attend his seminar in 1931, some five months before I took the final examinations. It was a revelation. He quoted Sir Arthur Salter: "The normal economic system works itself". And he explained how a competitive economic system coordinated by prices would lead to the production of goods and services which consumers valued most

[3] Richard Schmalensee and Robert D. Willig (editors), *Handbook of Industrial Organization*, page 126.

[4] Sam Peltzman, "The Handbook of Industrial Organization: A Review Article", *Journal of Political Economy*, February, 1991, pages 201–217.

highly. Before being exposed to Plant's teaching, my notions on how the economy worked were extremely woolly. After Plant's seminar I had a coherent view of the economic system. He introduced me to Adam Smith's "invisible hand". As I had taken the first year of University work while still at High School, I managed to complete the requirements for a degree in two years. However, university regulations required three years of residence before a degree could be granted. I had therefore a year to spare. I then had another stroke of luck. I was awarded a Cassel travelling scholarship by the University of London. I decided to spend the year in the United States, this being treated as a year's residence at the London School of Economics, the regulations being somewhat loosely interpreted.

I decided to study vertical and lateral integration of industry in the United States. Plant had described in his lectures the different ways in which various industries were organised, but we seemed to lack any theory which would explain these differences. I set out to find it. There was also another puzzle which, in my mind, needed to be solved and which seemed to be related to my main project. The view of the pricing system as a co-ordinating mechanism was clearly right but there were aspects of the argument which troubled me. Plant was opposed to all schemes, then very fashionable during the Great Depression, for the co-ordination of industrial production by some form of planning. Competition, according to Plant, acting through a system of prices, would do all the co-ordination necessary. And yet we had a factor of production, management, whose function was to co-ordinate. Why was it needed if the pricing system provided all the co-ordination necessary? The same problem presented itself to me at that time in another guise. The Russian Revolution had taken place only fourteen years earlier. We knew then very little about how planning would actually be carried out in a communist system. Lenin had said that the economic system in Russia would be run as one big factory. However, many economists in the West maintained that this was an impossibility. And yet there were factories in the West and some of them were extremely large. How did one reconcile the views expressed by economists on the role of the pricing system and the impossibility of successful central economic planning with the existence of management and of these apparently planned societies, firms, operating within our own economy?[5]

I found the answer by the summer of 1932. It was to realise that there were costs of using the pricing mechanism. What the prices are has to be discovered. There are negotiations to be undertaken, contracts have to be drawn up, inspections have to be made, arrangements have to be made to settle disputes, and so on. These costs have come to be known as transaction costs. Their existence implies that methods of co-ordination, alternative to the market, which are themselves costly and in various ways imperfect, may nonetheless be preferable to relying on the pricing mechanism, the only

[5] A fuller account of these events will be found in Oliver E. Williamson and Sidney G. Winter (editors), *The Nature of the Firm, Origins, Evolution and Development*, pages 34–47.

method of co-ordination normally analysed by economists. It was avoidance of the costs of carrying out transactions through the market that could explain the existence of the firm in which the allocation of factors came about as a result of administrative decisions (and I thought it did). In my 1937 article, I argued that in a competitive system there would be an optimum of planning since a firm, that little planned society, could only continue to exist if it performed its co-ordination function at a lower cost than would be incurred if it were achieved by means of market transactions and also at a lower cost than this same function could be performed by another firm. To have an efficient economic system it is necessary not only to have markets but also areas of planning within organizations of the appropriate size. What this mix should be we find as a result of competition. This is what I said in my article of 1937. However, as we know from a letter I wrote in 1932, which has been preserved, all the essentials of this argument had been presented in a lecture I gave in Dundee at the beginning of October, 1932[6]. I was then twenty-one years of age and the sun never ceased to shine. I could never have imagined that these ideas would become some 60 years later a major justification for the award of a Nobel Prize. And it is a strange experience to be praised in my eighties for work I did in my twenties.

There is no doubt that the recognition by economists of the importance of the role of the firm in the functioning of the economy will prompt them to investigate its activities more closely. The work of Oliver Williamson and others has led to a greater understanding of the factors which govern what a firm does and how it does it. And we can also hope to learn much more in future from the studies of the activities of firms which have recently been initiated by the Center for Economic Studies of the Bureau of the Census of the United States. But it would be wrong to think that the most important consequence for economics of the publication of *The Nature of the Firm* has been to direct attention to the importance of the firm in our modern economy, a result which, in my view, would have come about in any case. What I think will be considered in future to have been the important contribution of this article is the explicit introduction of transaction costs into economic analysis. I argued in *The Nature of the Firm* that the existence of transaction costs leads to the emergence of the firm. But the effects are pervasive in the economy. Businessmen in deciding on their ways of doing business and on what to produce have to take into account transaction costs. If the costs of making an exchange are greater than the gains which that exchange would bring, that exchange would not take place and the greater production that would flow from specialisation would not be realised. In this way, transaction costs affect not only contractual arrangements but also what goods and services are produced. Not to include transaction costs in the theory leaves many aspects of the working of the economic system unexplained, including the emergence of the firm, but much else

[6] *Ibid*, pages 34–35.

besides. In fact, a large part of what we think of as economic activity is designed to accomplish what high transaction costs would otherwise prevent or to reduce transaction costs so that individuals can freely negotiate and we can take advantage of that diffused knowledge of which Hayek has told us.

I know of only one part of economics in which transaction costs have been used to explain a major feature of the economic system and that relates to the evolution and use of money. Adam Smith pointed out the hindrances to commerce that would arise in an economic system in which there was a division of labour but in which all exchange had to take the form of barter. No-one would be able to buy anything unless he possessed something that the producer wanted. This difficulty, he explained, could be overcome by the use of money. A person wishing to buy something in a barter system has to find someone who has this product for sale but who also wants some of the goods possessed by the potential buyer. Similarly, a person wishing to sell something has to find someone who both wants what he has to offer and also possesses something that the potential seller wants. Exchange in a barter system requires what Jevons called "this double coincidence". Clearly the search for partners in exchange with suitable qualifications is likely to be very costly and will prevent many potentially beneficial exchanges from taking place. The benefit brought about by the use of money consists of a reduction in transaction costs. The use of money also reduces transaction costs by facilitating the drawing up of contracts as well as by reducing the quantity of goods that need to be held for purposes of exchange. However, the nature of the benefits secured by the use of money seems to have faded into the background so far as economists are concerned and it does not seem to have been noticed that there are other features of the economic system which exist because of the need to mitigate transaction costs.

I now turn to that other article cited by the Swedish Academy, *The Problem of Social Cost,* published some 30 years ago. I will not say much here about its influence on legal scholarship which has been immense but will mainly consider its influence on economics, which has not been immense, although I believe that in time it will be. It is my view that the approach used in that article will ultimately transform the structure of microeconomics—and I will explain why. I should add that in writing this article I had no such general aim in mind. I thought that I was exposing the weaknesses of Pigou's analysis of the divergence between private and social products, an analysis generally accepted by economists, and that was all. It was only later, and in part as a result of conversations with Steven Cheung in the 1960s that I came to see the general significance for economic theory of what I had written in that article and also to see more clearly what questions needed to be further investigated.

Pigou's conclusion and that of most economists using standard economic theory was, and perhaps still is, that some kind of government action (usually the imposition of taxes) was required to restrain those whose actions had harmful effects on others, often termed negative externalities.

What I showed in that article, as I thought, was that in a regime of zero transaction costs, an assumption of standard economic theory, negotiations between the parties would lead to those arrangements being made which would maximise wealth and this irrespective of the initial assignment of rights. This is the infamous *Coase Theorem,* named and formulated by Stigler, although it is based on work of mine. Stigler argues that the Coase Theorem follows from the standard assumptions of economic theory. Its logic cannot be questioned, only its domain[7]. I do not disagree with Stigler. However, I tend to regard the Coase Theorem as a stepping stone on the way to an analysis of an economy with positive transaction costs. The significance to me of the Coase Theorem is that it undermines the Pigovian system. Since standard economic theory assumes transaction costs to be zero, the Coase Theorem demonstrates that the Pigovian solutions are unnecessary in these circumstances. Of course, it does not imply, when transaction costs are positive, that government actions (such as government operation, regulation or taxation, including subsidies) could not produce a better result than relying on negotiations between individuals in the market. Whether this would be so could be discovered not by studying imaginary governments but what real governments actually do. My conclusion; let us study the world of positive transaction costs.

If we move from a regime of zero transaction costs to one of positive transaction costs, what becomes immediately clear is the crucial importance of the legal system in this new world. I explained in *The Problem of Social Cost* that what are traded on the market are not, as is often supposed by economists, physical entities but the rights to perform certain actions and the rights which individuals possess are established by the legal system. While we can imagine in the hypothetical world of zero transaction costs that the parties to an exchange would negotiate to change any provision of the law which prevents them from taking whatever steps are required to increase the value of production, in the real world of positive transaction costs such a procedure would be extremely costly, and would make unprofitable, even where it was allowed, a great deal of such contracting around the law. Because of this, the rights which individuals possess, with their duties and privileges, will be, to a large extent what the law determines. As a result the legal system will have a profound effect on the working of the economic system and may in certain respects be said to control it. It is obviously desirable that these rights should be assigned to those who can use them most productively and with incentives that lead them to do so and that, to discover and maintain such a distribution of rights, the costs of their transference should be low, through clarity in the law and by making the legal requirements for such transfers less onerous. Since this can come about only if there is an appropriate system of property rights, and they are enforced, it is easy to understand why so many academic lawyers (at least in

[7] George J. Stigler, "Two Notes on the Coase Theorem", *Yale Law Journal,* December, 1989, pages 631 – 633.

the United States) have found so attractive the task of uncovering the character of such a property rights system and why the subject of "law and economics" has flourished in American law schools. Indeed, work is going forward at such a pace that I do not consider it over-optimistic to believe that the main outlines of the subject will be drawn within five or ten years.

Until quite recently most economists seem to have been unaware of this relationship between the economic and legal systems except in the most general way. Stock and produce exchanges are often used by economists as examples of perfect or near-perfect competition. But these exchanges regulate in great detail the activities of traders (and this quite apart from any public regulation there may be). What can be traded, when it can be traded, the terms of settlement and so on are all laid down by the authorities of the exchange. There is, in effect, a private law. Without such rules and regulations, the speedy conclusion of trades would not be possible. Of course, when trading takes place outside exchanges (and this is almost all trading) and where the dealers are scattered in space and have very divergent interests, as in retailing and wholesaling, such a private law would be difficult to establish and their activities will be regulated by the laws of the State. It makes little sense for economists to discuss the process of exchange without specifying the institutional setting within which the trading takes place since this affects the incentives to produce and the costs of transacting. I think this is now beginning to be recognized and has been made crystal-clear by what is going on in Eastern Europe today. The time has surely gone in which economists could analyze in great detail two individuals exchanging nuts for berries on the edge of the forest and then feel that their analysis of the process of exchange was complete, illuminating though this analysis may be in certain respects. The process of contracting needs to be studied in a real world setting. We would then learn of the problems that are encountered and of how they are overcome and we would certainly become aware of the richness of the institutional alternatives between which we have to choose.

Oliver Williamson has ascribed the non-use or limited use of my thesis in *The Nature of the Firm* to the fact that it has not been made "operational", by which he means that the concept of transaction costs has not been incorporated into a general theory. I think this is correct. There have been two reasons for this. First, incorporating transaction costs into standard economic theory which has been based on the assumption that they are zero, would be very difficult and economists who, like most scientists, as Thomas Kuhn has told us, are extremely conservative in their methods, have not been inclined to attempt it. Second, Williamson has also pointed out that although I was correct in making the choice between organization within the firm or through the market the center piece of my analysis, I did not indicate what the factors were that determined the outcome of this choice and thus made it difficult for others to build on what is often described as a "fundamental insight". This also is true. But the interrelationships which govern the mix of market and hierarchy, to use Williamson's terms, are extremely complex and in our present state of ignorance it will not be easy to discover what these factors are. What we need is more empirical work. In a paper written for a conference of the National Bureau of Economic Research I explained why I thought this was so. This is what I said: "An inspired theoretician might do as well without such empirical work, but my own feeling is that the inspiration is most likely to come through the stimulus provided by the patterns, puzzles and anomalies revealed by the systematic gathering of data, particularly when the prime need is to break our existing habits of thought"[8]. This statement was made in 1970. I still think that in essentials it is true today. Although much interesting and important research was done in the seventies and eighties and we certainly know much more than we did in 1970, there is little doubt that a great deal more empirical work is needed. However, I have come to the conclusion that the main obstacle faced by researchers in industrial organization is the lack of available data on contracts and the activities of firms. I have therefore decided to do something about it.

Believing that there is a great deal of data on contracts and the activities of firms in the United States available in government departments and agencies in Washington, D.C., and that this information is largely unknown to economists, I organized a conference at the University of Chicago Law School in the Summer of 1990 at which government officials presented papers in which they described what data was available and how to get access to it and also reported on some of the research being carried out within their departments. The audience consisted of academic economists. It was, as a colleague remarked, a case of supply meeting demand. The proceedings of this conference will be published in a special issue of the *Journal of Law and Economics*. Another development with which I am associated is the establishment of the Center for the Study of Contracts and the Structure of Enterprise at the Business School of the University of Pittsburgh. This Center will make large-scale collections of business contracts and will prepare databases which will be made available to all researchers, whatever their institution. Nor should we forget the work now getting started at the Center for Economic Studies of the Bureau of the Census. This greater availability of data and the encouragement given to all researchers working on the institutional structure of production by the award to me of the Nobel Prize, should result in a reduction in that elegant but sterile theorizing so commonly found in the economics literature on industrial organization and should lead to studies which increase our understanding of how the real economic system works.

My remarks have sometimes been interpreted as implying that I am hostile to the mathematization of economic theory. This is untrue. Indeed, once we begin to uncover the real factors affecting the performance of the economic system, the complicated interrelations between them will clearly necessitate a mathematical treatment, as in the natural sciences, and econo-

[8] R. H. Coase, *The Firm, the Market and the Law*, page 71.

mists like myself, who write in prose, will take their bow. May this period soon come.

I am very much aware that many economists whom I respect and admire will not agree with the opinions I have expressed and some may even be offended by them. But a scholar must be content with the knowledge that what is false in what he says will soon be exposed and, as for what is true, he can count on ultimately seeing it accepted, if only he lives long enough.

ECONOMIC SCIENCES 1992

GARY S. BECKER

for having extended the domain of microeconomic analysis to a wide range of human behaviour and interaction, including nonmarket behaviour

THE SVERIGES RIKSBANK (BANK OF SWEDEN) PRIZE IN ECONOMIC SCIENCES IN MEMORY OF ALFRED NOBEL

Speech by Professor Assar Lindbeck of the Royal Swedish Academy of Sciences.
Translation from the Swedish text.

Your Majesties, Your Royal Highnesses, Ladies and Gentlemen,

Gary Becker has made it his task to extend the analytical domain of what he calls "an economic approach" to various social issues. Now it is important to bear in mind that what Becker calls "an economic approach" does *not* mean that individuals are assumed to strive solely for economic gain. Non-pecuniary, and indeed also altruistic, aspects are part of Becker's analysis alongside of pecuniary aspects. Therefore, the analysis should perhaps more appropriately be characterized as a theory of rational choice, i.e. of *purposeful behavior,* rather than as a traditional "economic approach."

Such a concept of research might perhaps, when looked at superficially, seem trivial. But that is precisely what it is *not.* Human behavior in the areas where Becker has conducted his studies has hitherto often been assumed to be unexplained, *habitual* behavior, rather than founded on rational calculations. Moreover, had Becker's approach been trivial, it would hardly have given rise to the amount of criticism and protest it was plagued with when first launched.

An important application of Becker's model of analysis is his studies of education and on-the-job training, i.e. investments in human capital, as they are now called. With the aid of this concept, Becker has developed, and empirically tested, an explicit theory of the wage structure in society and its development over time. Researchers after Becker have used the same method of analysis, to explain among other things, such as diverse phenomena as economic growth, the composition of trade, and investment in the sphere of health.

Another of Becker's important contributions is his analysis of the role of the family, or the household, in society. In traditional theory, the household was supposed to have a choice between income, and by means of this income, consumption of purchased consumer goods on the one hand, and leisure on the other hand. Becker's basic idea is rather to look upon the household as "a small factory" producing services for the members of the household with an input of time and purchased consumer goods, the latter being regarded as intermediate inputs in the production process taking place in the household.

This analysis is an interesting example of how a *new* angle to an old question can lead to completely new insights. In the context of this alternative approach, a wage rise for example, leads to a shift to less time-consuming production of the services produced within the household. Rising wages on the open market make it more costly to have one member of the family specializing in household production (e.g. child care). Therefore, parts of the earlier social and economic functions of the family are moved to other institutions such as businesses, schools, day care centers for children and various public institutions. This development constitutes a stimulus to work outside the home, a stimulus that also makes parents choose to have fewer children, investing rather in more education for the children they choose to have. Becker uses his theory to explain the historical decline of fertility in the industrialized countries, and the differences in fertility between countries, and between urban and rural areas.

Becker has also applied his theory to the area of "crime and punishment." He assumes that, except for a limited number of psychopaths, individuals who behave criminally react in predictable ways to different stimuli in the form of benefits and costs of criminal activities. This theory seems to provide realistic predictions about what groups of citizens can be expected to commit specific types of crime. The empirical studies conducted in connection with this theory also indicate that an increase in the probability of being convicted has a more discouraging effect on criminality than has the harshness of the punishment.

Yet another application concerns discrimination, with regard to race and sex, on the job and housing markets. Becker shows that such behavior works, purely analytically, as a "tax wedge," i.e. a marginal tax, between social and private economic returns. Discrimination, therefore, tends to harm economically, not only the party subjected to discrimination but also the party carrying out discrimination.

I now turn to you, Professor Becker: You have always chosen important *social* issues for your research agenda, such as population growth, the role of the family in society, the importance of education and on-the-job training, crime and punishment, and discrimination. You have, thanks to your creative and often provocative research strategy, widened the domain of models of "rational choice." It is a pleasure to convey to you the warmest congratulations from the Royal Swedish Academy of Sciences and to ask you to receive, from the hands of His Majesty the King, the 1992 Prize in Economic Sciences in Memory of Alfred Nobel.

Gary S Becker

GARY S. BECKER

I was born in Pottsville, Pennsylvania, a little coal mining town in Eastern Pennsylvania, where my father owned a small business. He had first gone into business for himself after leaving Montreal and his family for the United States when he was only sixteen years old. He moved many times in the eastern United States before settling in Pottsville in the mid-1920s. My two sisters, Wendy and Natalie, and brother, Marvin, were also born there. However, when I was four or five we moved to Brooklyn, New York, where my father became a partner in another business.

I went to elementary school and high school in Brooklyn. I was a good student, but until age sixteen was more interested in sports than intellectual activities. At that time I had to decide between being on the handball and math teams since they met during the same time period. It was indicative of my shift in priorities that I chose math, although I was better at handball.

My father had left school in Montreal after the 8th grade because he was eager to make money. My mother — whose family emigrated from Eastern Europe to New York City when she was six months old — also left after the 8th grade because girls were not expected to get much education. There were only a few books in our house, but my father kept up with the political and financial news, and my older sister read a lot. After my father lost most of his sight I had the task of reading him stock quotations and other reports on financial developments. Perhaps that stimulated my interest in economics, although I was rather bored by it.

We had many lively discussions in the house about politics and justice. I believe this does help explain why by the time I finished high school, my interest in mathematics was beginning to compete with a desire to do something useful for society. These two interests came together during my freshman year at Princeton, when I accidentally took a course in economics, and was greatly attracted by the mathematical rigor of a subject that dealt with social organization. During the following summer I read several books on economics.

To be financially independent more quickly, I decided at the end of my first year to graduate in three years, a seldom used option at Princeton. I had to take a few extra courses during the next year, and I chose reading courses in modern algebra and differential equations for the summer afterwards. For the equations course, I was given a set of unpublished lectures that emphasized existence proofs and uniqueness of solutions to differential equations. I learned a lot about such proofs, but very little about actually solving one of these equations. Still, my heavy investment in mathematics at Princeton prepared me well for the increasing use of mathematics in economics.

I began to lose interest in economics during my senior (third) year because it did not seem to deal with important social problems. I contemplated transferring to sociology, but found that subject too difficult. Fortunately, I decided to go to the University of Chicago for graduate work in economics. My first encounter in 1951 with Milton Friedman's course on microeconomics renewed my excitement about economics. He emphasized that economic theory was not a game played by clever academicians, but was a powerful tool to analyze the real world. His course was filled with insights both into the structure of economic theory and its application to practical and significant questions. That course and subsequent contacts with Friedman was had a profound effect on the direction taken by my research.

While Friedman was clearly the intellectual leader, Chicago had a first class group of economists who were doing innovative research. Especially important to me were Gregg Lewis's use of economic theory to analyze labor markets, T.W. Schultz's pioneering research on human capital, Aaron Director's applications of economics to anti-trust problems, and industrial organization more generally, and L.J. Savage's research on subjective probability and the foundation of statistics.

I published two articles in 1952, based on my research at Princeton. But I realized shortly after arriving in Chicago that I had to begin to learn again what economics is all about. I published nothing else until an article written with Friedman and a book based on my Ph.D. dissertation came out in 1957. The book contains the first systematic effort to use economic theory to analyze the effects of prejudice on the earnings, employment and occupations of minorities. It started me down the path of applying economics to social issues, a path that I have continued to follow.

The book was very favorably reviewed in a few major journals, but for several years it had no visible impact on anything. Most economists did not think racial discrimination was economics, and sociologists and psychologists generally did not believe I was contributing to their fields. However, Friedman, Lewis, Schultz, and others at Chicago were confident I had written an important book. Support by the people I respected so highly was crucial to my willingness to persevere in the face of much hostility.

After my third year of graduate study I became an assistant professor at Chicago. I had a light teaching load and could concentrate mainly on research. However, I felt that I would become intellectually more independent if I left the nest and had to make it on my own. After three years in that position, I turned down a much larger salary from Chicago to take a similar appointment at Columbia combined with one at the National Bureau of Economic Research, then also located in Manhattan. I have always believed this was the correct decision, for I developed greater independence and self-confidence than seems likely if I remained at Chicago.

For twelve years I divided my time between teaching at Columbia and doing research at the Bureau. My book on human capital was the outgrowth of my first research project for the Bureau. During this period I also wrote frequently cited articles on the allocation of time, crime and punishment, and irrational behavior.

At Columbia I began a workshop on labor economics and related subjects — anything that interested us was "related." This involved transplanting the workshop system of supervising doctoral research from Chicago — where it originated. After a few years, Jacob Mincer joined the Columbia department and became co-director of the workshop. We had a very exciting atmosphere and attracted most of the best students at Columbia. Both Mincer and I were doing research on human capital before this subject was adequately appreciated in the profession at large, and the students found it fascinating. We were also working on the allocation of time, and other subjects in the forefront of research.

I married for the first time in 1954, and have two daughters from that marriage, Judy and Catherine. To provide a better family atmosphere I lived in the suburbs and commuted to Columbia and the Bureau. Eventually, I began to tire of commuting and decided either to move into New York or to leave Columbia for another university. I also was beginning to feel intellectually stale.

My decision to leave was hastened by the student riots in 1968. I believed that Columbia should take a firm hand and uphold the right to free inquiry without student intimidation. The central administration wanted to do this, but it was incompetent, and was opposed by many faculty who behaved no better than the students.

In 1970, I returned to Chicago, and found the atmosphere there very stimulating. The department was still powerful, especially after it had added George Stigler and Harry Johnson. Stigler and I soon became close friends, and he had a very large effect on my subsequent intellectual development. We wrote two influential papers together: a controversial one on the stability of tastes, and an early treatment of the principle-agent problem. Stigler also renewed my interest in the economics of politics; I had published a short paper on this subject in 1958. In the 1980s I published two articles that developed a theoretical model of the role of special interest groups in the political process.

But mainly I worked on the family after returning to Chicago. I had much earlier used economic theory to try to understand birth rates and family size. I now began to consider the whole range of family issues: marriage, divorce, altruism toward other members, investments by parents in children, and long term changes in what families do. A series of articles in the 1970s culminated in 1981 in *A Treatise on the Family.* Since I continued to work on this subject, a greatly expanded edition was published in 1991. I have tried not only to understand the determinants of divorce, family size, and the like, but also the effects of changes in family composition and structure on inequality and economic growth. Most of my research on the family and that by students and faculty at Chicago and elsewhere was presented at the Workshop in Applications of Economics that Sherwin Rosen and I run.

For a long time my type of work was either ignored or strongly disliked by most of the leading economists. I was considered way out and perhaps not really an economist. But younger economists were more sympathetic. They may disagree with my analysis, but accept the kind of problems, studied as perfectly legitimate. During the past ten years I have received much tangible evidence of this shift in professional opinion, including the presidency of the American Economic Association, the Seidman Award, and the first social science Award of Merit from the National Institute of Health.

In 1983, the sociology department at Chicago offered me a joint appointment. I was happy to accept because this was an outstanding department. Its invitation to me gave a signal to the sociology profession that the rational choice approach was a respectable theoretical paradigm. James Coleman and I shortly thereafter began an interdisciplinary faculty seminar on rational choice in the social sciences that has been far more successful than we anticipated.

Until 1985, I had published only technical books and technical articles in professional journals. At that time, I was surprised by being asked to write a monthly column for *Business Week* magazine. Since I feared that I could not write for a general audience, I was inclined to turn the offer down. Finally, however, I agreed to do some columns on an experimental basis. It was a wise decision, for I was forced to learn how to write about economic and social issues without using technical jargon, and in about 800 words per column. Doing this has enormously improved my capacity to discuss important subjects briefly and in simple language. The pressure of having to do a column every month also makes me stay abreast of many subjects that interest the business and professional readers of the magazine.

I married for the second time in 1980 to Guity Nashat – my first wife died in 1970. This gave me two stepsons, Michael and Cyrus, to go with two daughters. Guity is the one who overcame my reluctance to do the Business Week columns. She is an historian of the Middle East with professional interests that overlap my own: on the role of women in economic and social life, and the causes of economic growth. The personal and professional compatibility she provides has made my life so much better.

CURRICULUM VITAE

Name: Gary Stanley Becker

Born: December 2, 1930
Pottsville, Pennsylvania

Marital Status: Married

Address: Department of Economics
University of Chicago
1126 East 59th Street
Chicago, Illinois 60637

Phone: 773-702-8168
Fax: 773-702-8490
e-mail: myrn@cicero.spc.uchicago.edu

Academic Degrees

A.B. Princeton University, 1951 (Summa cum Laude)
A.M. University of Chicago, 1953
Ph.D. University of Chicago, 1955

Honorary Degrees

Doctor Philosophae Honoris Causa, Hebrew University, Jerusalem, Israel, 1985
Doctor of Laws, Knox College, Galesburg, Illinois, 1985
Doctor of Arts, University of Illinois at Chicago, Chicago, Illinois, 1988
Doctor of Science, State University of New York at Stony Brook, Stony Brook, New York, 1990
Doctor of Humane Letters, Princeton University, Princeton, New Jersey, 1991
Doctor Philosophae Honoris Causa, University of Palermo, Buenos Aires, Argentina, 1993
Doctor of Humane Letters, Columbia University in the City of New York, 1993
Doctoris Honoris Causa Scientiarum Oeconomicarum, Warsaw School of Economics, 1995
Doctoris Honoris Causa, University of Economics, Prague, 1995
Doctor of Business Administration, University of Miami, 1995
Doctor of Science, University of Rochester, 1995

Academic Appointments

University Professor, University of Chicago, Departments of Economics and Sociology, 1983–present

Department of Economics, 1970–1983; Chairman, Department of Economics, 1984–1985

Ford Foundation Visiting Professor of Economics, University of Chicago, 1969–70

Arthur Lehman Professor of Economics, Columbia University, 1968–69

Professor of Economics, Columbia University, 1960–1968

Assistant and Associate Professor of Economics, Columbia University, 1957–60

Assistant Professor, University of Chicago, 1954–57

Other Professional Appointments

Columnist, *Business Week*, 1985–present

Economic advisor to Presidential Candidate Robert Dole – 1996

Research Associate, Economics Research Center, N.O.R.C., 1980–present

Senior Fellow, Hoover Institution, 1990–present

Member, Domestic Advisory Board, Hoover Institution, 1973–1991

Member, Academic Advisory Board, American Enterprise Institute for Public Policy Research, 1987–1991

Associate Member, Institute of Fiscal and Monetary Policy, Ministry of Finance, Japan, 1988–present

Member, Senior Research Associate and research policy advisor to the Center for Economic Analysis of Human Behavior and Social Institutions, National Bureau of Economic Research, 1957–79

Board of Publications, University of Chicago Press, 1971–75

Professional Societies

American Economic Association (Distinguished Fellow, 1988; President, 1987; Vice-President, 1974; Editorial Board, *American Economic Review*, 1968–71)

American Statistical Association, 1955

Econometric Society

Economic History Association

Western Economic Association (Vice-President, 1995–96; President, 1996–97)

American Sociological Society

Elected Societies

Mont Pelerin Society, 1971; Executive Board, 1985–; Vice-President, 1989, President, 1990–92

Member, National Academy of Sciences, 1975–

Member, American Philosophical Society, 1986–

Fellow, American Statistical Association, 1965

Fellow, Econometric Society, 1967

Founding Member, National Academy of Education, 1965 (Vice-President, 1965–67)

Fellow, American Academy of Arts and Sciences, 1972–

Member, International Union for the Scientific Study of Population, 1982–

Fellow, National Association of Business Economists, 1993–

Phi Beta Kappa, Princeton University, 1950

Awards

W.S. Woytinsky Award, for Human Capital, University of Michigan, 1964
John Bates Clark Medal, American Economic Association, 1967
Professional Achievement Award, University of Chicago Alumni Association, 1968
Frank E Seidman Distinguished Award in Political Economy, 1985
MERIT Award, National Institutes of Health, US Department of Health and Human Services, 1986
John R. Commons Award, Omicron Delta Epsilon, 1987
Nobel Prize for Economic Sciences, 1992
Lord Foundation Award, 1995
50 Great Americans, Marquis *Who's Who*, 1995

PUBLICATIONS

Monographs

Accounting for Tastes, Harvard University Press, 1996

A Treatise on the Family, Harvard University Press, 1981; expanded edition, 1991; Spanish translation, 1987; Chinese translation, 1988

The Economic Approach to Human Behavior, University of Chicago Press, 1976; German translation, 1982; Polish translation, 1990; Chinese translation, 1993; Romanian translation, 1994

Essays in Labor Economics in Honor of H. Gregg Lewis, edited, Special Supplement to the *Journal of Political Economy* 84, no 2, part 2, August 1976

The Allocation of Time and Goods Over the Lift Cycle, with Gilbert Ghez, Columbia University Press for the National Bureau of Economic Research, 1975

Essays in the Economics of Crime and Punishment, edited with William M. Landes, Columbia University Press for the National of Economic Research, 1974

Economic Theory, A. Knopf, 1971; Japanese translation, 1976

Human Capital and the Personal Distribution of Income: An Analytical Approach, University of Michigan, 1967

Human Capital, Columbia University Press, 1964; second edition, 1975; third edition, 1993; Japanese translation, 1975; Spanish translation, 1984

The Economics of Discrimination, University of Chicago Press, 1957; second edition, 1971

Forthcoming

The Economics of Everyday Life, McGraw-Hill, Inc., October 1996

Family, Society, and State (in German), J.C.B. Mohr (Paul Siebeck), October 1996

Selected Articles

"An Empirical Analysis of Cigarette Addiction", with Michael Grossman and Kevin M. Murphy, *American Economic Review* 84 (no. 3): 396–418, June 1994

"A Simple Theory of Advertising as a Good or Bad", with Kevin M. Murphy, *Quarterly Journal of Economics* CVIII (no. 4): 941–964, November 1993

"George Joseph Stigler: January 17, 1911–December 1, 1991", *Journal of Political Economy* 101 (no. 5): 761–767, October 1993

"Cross-Cultural Differences in Family and Sexual Life: An Economic Analysis", with Richard Posner, *Rationality and Society* 5 (no. 4): 421–31, October 1993

"Nobel Lecture: The Economic Way of Looking at Behavior", *Journal of Political Economy* 101 (no. 3): 385–409, June 1993

"Government, Human Capital, and Economic Growth", Presidential Address to the Mont Pelerin Society, Vancouver General Meeting, September, 1992, *Industry of Free China* 79 (no. 6): 47–56, June 1993

"Rational Addiction and the Effect of Price on Consumption", with Michael Grossman and Kevin Murphy, in George Loewenstein and Jon Elster (eds.), *Choice over Time*, Russell Sage Foundation, 1992

"George Joseph Stigler", *Journal des Economistes et des Etudes Humaines* 3 (no. 1): 5–9, March 1992

"The Division of Labor, Coordination Costs, and Knowledge", with Kevin Murphy, *Quarterly Journal of Economics* CVII (no. 4): 1137–1160, November 1992

"Fertility and the Economy", *Journal of Population Economics* 5 (no. 3): 185–201, 1992

"Habits, Addictions and Traditions", *Kyklos* 45 (Fasc. 3): 327–346, 1992

"Human Capital and the Economy", *Proceedings of the American Philosophical Society* 136 (no. 1): 85–92, March 1992

"Education, Labor Force Quality and the Economy", *Business Economics* XXVII (no. 1): 7–12, January 1992

"Milton Friedman", in Edward Shils (ed.), *Remembering the University of Chicago: Teachers, Scientists, and Scholars*, University of Chicago Press, 1991

"A Note on Restaurant Pricing and Other Examples of Social Influences on Price", *Journal of Political Economy* 99 (no. 1): 1109–1116, October 1991

"Rational Addiction and the Effect of Price on Consumption", with Michael Grossman and Kevin M. Murphy, *AEA Papers and Proceedings* 81 (no. 2): 237–241, May 1991

"Human Capital, Fertility, and Economic Growth", with Kevin M. Murphy and Robert Tamura, *Journal of Political Economy* 98 (no. 5, pt. 2): S12–S70, October 1990

"Fertility Choice in a Model of Economic Growth", with Robert Barro, *Econometrica* 57: 481–501, March 1989

"A Theory of Rational Addiction", with Kevin M. Murphy, *Journal of Political Economy* 96: 675–700, August 1988

"The Family and the State", with Kevin M. Murphy, *Journal of Law and Economics* 31: 1–18, April 1988

"Family Economics and Macro Behavior", Presidential Address to the American Economic Association, December 29, 1988, *American Economic Review* 86 (no. 1): March 1989

"A Reformulation of the Economic Theory of Fertility", with Robert J. Barro, *Quarterly Journal of Economics* CIII (no. 1): 1–25, February 1988

"Human Capital and the Rise and Fall of Families," with Nigel Tomes, *Journal of Labor Economics* 4 (no. 3, pt. 2): S1–S39, July 1986

"Special Interests and Public Policies", Acceptance Paper, The Frank E. Seidman Distinguished Award in Political Economy, Rhodes College, September 26, 1985

"Public Policies, Pressure Groups, and Dead Weight Costs", *Journal of Public Economics* 28 (1985): 329–47

"Pressure Groups and Political Behavior", in R. D. Coe and C. K. Wilbur, eds., *Capitalism and Democracy: Schumpeter Revisited* (Notre Dame, IN: University of Notre Dame Press, 1985)

"An Economic Analysis of the Family", Seventeenth Geary Lecture, The Economic and Social Research Institute, Dublin, Ireland, 1985

"Human Capital, Effort, and the Sexual Division of Labor", *Journal of Labor Economics* 3 (no. 1, pt. 2): S33–S58, January 1985

"A Theory of Competition Among Pressure Groups for Political Influence", *Quarterly Journal of Economics* XCVII (no. 3): 371–400, August 1983

"Altruism in the Family and Selfishness in the Market Place", *Economica* 48: 1–15, February 1981

"An Equilibrium Theory of the Distribution of Income and Intergenerational Mobility", with Nigel Tomes, *Journal of Political Economy* 87 (no. 6): 1153–89, December 1979

"Economic Analysis and Human Behavior", in L. Levy-Garboua, ed., *Sociological Economics* (Beverly Hills, CA: Sage, 1979)

"An Economic Analysis of Marital Instability", with E. M. Landes and R. T. Michael, *Journal of Political Economy* 85 (no. 6): 1153–89, December 1977

"De Gustibus Non Est Disputandum", with G. J. Stigler, *The American Economic Review* 67 (no. 2): 76–90, March 1977

"Altruism, Egoism, and Genetic Fitness: Economics and Sociobiology", *Journal of Economic Literature* XIV (no. 3): 817–26, September 1976

"Child Endowments and the Quantity and Quality of Children", with Nigel Tomes, in G. S. Becker, ed., *Essays in Labor Economics in Honor of H. Gregg Lewis, Journal of Political Economy* 84 (no. 4, part 2): S143–62, August 1976

"A Theory of Social Interactions", *Journal of Political Economy* 82 (no. 6): 1063–93, November/December 1974

"A Theory of Marriage, Part II", *Journal of Political Economy* 82 (no. 2, part 2): S11–S26, March/April, 1974. Reprinted in T. W. Schultz, ed., *Economics of the Family* (Chicago: University of Chicago Press, 1974)

"Law Enforcement, Malfeasance, and Compensation of Enforcers", with G. J. Stigler, *Journal of Legal Studies* III (no. 1): 1–8, January 1974

"On the New Theory of Consumer Behavior", with R. T. Michael, *Swedish Journal of Economics* 75: 378–96, 1973

"A Theory of Marriage: Part I", *Journal of Political Economy* 81 (no. 4): 813–46, July/August 1973. Reprinted in T. W. Schultz, ed., *Economics of the Family* (Chicago: University of Chicago Press, 1974)

"On the Interaction Between the Quantity and Quality of Children", with H. G. Lewis, *Journal of Political Economy* 81 (no. 2, part 2): S279–S288, March/April 1973

"Market Insurance, Self-Insurance, and Self-Protection", with I. Ehrlich, *Journal of Political Economy* 80 (no. 4): 623–48, July/August 1972

"Crime and Punishment: An Economic Approach", *Journal of Political Economy* 76 (no. 2): 169–217, March/April 1968

"Education and the Distribution of Earnings", with B. Chiswick, *American Economic Review* LVI (no. 2): 358–69, May 1966

"A Theory of the Allocation of Time", *Economic Journal* LXXV (no. 299): 493–508, September 1965

"Underinvestment in College Education?", *American Economic Review* 50 (no. 2): 346–54, 1960. Reprinted in E. Phelps, ed., *Problems of Economic Growth* (New York: W. W. Norton, 1962)

"Investment in Human Capital: A Theoretical Analysis", *Journal of Political Economy* LXX (no. 5, part 2): 9–49, October 1962

"Irrational Behavior and Economic Theory", *Journal of Political Economy* LXX (no. 1): 1–13, February 1962

"The Classical Monetary Theory: The Outcome of the Discussion", with W. J. Baumol, revised and published in J. Spengler and W. Allen, eds., *Essays in Economic Thought,* (Chicago: Rand McNally and Co, 1960)

"An Economic Analysis of Fertility", in *Demographic and Economic Change in Developed Countries, Conference of the Universities-National Bureau Committee for Economic Research, a Report of the National Bureau of Economic Research* (Princeton, NJ: Princeton University Press, 1960), pp. 209–40

"Union Restrictions on Entry", in *The Public Stake in Union Power*, Philip D. Bradley, ed., Charlottesville, VA: University of Virginia Press, 1959

"Competition and Democracy", *Journal of Law and Economics* 1:105–09, 1958

"A Statistical Illusion in Judging Keynesian Models", with M. Friedman, *Journal of Political Economy* LXV (no. 1): 64–75, February 1957

"The Classical Monetary Theory: The Outcome of the Discussion", with W. J. Baumol, *Economica* XIX (76): 355–76, November 1952

"A Note on Multi-Country Trade", *American Economic Review*, XLII (no. 4): 558–68, September 1952

THE ECONOMIC WAY OF LOOKING AT LIFE*

Nobel Lecture, December 9, 1992

by

GARY S. BECKER

Department of Economics, University of Chicago, Chicago, IL. 60637, USA

1. *The Economic Approach*

My research uses the economic approach to analyze social issues that range beyond those usually considered by economists. This lecture will describe the approach, and illustrate it with examples drawn from past and current work.

Unlike Marxian analysis, the economic approach I refer to does not assume that individuals are motivated solely by selfishness or gain. It is a *method* of analysis, not an assumption about particular motivations. Along with others, I have tried to pry economists away from narrow assumptions about self interest. Behavior is driven by a much richer set of values and preferences.

The analysis assumes that individuals maximize welfare *as they conceive it*, whether they be selfish, altruistic, loyal, spiteful, or masochistic. Their behavior is forward-looking, and it is also consistent over time. In particular, they try as best they can to anticipate the uncertain consequences of their actions. Forward-looking behavior, however, may still be rooted in the past, for the past can exert a long shadow on attitudes and values.

Actions are constrained by income, time, imperfect memory and calculating capacities, and other limited resources, and also by the available opportunities in the economy and elsewhere. These opportunities are largely determined by the private and collective actions of other individuals and organizations.

Different constraints are decisive for different situations, but the most fundamental constraint is limited time. Economic and medical progress have greatly increased length of life, but not the physical flow of time itself, which always restricts everyone to twenty-four hours per day. So while goods and services have expended enormously in rich countries, the total time available to consume has not.

Thus, wants remain unsatisfied in rich countries as well as in poor ones.

* This lecture is dedicated to the memory of George J. Stigler, who died almost exactly one year ago. Nobel Laureate, outstanding economist, very close friend and mentor, he would be as happy as I am had he lived to see me deliver the 1992 Nobel Lecture in Economics.

For while the growing abundance of goods may reduce the value of additional goods, time becomes more valuable as goods become more abundant. Utility maximization is of no relevance in a Utopia where everyone's needs are fully satisfied, but the constant flow of time makes such a Utopia impossible. These are some of the issues analyzed in Becker [1965], and Linder [1970].

The following sections illustrate the economic approach with four very different subjects. To understand discrimination against minorities, it is necessary to widen preferences to accommodate prejudice and hatred of particular groups. The economic analysis of crime incorporates into rational behavior illegal and other antisocial actions. The human capital approach considers how the productivity of people in market and non-market situations is changed by investments in education, skills, and knowledge. The economic approach to the family interprets marriage, divorce, fertility, and relations among family members through the lens of utility-maximizing forward-looking behavior.

2. *Discrimination Against Minorities*

Discrimination against outsiders has always existed, but with the exception of a few discussions of the employment of women (see Edgeworth [1922], and Faucett [1918]), economists wrote little on this subject before the 1950s. I began to worry about racial, religious, and gender discrimination while a graduate student, and used the concept of discrimination coefficients to organize my approach to prejudice and hostility to members of particular groups.

Instead of making the common assumptions that employers only consider the productivity of employees, that workers ignore the characteristics of those with whom they work, and that customers only care about the qualities of the goods and services provided, discrimination coefficients incorporate the influence of race, gender, and other personal characteristics on tastes and attitudes. Employees may refuse to work under a woman or a black even when they are well paid to do so, or a customer may prefer not to deal with a black car salesman. It is only through *widening* of the usual assumptions that it is possible to begin to understand the obstacles to advancement encountered by minorities.

Presumably, the amount of observable discrimination against minorities in wages and employment depends not only on tastes for discrimination, but also on other variables, such as the degree of competition and civil rights legislation. However, aside from the important theory of compensating differentials originated by Adam Smith, and a few major studies like Myrdal's *American Dilemma* [1944], there was little else available in the 1950s to build on to analyze how prejudice and other variables interact. I spent several years working out a theory of how actual discrimination in earnings and employment is determined by tastes for discrimination, along with the degree of competition in labor and product markets, the distribution of discrimination coefficients among members of the majority group, the access of minorities to education and training, the outcome of median voter and other voting mechanisms that determine whether legislation favors or is hostile to minorities, and other considerations. Since there was so much to be done in this field, my advisors encouraged me to convert my doctoral dissertation (Becker [1955]) into a book (Becker [1957]).

The actual discrimination in the market place against a minority group depends on the combined discrimination of employers, workers, consumers, schools, and governments. The analysis shows that sometimes the environment greatly softens, while at other times it magnifies, the impact of a given amount of prejudice. For example, the discrepancy in wages between equally productive blacks and whites, or women and men, would be much smaller than the degree of prejudice against blacks and women when many companies can efficiently specialize in employing mainly blacks or women.

Indeed, in a world with constant returns to scale in production, two segregated economies with the same distribution of skills would completely bypass discrimination and would have equal wages and equal returns to other resources, regardless of the desire to discriminate against the segregated minorities. Therefore, discrimination by the majority in the marketplace is effective because minority members cannot provide various skills in sufficient quantities to companies that would specialize in using these workers.

When the majority is very large compared to the minority – in the United States whites are nine times as numerous and have much more human and physical capital per capita than blacks – market discrimination by the majority hardly lowers their incomes, but may greatly reduce the incomes of the minority. However, when minority members are a sizable fraction of the total, discrimination by the majority injures them as well.

This proposition can be illustrated with an analysis of discrimination in South Africa, where blacks are four to five times as numerous as whites. Discrimination against blacks has also significantly hurt whites, although some white groups have benefitted (see Becker [1971, pages 30–31], and Hutt [1964]). Its sizable cost to whites suggests why apartheid and other blatant forms of Afrikaaner discrimination eventually broke down.

A literature has developed on whether discrimination in the marketplace due to prejudice disappears in the long run. Whether employers who do not want to discriminate will eventually compete away all discriminating employers depends not only on the distribution of tastes for discrimination among potential employers, but critically also on the nature of firm production functions.

Of greater significance empirically is the long run discrimination by employees and customers, who are far more important sources of market discrimination than employers. There is no reason to expect discrimination by these groups to be competed away in the long run unless it is possible to have enough efficient segregated firms and effectively segregated markets for goods.

A novel theoretical development in recent years is the analysis of the consequences of stereotyped reasoning or statistical discrimination (see Phelps [1972], and Arrow [1973]). This analysis suggests that the *beliefs* of employers, teachers, and other influential groups that minority members are less productive *can* be self-fulfilling, for these beliefs may cause minorities to underinvest in education, training, and work skills, such as punctuality. The underinvestment does make them less productive (see a good recent analysis by Loury [1992]).

Evidence from many countries on the earnings, unemployment, and occupations of blacks, women, religious groups, immigrants, and others has expanded enormously during the past twenty-five years. This evidence more fully documents the economic position of minorities and how that changes in different environments. However, the evidence has not dispelled some of the controversies over the source of lower incomes of minorities (see Cain's [1986] good review of both the theoretical literature and empirical analysis.)

3. *Crime and Punishment*

I began to think about crime in the 1960s after driving to Columbia University for an oral examination of a student in economic theory. I was late and had to decide quickly whether to put the car in a parking lot or risk getting a ticket for parking illegally on the street. I calculated the likelihood of getting a ticket, the size of the penalty, and the cost of putting the car in a lot. I decided it paid to take the risk and park on the street. (I did not get a ticket.)

As I walked the few blocks to the examination room, it occurred to me that the city authorities had probably gone through a similar analysis. The frequency of their inspection of parked vehicles and the size of the penalty imposed on violators should depend on their estimates of the type of calculations potential violators like me would make. Of course, the first question I put to the hapless student was to work out the optimal behavior of both the offenders and the police, something I had not yet done.

In the 1950s and 1960s, intellectual discussions of crime were dominated by the opinion that criminal behavior was caused by mental illness and social oppression, and that criminals were helpless "victims." A book by a well-known psychiatrist was entitled *The Crime of Punishment* (see Menninger [1966]). Such attitudes began to exert a major influence on social policy, as laws changed to expand criminals' rights. These changes reduced the apprehension and conviction of criminals, and provided less protection to the law-abiding population.

I was not sympathetic to the assumption that criminals had radically different motivations from everyone else. I explored instead the theoretical and empirical implications of the assumption that criminal behavior is rational (see the early pioneering work by Bentham [1931] and Beccaria [1986]), but again "rationality" did not necessarily imply narrow materialism. It recognized that many people are constrained by moral and ethical considerations, and did not commit crimes even when they were profitable and there was no danger of detection.

However, police and jails would be unnecessary if such attitudes always prevailed. Rationality implied that some individuals become criminals because of the financial rewards from crime compared to legal work, taking account of the likelihood of apprehension and conviction, and the severity of punishment.

The amount of crime is determined not only by the rationality and preferences of would-be criminals, but also by the economic and social environment created by public policies, including expenditures on police, punishments for different crimes, and opportunities for employment, schooling, and training programs. Clearly, the type of legal jobs available as well as law, order, and punishment are an integral part of the economic approach to crime.

Total public spending on fighting crime can be reduced, while keeping the mathematically expected punishment unchanged, by offsetting a cut in expenditures on catching criminals with a sufficient increase in the punishment to those convicted. However, risk-preferring individuals are more deterred from crime by a higher probability of conviction than by severe punishments. Therefore, optimal behavior by the State would balance the reduced spending on police and courts from lowering the probability of conviction against the preference of risk-preferring criminals for a lesser certainty of punishment. The State should also consider the likelihood of punishing innocent persons.

In the early stages of my work on crime, I was puzzled by why theft is socially harmful since it appears merely to redistribute resources, usually from wealthier to poorer individuals. I resolved the puzzle (Becker [1968, fn. 3] by recognizing that criminals spend on weapons and on the value of the time in planning and carrying out their crimes, and that such spending is socially unproductive — it is what is now called "rent-seeking" — because it does not create wealth, only forcibly redistributes it. The social cost of theft was approximated by the number of dollars stolen since rational criminals would be willing to spend up to that amount on their crimes. (I should have added the resources spent by potential victims protecting themselves against crime.)

One reason why the economic approach to crime became so influential is that the same analytic apparatus can be used to study enforcement of all laws, including minimum wage legislation, clean air acts, insider trader and other violations of security laws, and income tax evasions. Since few laws are self-enforcing, they require expenditures on conviction and punishment to deter violators. The United States Sentencing Commission has explicitly used the economic analysis of crime to develop rules to be followed by judges in punishing violators of Federal statutes (United States Sentencing Commission [1988]).

Studies of crime that use the economic approach have become common during the past quarter century. These include analysis of the optimal marginal punishments to deter increases in the severity of crimes – for example, to deter a kidnapper from killing his victim (the modern literature starts with Stigler [1970]), and the relation between private and public enforcement of laws (see Becker and Stigler [1974], and Landes and Posner [1975]).

Fines are preferable to imprisonment and other types of punishment because they are more efficient. With a fine, the punishment to offenders is also revenue to the State. The early discussions of the relations between fines and other punishments have been clarified and considerably improved (see, e.g., Polinsky and Shavell [1984], and Posner [1986]).

Empirical assessments of the effects on crime rates of prison terms, conviction rates, unemployment levels, income inequality, and other variables have become more numerous and more accurate (the pioneering work is by Ehrlich [1973], and the subsequent literature is extensive). The greatest controversies surround the question of whether capital punishment deters murders, a controversy that is far from being resolved (see, e.g., Ehrlich [1975], and National Research Council [1978]).

4. *Human Capital*

Until the 1950s economists generally assumed that labor power was given and not augmentable. The sophisticated analyses of investments in education and other training by Adam Smith, Alfred Marshall, and Milton Friedman were not integrated into discussions of productivity. Then T. W. Schultz and others began to pioneer the exploration of the implications of human capital investments for economic growth and related economic questions.

Human capital analysis starts with the assumption that individuals decide on their education, training, medical care, and other additions to knowledge and health by weighing the benefits and costs. Benefits include cultural and other non-monetary gains along with improvement in earnings and occupations, while costs usually depend mainly on the foregone value of the time spent on these investments.

Human capital is so uncontroversial nowadays that it may be difficult to appreciate the hostility in the 1950s and 1960s toward the approach that went with the term. The very concept of *human* capital was alleged to be demeaning because it treated people as machines. To approach schooling as an investment rather than a cultural experience was considered unfeeling and extremely narrow. As a result, I hesitated a long time before deciding to call my book *Human Capital*, and hedged the risk by using a long subtitle. Only gradually did economists, let alone others, accept the concept of human capital as a valuable tool in the analysis of various economic and social issues.

My work on human capital began with an effort to calculate both private and social rates of return to men, women, blacks, and other groups from investments in different levels of education. After a while it became clear that the analysis of human capital could help explain many regularities in labor markets and the economy at large. It seemed possible to develop a more general theory of human capital that includes firms as well as individuals, and that could consider its macro-economic implications.

The empirical analysis tried to correct data on the higher earnings of more educated persons for the fact that they are abler: they have higher I.Q.s and score better on other aptitude tests. It also considered the effects on rates of return to education of mortality, income taxes, foregone earnings, and economic growth. Ability corrections did not seem very important, but large changes in adult mortality and sizeable rates of economic growth did have big effects.

The empirical study of investments in human capital received a major boost from Mincer's classic work [see 1974]. He extended a simple regression analysis that related earnings to years of schooling (Becker and Chiswick [1966]) to include a crude but very useful measure of on-the-job training and experience – years after finishing school; he used numerous individual observations rather than grouped data, and he carefully analyzed the properties of residuals from earnings-generating equations. There are now numerous estimated rates of return to education and training for many countries (for a summary of some of this literature, see Psacharopoulos [1975]).

The accumulating evidence on the economic benefits of schooling and training also promoted the importance of human capital in policy discussions. This new faith in human capital has reshaped the way governments approach the problem of stimulating growth and productivity, as was shown by the emphasis on human capital in the recent presidential election in the United States.

One of the most influential theoretical concepts in human capital analysis is the distinction between general and specific training or knowledge (see Becker [1962], and Oi [1962]). By definition, firm-specific knowledge is useful only in the firms providing it, whereas general knowledge is useful also in other firms. Teaching someone to operate an IBM-compatible personal computer is general training, while learning the authority structure and the talents of employees in a particular company is specific knowledge. This distinction helps explain why workers with highly specific skills are less likely to quit their jobs and are the last to be laid off during business downturns. It also explains why most promotions are made from within a firm rather than through hiring – workers need time to learn about a firm's structure and "culture" – and why better accounting methods would include the specific human capital of employees among the principle assets of most companies.

Firm-specific investments produce rents that must be shared between employers and employees, a sharing process that is vulnerable to "opportunistic" behavior because each side may try to extract most of the rent after investments are in place. Rents and opportunism due to specific investments play a crucial role in the modern economic theory of organizations (see Williamson [1985]), and in many discussions of principal-agent problems (see, for example, Grossman and Hart [1983]). The implications of specific capital for sharing and turnover have also been used in analyzing marriage "markets" to explain divorce rates and bargaining within a marriage (see Becker, Landes and Michael [1977], and McElroy and Horney [1981]), and in analyzing political "markets" to explain the low turnover of politicians (see Cain, Ferejohn and Firoina [1987]).

The theory of human capital investment relates inequality in earnings to differences in talents, family background, and bequests and other assets (see Becker and Tomes [1986]). Many empirical studies of inequality also rely on human capital concepts, especially differences in schooling and training (see Mincer [1974]). The sizeable growth in earnings inequality in the United States during the 1980s that has excited so much political discussion is largely explained by higher returns to the more educated and better trained (see, e.g., Murphy and Welch [1992]).

Human capital theory gives a provocative interpretation of the so-called "gender gap" in earnings. Traditionally, women have been far more likely than men to work part-time and intermittently partly because they usually withdrew from the labor force for a while after having children. As a result, they had fewer incentives to invest in education and training that improved earnings and job skills.

During the past twenty years all this changed. The decline in family size, the growth in divorce rates, the rapid expansion of the service sector where most women are employed, the continuing economic development that raised the earnings of women along with men, and civil rights legislation encouraged greater labor force participation by women, and hence greater investment in market-oriented skills. In practically all rich countries, these forces significantly improved both the occupations and relative earnings of women.

The United States' experience is especially well-documented. The gender gap in earnings among full-time men and women remained at about 35 percent from the mid-fifties to the mid-seventies. Then women began the steady economic advance which is still continuing; it narrowed the gap to under 25 percent. Women are flocking to business, law, and medical schools, and are working at skilled jobs that they formerly shunned, or were excluded from.

Schultz and others (see, e.g., Schultz [1963], and Denison [1962]) early on emphasized that investments in human capital were a major contributor to economic growth. But after a while the relation of human capital to growth was neglected, as economists became discouraged about whether the available growth theory gave many insights into the progress of different countries. The revival of more formal models of endogenous growth has brought human capital once again to the forefront of the discussions (see e.g., Romer [1986], Lucas [1988], Barro and Sala-i-Martin [1992], and Becker, Murphy and Tamura [1990]).

5. *Formation, Dissolution, and Structure of Families*

The rational choice analysis of family behavior builds on maximizing behavior, investments in human capital, the allocation of time, and discrimination against women and other groups. The rest of the lecture focuses on this analysis since it is still quite controversial.

Writing *A Treatise on the Family* is the most difficult sustained intellectual effort I have undertaken. The family is arguably the most fundamental and oldest of institutions – some authors trace its origin to more than 50,000 years ago. The *Treatise* tries to analyze not only modern Western families, but also those in other cultures and the changes in family structure during the past several centuries.

Trying to cover this broad subject required a degree of mental commitment over more than six years, during many nighttime as well as daytime hours, that left me intellectually and emotionally exhausted. In his autobiography, Bertrand Russell says that writing the *Principia Mathematica* used up so much of his mental powers that he was never again fit for really hard intellectual work. It took about two years after finishing the *Treatise* to regain my intellectual zest.

The analysis of fertility has a long and honorable history in economics, but until recent years marriage and divorce, and the relations between husbands, wives, parents, and children had been largely neglected by economists (although see the important study by Mincer [1962]). The point of departure of my work on the family is the assumption that when men and women decide to marry or have children or divorce, they attempt to maximize their utility by comparing benefits and costs. So they marry when they expect to be better off than if they remained single, and they divorce if that is expected to increase their welfare.

People who are not intellectuals are often surprised when told that this approach is controversial since it seems obvious to them that individuals try to raise their welfare by marriage and divorce. The rational choice approach to marriage and other behavior is in fact often consistent with the instinctive economics "of the common man" (Farrell and Mandel [1992]).

Still, intuitive assumptions about behavior is only the *starting point* of systematic analysis, for alone they do not yield many interesting implications. The rational choice approach embeds them in a framework that combines maximizing behavior with analysis of marriage and divorce markets, specialization and the division of labor, old-age support, investments in children, and legislation that affects families. The implications of the full model are often not so obvious, and sometimes run sharply counter to received opinion.

For example, contrary to a common belief about divorce among the rich, the economic analysis of family decisions shows that wealthier couples are *less* likely to divorce than poorer couples. According to this theory, richer couples tend to gain a lot from remaining married, whereas many poorer couples do not. A poor woman may well doubt whether it is worth staying married to someone chronically unemployed. Empirical studies for many countries do indicate that the marriages of richer couples are much more stable (see Becker, Landes and Michael [1977]).

Efficient bargaining between husbands and wives implies that the trend in Europe and the United States toward no-fault divorce during the past two decades would not raise divorce rates,and, therefore, that contrary to many claims, it could not be responsible for the rapid rise in these rates. However, the theory does indicate that no-fault divorce hurts women with children whose marriages are broken up by their husbands. Households headed by unmarried women with children now comprise about one-fifth of all households with children in the United States and other advanced countries.

Economic models of behavior have been used to study fertility ever since Malthus's classic essay; the great Swedish economist, Knut Wicksell, was attracted to economics by his belief in the Malthusian predictions of overpopulation. But Malthus's conclusion that fertility would rise and fall as incomes increased and decreased was contradicted by the large decline in birth rates after some countries became industrialized during the latter part of the nineteenth century and the early part of this century.

The failure of Malthus's simple model of fertility persuaded economists that family-size decisions lay beyond economic calculus. The neo-classical growth model reflects this belief, for in most versions it takes population growth as exogenous and given (see, for example, Cass [1965], or Arrow and Kurz [1970]).

However, the trouble with the Malthusian approach is not its use of economics per se, but an economics inappropriate for modern life. It neglects that the time spent on child care becomes more expensive as countries become more productive. The higher value of time raises the cost of children, and thereby reduces the demand for large families. It also fails to consider that the greater importance of education and training in industrialized economies encourages parents to invest more in the skills of their children, which also raises the cost of large families. The growing value of time and the increased emphasis on schooling and other human capital explain the decline in fertility as countries develop, and many features of birth rates in modern economies.

Why in almost all societies have married women specialized in bearing and rearing children and in certain agricultural activities, whereas married men have done most of the fighting and market work? The explanation, presumably, is a combination of biological differences between men and women – especially differences in their innate capacities to bear and rear children – and discrimination against women in market activities, partly through cultural conditioning. Large and highly emotional differences of opinion exist over the relative importance of biology and discrimination in generating the traditional division of labor in marriages (see, for example, Boserup [1970]).

The economic analysis of this division of labor does not determine the relative importance of biology and discrimination, but it shows how sensitive the division is to *small* differences in either. Since the return from investing in a skill is greater when more time is spent utilizing the skill, a married couple could gain a lot from a sharp division of labor because the husband could specialize in some types of human capital and the wife in others. Given such a large gain from specialization within a marriage, only a *little* discrimination against women or *small* biological differences in child-rearing skills would cause the division of labor between household and market tasks to be systematically related to gender. The sensitivity to small differences explains why the empirical evidence cannot readily choose between biological and "cultural" interpretations. This theory also explains why many women entered the labor force as families became smaller, divorce more common, and earning opportunities for women improved.

Relations among family members differ radically from those among employees of firms and members of other organizations. The interactions between husbands, wives, parents, and children are more likely to be motivated by love, obligation, guilt, and a sense of duty than by self-interest narrowly interpreted.

It was demonstrated about twenty years ago that altruism within families enormously alters how they respond to shocks and public policies that redistribute resources among members. Becker [1974] showed that exogenous redistributions of resources from an altruist to her beneficiaries (or vice versa) may not affect the welfare of anyone because the altruist would try to reduce her gifts by the amount redistributed. Barro [1974] derived this result in an intergenerational context, which cast doubt on the common assumption that government deficits and related fiscal policies have real effects on the economy.

The "Rotten-Kid Theorem" – the name is very popular even when critics disagree with the result – carries the analysis of altruism further, for it shows how the behavior of selfish individuals is affected by altruism. Under some conditions, even selfish beneficiaries – of course, most parents believe that the best example of this is selfish children with altruistic parents – are induced to act *as if* they are altruistic toward their benefactors because that raises their own selfish welfare. They act this way because otherwise gifts from their benefactors would be reduced enough to make them worse off (see Becker [1974], and the elaboration and qualifications to the analysis in Lindbeck and Weibull [1987], Bergstrom [1989], and Becker [1991, pp. 9–13]).

The Bible, Plato's *Republic*, and other early writings discussed the treatment of young children by their parents, and of elderly parents by adult children. Both the elderly and children need care – in one case because of declining health and energy, and in the other because of biological growth and dependency. A powerful implication of the economic analysis of relations within families is that these two issues are closely related.

Parents who leave sizable bequests do not need old-age support because instead they help out their children. I mentioned earlier one well-known implication of this: under certain conditions, budget deficits and social security payments to the elderly have no real effects because parents simply offset the bigger taxes in the future on their children through larger bequests.

It is much less appreciated that altruistic parents who leave bequests also tend to invest more in their children's skills, habits, and values. For they gain from financing all investments in the education and skills of children that yield a higher rate of return than the return on savings. They can indirectly save for old age by investing in children, and then reducing bequests when elderly. Both parents and children would be better off when parents make all investments in children that yield a higher return than that on savings, and then adjust bequests to the efficient level of investment (see section 1 of the Appendix for a formal demonstration).

Even in rich countries many parents do not plan on leaving bequests. These parents want old-age support, and they "underinvest" in their children's education and other care. They underinvest because they cannot compensate themselves for greater spending on children by reducing bequests since they do not plan on leaving any.

Both the children and parents would be better off if the parents agreed to invest more in the children in return for a commitment by the children to care for them when they need help. But how can such a commitment be enforced? Economists and lawyers usually recommend a written contract to insure commitment, but it is absurd to contemplate that a society will enforce contracts between adults and ten-year-olds or teenagers.

Part of my current research considers an indirect way to generate commitments when promises and written agreements are not binding. I will describe briefly some of this new work because it carries the economic approach to the family unto uncharted ground related to the rational formation of preferences within families.

Parental attitudes and behavior have an enormous influence on their children. Parents who are alcoholic or are addicted to crack create a bizarre atmosphere for impressionable youngsters, whereas parents with stable values who transmit knowledge and inspire their children favorably influence both what their children are capable of and what they want to do. The economic approach can contribute insights into the formation of preferences through childhood experiences without necessarily adopting the Freudian emphasis on the primacy of what happened during the first few months of life.

Again, I am trying to model a common sense idea; namely, that the attitudes and values of adults are enormously influenced by their childhood experiences. An Indian doctor living in the United States may love curry because he acquired a strong taste for it while growing up in India, or a woman may forever fear men because she was sexually abused as a child.

Through its assumption of forward-looking behavior, the economic point of view implies that parents try to anticipate the effect of what happens to children on their attitudes and behavior when adults. These effects help determine the kind of care parents provide. For example, parents worried about old-age support may try to instill in their children feelings of guilt, obligation, duty, and filial love that indirectly, but still very effectively, can "commit" children to helping them out.

Economists have too narrow a perspective on commitments. "Manipulating" the experiences of others to influence their preferences may appear to be inefficient and fraught with uncertainty, but it can be the most effective way to obtain commitment. Economic theory needs to incorporate guilt, affection, and related attitudes into preferences in order to have a deeper understanding of when commitments are "credible" (see section 2 of the appendix for a formal discussion).

Parents who do not leave bequests may be willing to make their children feel guiltier precisely because they gain more utility from greater old-age consumption than they lose from an equal reduction in children's consumption. This type of behavior may be considerably more common than suggested by the number of families that leave bequests, for parents with young children often do not know whether they will be financially secure when they are old. They may try to protect themselves against ill health, unemployment, and other hazards of old age by instilling in their children a willingness to help out if that becomes necessary.

This analysis of the link between childhood experiences and adult preferences is closely related to work on rational habit formation and addictions (see Becker and Murphy [1988]). The formation of preferences is rational in the sense that parental spending on children partly depends on the anticipated effects of childhood experiences on adult attitudes and behavior. I do not have time to consider the behavior of children – such as crying and acting "cute" – that tries in turn to influence the attitudes of parents.

Many economists, including myself, have excessively relied on altruism to tie together the interests of family members. Recognition of the connection between childhood experiences and future behavior reduces the need to rely on altruism in families. But it does not return the analysis to a narrow focus on self-interest, for it partially replaces altruism by feelings of guilt, obligation, anger, and other attitudes usually neglected by models of rational behavior.

If parents anticipate that children will help out in old age – perhaps because of guilt or related motivations – even parents who are not very loving toward their children would invest more in the children's human capital, and save less to provide for their old age. (For a proof, see section 3 of the Appendix.)

Equation (12) of the Appendix shows that parents always prefer small increases in their own consumption to equal increases in their children's *if* the only way they can get greater consumption is by making children feel guiltier. This means that altruistic parents who take steps to make their children feel guiltier always underinvest in the children's human capital. This shows directly why creating guilt has costs and is not fully efficient.

Altruistic family heads who do not plan to leave bequests try to create a "warm" atmosphere in their families, so that members are willing to come to the assistance of those experiencing financial and other difficulties. This conclusion is relevant to discussions of so-called "family values," a subject that received attention during the recent presidential campaign in the United States. Parents help determine the values of children – including their feelings of obligation, duty, and love – but what parents try to do can be greatly affected by public policies and changes in economic and social conditions.

Consider, for example, a program that transfers resources to the elderly, perhaps especially to poorer families who do not leave bequests, that reduces the elderly's dependence on children. According to the earlier analysis, parents who do not need support when they become old do not try as hard to make children more loyal, guiltier, or otherwise feel as well-disposed toward their parents. This means that programs like social security that significantly help the elderly would encourage family members to drift apart emotionally, not by accident but as maximizing responses to those policies.

Other changes in the modern world which have altered family values include increased geographical mobility, the greater wealth that comes with economic growth, better capital and insurance markets, higher divorce rates, smaller families, and publicly-funded health care. These developments have generally made people better off, but they also weakened the personal relations within families between husbands and wives, parents and children, and among more distant relatives, partly by reducing the incentives to invest in *creating* closer relations.

6. *Concluding Comments*

An important step in extending the traditional analysis of individual rational choice is to incorporate into the theory a much richer class of attitudes, preferences, and calculations. This step is prominent in all the examples that I consider. The analysis of discrimination includes in preferences a dislike of – prejudice against – members of particular groups, such as blacks or women. In deciding whether to engage in illegal activities, potential criminals are assumed to act as if they consider both the gains and the risks – including the likelihood they will be caught and severity of punishments. In human capital theory, people rationally evaluate the benefits and costs of activities, such as education, training, expenditures on health, migration, and formation of habits that radically alter the way they are. The economic approach to the family assumes that even intimate decisions like marriage, divorce, and family size are reached through weighing the advantages and disadvantages of alternative actions. The weights are determined by preferences that critically depend on the altruism and feelings of duty and obligation toward family members.

Since the economic, or rational choice, approach to behavior builds on a theory of individual decisions, criticisms of this theory usually concentrate on particular assumptions about how these decisions are made. Among other things, critics deny that individuals act consistently over time, and question whether behavior is forward-looking, particularly in situations that differ significantly from those usually considered by economists — such as those involving criminal, addictive, family, or political behavior. This is not the place to go into a detailed response to the criticisms, so I simply assert that no approach of comparable generality has yet been developed that offers serious competition to rational choice theory.

While the economic approach to behavior builds on a theory of individual choice, it is not mainly concerned with individuals. It uses theory at the micro level as a powerful tool to derive implications at the group or macro level. Rational individual choice is combined with assumptions about technologies and other determinants of opportunities, equilibrium in market and nonmarket situations, and laws, norms, and traditions to obtain results concerning the behavior of groups. It is mainly because the theory derives implications at the macro level that it is of interest to policymakers and those studying differences among countries and cultures.

None of the theories considered in this lecture aims for the greatest generality; instead, each tries to derive concrete implications about behavior that can be tested with survey and other data. Disputes over whether punishments deter crime, whether the lower earnings of women compared to men are mainly due to discrimination or lesser human capital, or whether no-fault divorce laws increase divorce rates all raise questions about the empirical relevance of predictions derived from a theory based on individual rationality.

A close relation between theory and empirical testing helps prevent both the theoretical analysis and the empirical research from becoming sterile. Empirically oriented theories encourage the development of new sources and types of data, the way human capital theory stimulated the use of survey data, especially panels. At the same time, puzzling empirical results force changes in theory, as models of altruism and family preferences have been enriched to cope with the finding that parents in Western countries tend to bequeath equal amounts to different children.

I have been impressed by how many economists want to work on social issues rather than issues forming the traditional core of economics. At the same time, specialists from fields that do consider social questions are often attracted to the economic way of modelling behavior because of the analytical power provided by the assumption of individual rationality. Thriving schools of rational choice theorists and empirical researchers are active in sociology, law, political science, history, anthropology, and psychology. The rational choice model provides the most promising basis presently available for a unified approach to the analysis of the social world by scholars from the social sciences.

APPENDIX

1. To show this formally, suppose that each person lives for three periods: youth (y), middle age (m), and old age (o), and has one child at the beginning of period m. A child's youth overlaps his parents' middle age, and a child's

middle age overlaps his parents' old age. The utility parents get from altruism is assumed to be separable from the utilities produced by their own consumption.

A simple utility function of parents (V_p) incorporating these assumptions is

$$V_p = u_{mp} + \beta u_{op} + \beta a V_c, \tag{1}$$

where β is the discount rate. Selfish parents have an a = 0, while the degree of altruism rises with a. I do not permit parents to be sadistic toward children (a < 0), although the analysis is easily generalized to include sadists.

Each person works and earns income only during middle age. It is possible to save then to provide consumption for old age (Z_{op}) by accumulating assets with a yield of R_k. Parents influence children's earnings by investing in their human capital. The marginal yield on investments in human capital (R_h) is defined as

$$R_h = \frac{dE_c}{dh}, \tag{2}$$

where E_c is the earnings of children at middle age. This yield is assumed to decline as more is invested in children: $dR_h/dh \leq 0$, where h is the amount invested.

Parents must also decide whether to leave bequests, denoted by k_c. If parents can consume at different ages, leave bequests, or invest in the child's human capital, their budget constraint is

$$Z_{mp} + h + \frac{Z_{op}}{R_k} + \frac{k_c}{R_k} = A_p, \tag{3}$$

where A is the present value of resources.

One first order condition to maximize parental utility determines their optimal consumption at middle and old age

$$u'_{mp} = \beta R_k u'_{op} = \lambda_p, \tag{4}$$

where λ_p is the parents' marginal utility of wealth. Another condition determines whether they give bequests,

$$\beta a V'_c \leq \frac{\lambda_p}{R_k} = \beta u'_{op}; \tag{5}$$

and the last determines investments in the human capital of children

$$R_h \beta a V'_c = \lambda_p. \tag{6}$$

Equation (6) assumes that the first order condition for investment in human capital is a strict equality; that some human capital is always invested in children. This can be justified with an Inada-type condition that small investments in human capital yield very high rates of return. In rich economies like Sweden or the United States, investments in basic knowledge and nutrition of children presumably do yield a very good return. As long as parents are not completely selfish – as long as $a > 0$ – then such a condition does always imply positive investment in human capital. For completely selfish parents, equation (6) would be an inequality.

Equation (4) determines the accumulation of assets to finance old-age consumption. Whether parents leave bequests or want old-age support from their children is determined by the inequality in (5). If this is a strict inequality, parents want support and would not leave bequests.

That inequality can be written in a more revealing way. If children also maximize their utility, then the envelope theorem implies that

$$au'_{mc} < u'_{op} \text{ whenever } aV'_c < u'_{op} \text{ since } V'_c = u'_{mc}. \tag{7}$$

Equation (7) has the intuitive interpretation that parents do not give bequests when the utility they get from their children consuming a dollar more at middle age is less than the utility they get from a dollar more of their own consumption at old age. Obviously, such an inequality holds for completely selfish parents since the left-hand side of equations (5) and (7) are zero when a is zero. The weaker the altruism (the smaller a) the more parents want from children.

Combining equations (5) and (6) gives

$$\frac{\lambda_p}{R_h} \leq \frac{\lambda_p}{R_k}, \text{ or } R_h \geq R_k. \tag{8}$$

Equation (8) implies that the marginal rate of return on human capital equals the return on assets when parents give bequests, and it is greater than the asset return when parents do not give bequests. Parents can help children either by investing in their human capital or by leaving them assets. Since they want to maximize the advantage to children, given the cost to themselves – parents are not sadistic – they help in the most efficient form.

Consequently, if strict inequality holds in equation (8), they would not give bequests, for the best way to help children when the marginal return on human capital exceeds that on assets is to invest only in human capital. Parents leave bequests only when they get the same marginal return on both (some of these results have been derived in Becker and Tomes [1986]).

2. To analyze in a simple way the influence of parents over the formation of children's preferences, suppose parents can take actions x and y when children are young that affect children's preferences when adults. I use the assumption of separability to write the utility function of middle-aged children as

$$V_c = u_{mc} + H(y) - G(x,g) + \beta u_{oc} + \ldots. \tag{9}$$

I assume that $H' > 0$ and $G_x > 0$, which means that an increase in y raises the utility of children, but an increase in x lowers their utility. For concreteness, interpret H as "happiness," and G as the "guilt" children feel toward their parents, so that greater x makes children feel guiltier. The question is: why would non-sadistic parents want to make their children feel guilty?

The variable g is the key to understanding why. This measures the contribution of children to the old-age support of parents; let us assume that children feel less guilty when they contribute more ($G_g < 0$). If $G_{gx} > 0$, then greater x both raises children's guilt and stimulates more giving by them.

The budget constraint of parents becomes:

$$Z_{mp} + h + x + y + \frac{Z_{op}}{R_k} + \frac{k_c}{R_k} = A_p + \frac{g}{R_k}. \tag{10}$$

The first-order condition for the optimal y is

$$\beta a H' \leq \lambda_p. \tag{11}$$

Since $H' > 0$, it is easy to understand why an altruistic parent may try to affect children's preferences through y since an increase in y makes children happier.

The first order condition for x is more interesting, for even altruistic parents may want to make their children feel guilty if that sufficiently raises old-age support. This first order condition can be written as

$$\frac{dV_p}{dx} = \frac{dg}{dx}\beta(u'_{op} - au'_{mc}) - \beta a\frac{dG}{dx} \leq \lambda_p, \tag{12}$$

where dG/dx incorporates the induced change in g. The second term in the middle expression is negative to altruistic parents because greater x does raise children's guilt, which lowers the utility of these parents ($a > 0$). However, guilt also induces children to increase old-age support, as given by dg/dx. The magnitude of this response determines whether it is worthwhile for parents to make children feel guiltier.

Increased old-age support from children has two partially offsetting effects on the welfare of altruistic parents. On the one hand, it raises their old-age consumption and utility, as given by u'_{op}. On the other hand, it lowers children's consumption, and hence the utility of altruistic parents, as given by $-au'_{mc}$. This means that altruistic parents who leave bequests never try to make children feel guiltier, for $u'_{op} = au'_{mc}$ for these parents. Since $dG/dx > 0$, they must be worse off when their children feel guiltier.

3. Combine the first order conditions in Equations (5) and (6) to get

$$\frac{u'_{op}}{au'_{mc}} = \frac{R_h}{R_k} \tag{13}$$

Both sides of this equation exceed unity when parents do not give bequests. Since greater old-age support from children lowers the left-hand side by lowering the numerator and raising the denominator, the right-hand side must also fall to be in a utility maximizing equilibrium. But since R_k is given by market conditions, the right-hand side can fall only if R_h falls, which implies greater investment in children when parents expect greater old-age support from children. Even completely selfish parents (a=0) might invest in children if that would sufficiently increase the expected old-age support from guilty children.

BIBLIOGRAPHY

Arrow, Kenneth J., (1973) "The Theory of Discrimination," in Orley Ashenfelter and Albert Rees, eds., *Discrimination in Labor Markets* (Princeton NJ: Princeton University Press), pp. 3–33.

Arrow, Kenneth J. and Kurz, Mordecai, (1970) *Public Investment, the Rate of Return, and Optimal Fiscal Policy* (Baltimore: Published for Resources for the Future by Johns Hopkins University Press).

Barro, Robert J., (1974) "Are Government Bonds Net Wealth?" *Journal of Political Economy* 82: 1095–1117.

Barro, Robert J. and Sala-i-Martin, X., (1992) "Convergence," *Journal of Political Economy* 100: 223–51.

Beccaria, Cesare, marchese di, (1986) *On Crimes and Punishment*, 1st ed., translation of *Dei Delith e delle Pene* (Indianapolis: Hackett Publishing Co.).

Becker, Gary S., (1955) "Discrimination in the Market Place," Ph.D. dissertation, University of Chicago.

Becker, Gary S., (1957) *The Economics of Discrimination*, 1st ed. (Chicago: University of Chicago Press).

Becker, Gary S., (1962) "Investment in Human Capital: A Theoretical Analysis," *Journal of Political Economy* LXX: 9–49.

Becker, Gary S., (1964) *Human Capital*, 1st ed. (New York: Columbia University Press for the National Bureau of Economic Research).

Becker, Gary S., (1965) "A Theory of the Allocation of Time," *Economic Journal* 75 (299): 493–517.

Becker, Gary S., (1968) "Crime and Punishment: An Economic Approach," *Journal of Political Economy* 76: 169–217.

Becker, Gary S., (1971) *The Economics of Discrimination*, 2nd ed. (Chicago: University of Chicago Press).

Becker, Gary S., (1974) "A Theory of Social Interactions," *Journal of Political Economy* 82: 1063–93.

Becker, Gary S., (1991) *A Treatise on the Family*, expanded ed. (Cambridge MA: Harvard University Press).

Becker, Gary S. and Chiswick, Barry, (1966) "Education and the Distribution of Earnings," *American Economic Review* LVI: 358–69.

Becker, Gary S., Landes, Elisabeth M., and Michael, Robert T., (1977) "An Economic Analysis of Marital Instability," *Journal of Political Economy* 85: 1141–87.

Becker, Gary S. and Murphy, Kevin M., (1988) "The Family and the State," *Journal of Law and Economics* 31: 1–18.

Becker, Gary S., Murphy, Kevin M., and Tamura, Robert, (1990) "Human Capital, Fertility, and Economic Growth," *Journal of Political Economy* 98: S12–37.

Becker, Gary S. and Stigler, George J., (1974) "Law Enforcement, Malfeasance, and Compensation of Enforcers," *Journal of Legal Studies* 3: 1–18.

Becker, Gary S. and Tomes, Nigel, (1986) "Human Capital and the Rise and Fall of Families," *Journal of Labor Economics* 4: S1-S39.

Bentham, Jeremy, (1931) *Theory of Legislation* (New York: Harcourt, Brace).

Bergstrom, Theodore, (1989) "A Fresh Look at the Rotten-Kid Theorem—And Other Household Mysteries," *Journal of Political Economy* 97: 1138–59.

Boserup, Ester, (1970) *Women's Role in Economic Development* (London: Allen and Unwin).

Cain, Bruce E., Ferejohn, John, and Fiorina, Morris, (1987) *The Personal Vote: Constituency Service and Electoral Independence* (Cambridge MA: Harvard University Press).

Cain, Glen G., (1986) "The Economic Analysis of Labor Market Discrimination: A Survey," in O. Ashenfelter and R. Layard, eds., *Handbook of Labor Economics*, Handbooks in Labor Economics Series, no. 5 (New York: Elsevier Science): 693–785.

Cass, David, (1965) "Optimal Growth in an Aggregative Model of Capital Accumulation," *Review of Economic Studies* 32: 233–240.

Denison, Edward F., (1962) *Sources of Economic Growth in the United States* (Washington, D.C.: Committee for Economic Development).

Edgeworth, F. Y., (1922) "Equal Pay to Men and Women for Equal Work" *Economic Journal* XXXII: 431–57.

Ehrlich, Isaac, (1973) "Participation in Illegitimate Activities: A Theoretical and Empirical Investigation," *Journal of Political Economy* 81: 521–65.

Ehrlich, Isaac, (1975) "The Deterrent Effect of Capital Punishment: A Question of Life and Death," *American Economic Review* 85: 397–417.

Farrell, C. and Mandel, M., "Uncommon Sense," *Business Week*, October 26, 1992, pp. 36–37.

Faucett, M., (1918) "Equal Pay for Equal Work," *Economic Journal* XXVIII: 1–6.

Grossman, Sanford J. and Hart, Oliver D., (1983) "An Analysis of the Principal-Agent Problem," *Econometrica* 51: 7–45.

Hutt, William H., (1964) *The Economics of the Colour Bar: A Study of the Economic Origins and Consequences of Racial Segregation in South Africa* (London: Published for the Institute of Economic Affairs by A. Deutsch).

Landes, William M. and Posner, Richard A., (1975) "The Private Enforcement of Law," *Journal of Legal Studies* 4: 1–46.

Lindbeck, Assar and Weibull, Jorgen W., (1988) "Strategic Interaction with Altruism: The Economics of Fait Accompli," *Journal of Political Economy* 96: 1165 - 82. University of Stockholm.

Linder, Staffan Burenstam, (1970) *The Harried Leisure Class* (New York: Columbia University Press).

Loury, Glenn C., (1992) "Incentive Effects of Affirmative Action," *Annals of the American Academy of Political and Social Science* 523: 19–29.

Lucas, Robert E., Jr., (1988) "On the Mechanics of Economic Development," *Journal of Monetary Economics* 22: 3–42.

McElroy, Marjorie B. and Horney, Mary Jean, (1981) "Nash-Bargained Household Decisions: Toward a Generalizaton of the Theory of Demand," *International Economic Review* 22: 333–49.

Menninger, Karl, (1966) *The Crime of Punishment* (New York: The Viking Press).

Mincer, Jacob, (1962) "Labor Force Participation of Married Women," in *Aspects of Labor Economics*, a conference of the Universities – National Bureau Committee for Economic Research (Princeton NJ: Princeton University Press for the National Bureau of Economic Research).

Mincer, Jacob, (1974) *Schooling, Experience, and Earnings* (New York: Columbia University Press for the National Bureau of Economic Research).

Murphy, Kevin M. and Welch, Finis, (1992) "The Structure of Wages," *Quarterly Journal of Economics* 107: 285–326.

Myrdal, Gunnar, (1944) *An American Dilemma: The Negro Problem and Modern Democracy*, 2 vols. (New York: Random House).

National Research Council (U.S.), Panel of Research on Deterrent and Incapacitative Effects, (1978) *Deterrence and Incapacitation: Estimating the Effects of Criminal Sanctions on Crime Rates*, Alfred Blumstein, Jacqueline Cohen, and Daniel Nagin, eds. (Washington, D.C.: National Academy of Sciences).

Oi, Walter Y., (1962) "Labor as a Quasi-Fixed Factor," *Journal of Political Economy* 70: 538–55.
Phelps, Edmund S., (1972) "The Statistical Theory of Racism and Sexism," *American Economic Review* 62: 659–61.
Polinsky, A. Mitchell and Shavell, Steven, (1984) "The Optimal Use of Fines and Imprisonment," *Journal of Public Economics* 24: 89–99.
Posner, Richard A., (1986) *Economic Analysis of Law*, 3rd ed. (Boston: Little, Brown).
Psacharopoulos, George, (1975) *Earnings and Education in OECD Countries* (Paris: Organization for Economic Co-operation; Washington, D.C.: OECD Publications Center).
Romer, Paul M., (1986) "Increasing Returns and Long Run Growth," *Journal of Political Economy* 94: 1002–37.
Schultz, Theodore W., (1963) *The Economic Value of Education* (New York: Columbia University Press).
Stigler, George J., (1970) "The Optimum Enforcement of Laws," *Journal of Political Economy* 78: 526–36.
United States Sentencing Commission (1988) "Discussion Draft of Sentencing Guidelines and Policy Statement for Organizations: Proposed Chapter 8 for the Guidelines Manual."
Williamson, Oliver E., (1985) *The Economic Institutions of Capitalism: Firms, Markets, Relational Contracting* (New York: Free Press; London: Collier Macmillan).

ACKNOWLEDGEMENTS

I have had valuable comments from James Coleman, Richard Posner, Sherwin Rosen, Raaj Sah, Jose Scheinkman, Richard Stern, and Stephen Stigler.

ECONOMIC SCIENCES 1993

ROBERT W. FOGEL and DOUGLASS C. NORTH

for having renewed research in economic history by applying economic theory and quantitative methods in order to explain economic and institutional change

THE SVERIGES RIKSBANK (BANK OF SWEDEN) PRIZE IN ECONOMIC SCIENCES IN MEMORY OF ALFRED NOBEL

Speech by Professor Lennart Jörberg of the Royal Swedish Academy of Sciences.
Translation from the Swedish text.

Your Majesties, Your Royal Highnesses, Ladies and Gentlemen,

Robert Fogel and Douglass North have been awarded this year's Prize in Economics for having renewed research in economic history by applying economic theory and quantitative methods in order to explain economic and institutional change.

Why are some countries rich while the majority are poor? Why have some experienced rapid economic growth over several centuries while others have remained stagnant or even become worse off economically? This year's Prize-Winners have attempted to answer questions such as these by combining economics with history, and have pointed to new ways of studying and understanding economic growth and change. They have employed the best analytical techniques of economic science and combined them with historical data. In other words, they have combined economic theory, quantitative methods, the testing of hypotheses, counterfactual alternatives and traditional economic history methodology in order to analyze and understand profound questions and explain profound changes.

Fogel showed that railways were not the essential prerequisite of economic growth which many scholars had formerly asserted. Fogel's analysis of the part played by the railways in the economic development of the United States has caused today's scholars to be more restrained in ascribing a crucial role to sundry 'great innovations' in order to explain modern economic growth. Fogel's finding, arrived at with the aid of so-called counterfactual analyses and social cost-benefit analysis, has been corroborated by other scholars, all influenced by Fogel.

With the assistance of a prodigious body of data along with economic and statistical techniques, Fogel also showed that despite the moral heinousness of slavery, it was an efficient market solution. Slavery did not perish because of inefficiency but required political decisions to secure its abolition.

In his efforts to elucidate the problems of economic growth Fogel has also laid stress on demographic factors. Through their organization of largescale international research, he and his colleagues have not merely assembled and processed an enormous mass of data but have also shown that our knowledge of the correlation between nutritional standards and mortality has been fragmentary and has left many questions unanswered.

Douglass North has studied the economic growth of the United States, most notably in the period prior to the Civil War, and Europe's development in a very long perspective. Like Fogel, North has shown that technological change is far from being a sufficient explanation for increased productivity. In transoceanic shipping, for example, the rise in productivity arose to a high degree out of organizational changes.

He has also shown that traditional theoretical analysis must be combined with a study of the development of institutions. It is this combination which is the key to the understanding of economic change.

North has underlined the role which institutions play in reducing uncertainty by creating stable, if not always efficient, structures for human activity. Institutions are to be understood as connoting all the written and unwritten rules and usages which influence our mode of being and acting. Absence of institutional stability raises the cost both of producers and of consumers. A lack of clearly defined property rights and difficulties of concluding binding contracts hamper rational economic decisions. In order to understand Europe's long-term development, from the Middle Ages onwards, we must be able to analyze the role of institutions, both as a cause of economic growth and as obstacles to economic change.

One reason why the Industrial Revolution took place in England was that the regulatory role of the state was small and the guild system was weak. In France mercantilism developed, with strong regulation of economic life and foreign trade but with weak economic growth. Strong state regulation and strong institutional obstacles, such as vagueness in the rules relating to property rights, may explain Spain's weak economic development during the seventeenth and eighteenth centuries.

We can also explain the lack of economic dynamism in non-Western countries during past epochs, the collapse of the Eastern European societies, and the current economic problems of many countries in the so-called Third World, by studying the importance of precisely these institutional factors, which have narrowed the scope for economic change more frequently than they have broadened it.

In other words, it is their manner and method of tackling the problems of economic history which, more than anything else, have elevated this year's Prize-Winners to the front rank of scholars in the field called 'the new economic history'. Robert Fogel and Douglass North were pioneers of this research, which has had a lasting influence on the continuing development of economic history as a subject. In their different ways Fogel and North have regenerated the study of economic history by making it more stringent and more theoretically aware. At the same time they have demonstrated the need for a historical dimension in economic analysis.

Professor Fogel and Professor North,

It is my pleasure, on behalf of the Royal Swedish Academy of Sciences, to convey to you our warmest congratulations for your pioneering research in Economic History, and ask you to receive the Nobel Memorial Prize in Economic Sciences from the hands of His Majesty the King.

Robert W. Fogel

ROBERT WILLIAM FOGEL

I was born in New York City in 1926, four years after my parents and my brother migrated to the United States from the city of Odessa in Russia. Although they arrived in New York penniless, my parents scraped together enough savings to establish the first of several small businesses just after I was born. Despite the hard times of the Great Depression and the modest financial circumstances in which we lived, they created a joyful household and they encouraged my brother and me to be optimistic about the future.

My parents' reverence for learning encouraged both my brother and me toward academic pursuits. In many ways, however, it was my brother who was the main intellectual influence on me until he joined the armed forces in 1941. Almost six years my senior in age and nine years ahead of me in school, he inspired me with his intellectual brilliance. I still remember the intense discussions by my brother and his college classmates about the social and economic issues of the Depression that I overheard as I lay in my bed, supposedly asleep, in the next room.

My education in the public schools of New York City between 1932 and 1944 was an excellent preparation for a life in science. Because of the Depression, these schools were able to attract a remarkably talented and dedicated collection of teachers who encouraged their students to strive for the highest levels of accomplishment. That environment led me to aspire to a career in science, and also kindled my love for literature and history.

My professional training began at Cornell University (BA 1948) and continued at Columbia University where I obtained my MA (1960), and at Johns Hopkins University, where I obtained my Ph.D. (1963). It was at Cornell that my scientific interests shifted from physics and chemistry to economics and history. The switch in focus was precipitated by the widespread pessimism about the future of the economy during the second half of the 1940s, when forecasts about the imminent return to the massive unemployment of the Great Depression were rife.

I began my graduate training with the naive belief that by combining the study of history and economics I would quickly discover the fundamental forces that had determined technological and institutional changes over the ages and that such knowledge would point to solutions to the current problems of economic instability and inequity. As I became aware of how little was actually known about these large processes and their interconnections, I began to focus on more discrete issues: What did we really know about the role of the factory system in economic and institutional change during the nineteenth century? What was the nature and the magnitude of the contribution of particular new technologies, such as railroads or steel mills, to economic growth? I also concluded that to answer such questions, much greater use had to be made of quantitative evidence, so I set out to master the most advanced analytical and statistical methods that were then taught in the economics department. It was only later that I discovered that the training program I had worked out for myself was unorthodox for an economic historian.

The two teachers who influenced me the most during my year at Columbia were George J. Stigler, who taught the graduate microeconomics sequence, and Carter Goodrich, who taught the sequence in American economic history. Stigler made microeconomic theory come alive. He emphasized not its elegance but its applicability to a wide range of issues in economic policy. He continually moved between theory and evidence, carefully considering the empirical validity for the assumptions that theorists made abóut the slope or other aspects of the shape of key functions. He often considered when, with what model, and under what implicit assumptions one could draw a particular inference from a given body of data.

Goodrich impressed me not only with his knowledge of the literature of American economic history, but with his willingness to identify the gaps in the profession's collective knowledge of key issues. By the end of the course one not only had a good grasp of what was known about the process of American economic growth, but a list of potential projects. It was to Goodrich that I turned for advice on my master's thesis. He was then engaged in research for his book *Government Promotion of Canals and Railroads* and raised a number of issues that puzzled him about the financing, riskiness, and benefits of the Union Pacific Railroad. These questions became the subject matter of my master's thesis, which was also my first published book. Although Goodrich did not himself make use of the new mathematical and statistical methods of economics, he encouraged me to do so. He also suggested that, given my substantial interests and quantitative approaches to economic history, Simon Kuznets at Johns Hopkins was probably the best economist to guide my future training.

The teachers who taught me the most at Johns Hopkins, aside from Simon Kuznets, were Abba Lerner and Fritz Machlup in microeconomic theory; Evsey Domar in macroeconomic theory and the theory of economic growth; T.C. Liu in mathematical economics, and two teachers of mathematical statistics and of sampling design in the School of Public Health.

Simon Kuznets, who supervised my doctoral dissertation, was by far the most influential figure in my graduate training. Soft spoken and of moderate stature, one did not have to be in his class very long to discover that he was a towering intellect, erudite not only in economics, but also in history, demography, statistics, and the natural sciences. His course in economic growth covered the history of technological change during the modern era, demography and population theory, and the use of national income aggregates for the comparative study of economic growth and of the size distribution of income. It was not until some years later that I realized the course presented the substance of the research that later appeared in a series of 10 supplements to *Economic Development and Cultural Change* and in his 1966 monograph, *Modern Economic Growth: Rate, Structure, and Spread*—the work for which he was awarded the third Nobel Prize in economics. Kuznets's course was valuable not only for the substance of the material but also for the way that he used the material to transmit the art of measurement. He repeatedly demonstrated that the central statistical problem in economics was not random error but systematic biases in the data, and he conveyed a number of powerful approaches to coping with that problem, particularly emphasizing the role of sensitivity analysis.

By the time I left residence at Johns Hopkins, I had worked out a two-pronged research strategy that I thought could keep me going for a decade or more. The first was to measure the impact of key scientific and technological innovations, key governmental policies, and key environmental and institutional changes on the course of economic growth. The second was to promote the wider use of the mathematical models and statistical methods of economics in studying the complex, long-term processes that were the focus of economic historians. In my mind these two objectives were closely interrelated. The best argument for the new methods was the demonstration that in the study of particular issues, such as the contribution of railroads to economic growth, these methods were superior to traditional approaches. The new methods made it possible to lay out the key analytical issues in a manner that made them amenable to measurement, to identify the categories of evidence needed to resolve the points at issue, to develop techniques of measurement that were suitable for both the issues and the available evidence, and to assess the robustness of the results.

Several factors made the realization of my research program possible. One was the willingness of university administrators to provide me with a generous share of the limited research funds at their disposal, a *sine qua non* for work that was both labor and computer intensive. Even when I was still an unproven new assistant professor at Rochester, Lionel W. McKenzie provided several research assistants, a computer programmer, and all of the computer time I could use. Deans D. Gale Johnson and Robert McC. Adams made similar investments in my research at Chicago during the 1960s and early 1970s at levels that reflected as much their estimates of my promise as of accomplishments. This type of support was continued at Harvard by Henry Rosovsky during the last half of the 1970s.

Except for a small grant from the Social Science Research Council (SSRC) when I was still a student at Johns Hopkins, my work on railroads was supported exclusively from university funds. Since my later projects were based on ever-larger data sets, obtained primarily from manuscript sources at archives, these projects could not have been carried out without the generous support of foundations, particularly the National Science Foundation (NSF) and the National Institutes of Health (NIH), but to a significant degree also such private foundations as the Ford Foundation, the Exxon Educational Foundation, and the Walgreen Foundation Endowment Fund. University funding still remained crucial since it took considerable outlays of funds to bring a large project to a point that could win approval from peer review committees.

Another key factor was the plunging cost of data processing made possible by rapid advances in computer hardware and software. These technological developments made it feasible to work with ever-larger data sets. By linking together the data on individuals and households from a wide range of archival sources, data sets could be customized for particular economic issues. The sources include the manuscript schedules of decennial censuses, probate records, military and pension records, genealogies, tax rolls, death certificates, and public health records.

Still another important factor in making such research feasible was the cooperation of officials at the U. S. National Archives and of the Genealogical Library of the Church of Jesus Christ of Latter-Day Saints in Salt Lake City. The Genealogical Library is especially valuable because it is a depository for vast quantities of records from all over the United States, and from many other countries, relevant to economic, social, and biomedical research. Although collected for religious reasons, officials of the Library have made their holdings available to the scientific community, providing a resource that would otherwise have required enormous sums of money to reproduce.

No single organization has contributed more to the study of long-term economic growth than the National Bureau of Economic Research (NBER). The long-term approach figured prominently in NBER research programs conducted between the late 1930s and the late 1960s. That work, which was conducted mainly at the macro level, was a continuation of the Bureau's pioneering work in the development of national income accounts and related measures of macroeconomic behavior. However, during the 1970s the Bureau's work on long-term growth processes had waned. When Martin Feldstein became President of the NBER in 1977 he decided to undertake a new program on the long-term Development of the American Economy (DAE), and asked me to be its program director.

I appointed an executive committee consisting of Lance E. Davis, Stanley L. Engerman, Robert M. Gallman, Claudia D. Goldin, Clayne L. Pope, and myself to chart the direction of the new program. After reviewing the Bureau's past work, and the new direction it was taking under Feldstein's leadership, the committee sought to identify a set of current policy issues to which the DAE could contribute. In the course of this review we consulted with Simon Kuznets, Douglass C. North, Richard A. Easterlin, and Moses Abramovitz, among others.

After more than a year of investigation, we concluded that to understand the sources of the long-term decline in saving and investment rates, the factors influencing the rate of technological change, or the long-term shifts in the demographic structure of the population and the labor force, we needed to know much more about microeconomic behavior than was known at the time. Research at the microeconomic level, however, had been inhibited by the absence of suitable data. The DAE, therefore, turned its attention to the problem of constructing new data sets capable of illuminating the relationship between the current and the past behavior of families and firms.

The executive committee launched a series of pilot projects investigating the feasibility of creating several representative data sets consisting of intergenerationally linked families. Such data sets would open up entirely new possibilities for examining the interaction of economic and cultural factors and their mutual influence on such variables as the saving rate, the rate of female entry into the labor force, fertility and mortality rates, the inequality of the wealth distribution, migration rates, and rates of economic and social mobility. These data sets could not be created from a single set of records but required the linking of several different types of archival records. The executive committee also began a pilot study on the feasibility of constructing data sets based on firm records that would permit the analysis of the way that firms respond to the changing technological opportunities that are open to them, as well as to the changing institutional and legal environment in which they must operate. Dealing with such issues required the development of representative sets of firm records stretching over long periods of time that not only contained information on the decision-making processes of these firms, but also on the economic consequences of the decisions.

The DAE's review of the pilot projects concluded that the design of portable computers for data retrieval, and of software to manipulate large files, had developed to the point where the creation of such microeconomic data sets was feasible. A score of projects were set out by 1980 and investigators to lead them were chosen. Claudia Goldin, who became the director of the DAE in 1991, reported that there are now some forty DAE research associates. Since the start of the DAE, they have created over fifty longitudinal and cross-sectional data sets that span the period from the late 1700s to the present. These data sets have formed the basis for scores of papers, several conference volumes and a number of monographs.

My ability to work on the problem of creating and studying large life-cycle and intergenerational data sets reached a new level in 1981 when Richard N. Rosett, then Dean of the Graduate School of Business at The University of Chicago, invited me to succeed George J. Stigler as the Charles R. Walgreen Professor of American Institutions. In addition to the unusual research fund endowed by Walgreen, Rosett offered to establish a Center for Population Economics (CPE) that would focus on the interaction of economic, demographic, and biological processes over life-cycles and generations. The invitation was enthusiastically supported by Hanna Gray, who was then the President of The University of Chicago. The generous support of the CPE has been continued by John P. Gould, who succeeded Rosett as Dean, by Robert S. Hamada, the current Dean, and by Hugo F. Sonnenschein, President of The University of Chicago.

Without the resources of the Walgreen Chair and the CPE the current research projects on which I reported in the Prize Lecture would not have been possible. The data on health conditions, for example, comes from a project called "Early Indicators of Later Work Levels, Disease, & Death," which is tracing nearly 40,000 Union Army men from the cradle to the grave. It takes over 15,000 variables to describe the life-cycle history of one of these men. These life-cycle histories are created by linking about a score of data sets. It took more than half a decade of work to investigate the potential of these data sets, work out procedures for data retrieval and file management, and to establish the feasibility of the enterprise in our own minds.

The site committee of the National Institutes of Health which reviewed the original project proposal in 1986 agreed that such a project could in principle make a significant contribution to an understanding of the process of aging, but they were skeptical about the quality of some of the data, about whether the software and programming procedures we had developed by that time were adequate for the management of such a large data set, and about whether the project could be completed within the proposed budget. To resolve these doubts it was necessary to draw a six percent subsample which linked together all of the separate sources and which demonstrated the effectiveness of the software by analyzing the information in the subsample. It took an additional four years to complete the second phase of the justification of the project. Thus nearly a decade of preliminary research, much of it funded by Walgreen and the CPE, was required before the project was accepted by the peer reviewers of NIH and NSF.

No individual has done more to help me pursue a career in science than my wife of forty-five years. I met Enid Cassandra Morgan during the election campaign of 1948 when she was a Sunday school teacher, a leader of the youth organizations of St. Phillips Episcopal Church, and the head of Harlem Youth for the election of Henry Wallace. Over the years Enid has been both my most confident supporter and my keenest critic. During my graduate training her earnings contributed significantly to the income of our family. When I was an assistant professor she combined care of the children with many hours of unpaid labor as a research assistant in library archives. She helped boost my self-confidence when my unorthodox findings provoked controversy and criticisms, and she often provided insightful suggestions for the improvement of my lectures, papers, books, letters, and research proposals.

Throughout the years she has been the overseer of my social conscience, pulling me back to reality when she saw that my preoccupation with the abstract aspects of scientific issues had led me to extenuate their deeply human aspects. I also benefitted greatly from her experiences as Student Counselor, Dean of Students, and Director of Student Life at Rochester, Harvard, and Chicago. She has helped me to understand the administrator's point of view and to improve what she and my sons refer to as "people skills."

My sons, Michael and Steven, have shared in the joys and the tribulations of being raised by academic parents. They have encouraged me to adhere steadfastly to scholarly principles in the face of unfair criticisms. They have read my papers and books, offered helpful suggestions, and sometimes helped substantially in the process of editing, teaching me how to say more with fewer words.

One aspect of the plunging cost of data processing has been the emergence of large-scale collaborative projects in economic history. Such projects have been promoted partly by economies of scale in the retrieval and cleaning of the data sets and partly by the wide range of skills required to manipulate, analyze and interpret the data. There were, for example, thirty-five contributors to the three technical volumes of *Without Consent or Contract*, many of them former students who are now distinguished senior investigators. The research team for the "Early Indicators" project is even larger. It has been my good fortune to have had access not only to the pool of talented students at Chicago, but also to those at Harvard and Rochester. In both the slavery and aging projects these students were often far ahead of the senior investigators in recognizing major unanticipated findings, in proposing novel approaches to the analysis of the data, in discovering new data sets, and in offering probing criticisms.

It is known far and wide among economic historians that much of the credit for the success of my research enterprises goes to Marilyn Coopersmith who has worked with me for more than a quarter of a century. She was the administrative assistant of the DAE program from its inception until 1991, and she has been the associate director of the CPE since 1981. She is not only an effective coordinator but has been a diligent researcher and a friend to a legion of graduate research assistants, who often turned to her for help in overcoming bureaucratic obstacles.

The companionship of scholars and the thrill of continuous learning are two wonderful aspects of a life in science. When one is engaged with students who are both very curious and very bright, it is never quite clear who is teaching whom. I have also had the good fortune of collaborating with senior investigators who are all exceptional teachers with enthusiasm for their work and with great patience for the bewilderment of novices. Their guidance greatly facilitated my efforts to train myself for research involving the interconnections between economics, demography, and the biomedical sciences. James Trussell tutored me as I tried to master the mathematical models of demography and the art of applying them to incomplete data. J.M. Tanner has spent numerous hours teaching me the fundamentals of the branch of medicine called auxology (the study of human growth), looking at our data and helping to interpret them, guiding me through basic texts, calling my attention to the latest relevant papers, and reading and criticizing my work. I received a similar education from Nevin S. Scrimshaw in epidemiology (particularly of infectious diseases), in nutrition, and in some aspects of both physiology and clinical medicine.

ECONOMIC GROWTH, POPULATION THEORY, AND PHYSIOLOGY: THE BEARING OF LONG-TERM PROCESSES ON THE MAKING OF ECONOMIC POLICY

Nobel Lecture, December 9, 1993

by

ROBERT WILLIAM FOGEL

University of Chicago, Center for Population Economics, Chicago, IL 60637, USA

Economic history has contributed significantly to the formulation of economic theory.* Among the economists who have found history an important source for their ideas are Smith, Malthus, Marx, Marshall, Keynes, Hicks, Arrow, Friedman, Solow, and Becker. Failure to take account of history, as Simon Kuznets (1941) stressed, has often led to a misunderstanding of current economic problems by investigators who have not realized that their generalizations rested upon transient circumstances. Nowhere is the need to recognize the role of long-run dynamics more relevant than in such pressing current issues as medical care, pension policies, and development policies.

This lecture sketches a theory of the secular decline in morbidity and mortality that takes account of changes induced in physiological functioning since 1700. The synergism between technological and physiological improvements has produced a form of human evolution, biological though

* Prepared for presentation as the Prize Lecture in Economic Sciences in Memory of Alfred Nobel, December 9, 1993. Since this lecture is based on research still in progress, it is important to emphasize that the findings reported here are provisional and are subject to change as the current databases expand and as the analyses of these data are refined. Nevertheless, I believe that the general outlines of the emerging new theories of mortality, morbidity, and aging are likely to survive further research. Research reported in this paper was supported by grants from the National Institutes of Health (#PO1-AG10120–02), the National Science Foundation (#SES-9114981), and the Walgreen Foundation. I have benefitted from comments and criticisms by Christopher J. Acito, Robert McC. Adams, Gary S. Becker, Christine K. Cassel, Katherine A. Chavigny, Dora L. Costa, William J. Darby, Partha Dasgupta, Sidney Davidson, Stanley L. Engerman, Phyllis Eveleth, Enid M. Fogel, Milton Friedman, Victor R. Fuchs, Zvi Griliches, Robin M. Hogarth, Susan E. Jones, John M. Kim, Peter Laslett, Lionel W. McKenzie, Reynaldo Martorell, Douglass C. North, S. Jay Olshansky, Clayne L. Pope, Samuel H. Preston, Irwin Rosenberg, Roger A. Schofield, Nevin S. Scrimshaw, Robert M. Solow, Richard H. Steckel, David Surdam, Richard Suzman, James M. Tanner, Peter Temin, James Trussell, James W. Vaupel, Hans T. Waaler, Larry T. Wimmer, and E.A. Wrigley.

not genetic, rapid, culturally transmitted, and not necessarily stable, which is still ongoing in both OECD and developing countries. Thermodynamic and physiological aspects of economic growth are defined and their impact on growth rates is assessed. Implications of this theory for population forecasting, measurement of national income, demand for leisure, pension policies, and demand for health care are considered.

* * *

The attempt to explain the secular decline in mortality in a systematic way did not begin until after World War I because before that time it was uncertain whether such a decline was in progress. There were two reasons for the delay in recognizing the phenomenon. First, little was known about mortality rates before the end of the Napoleonic wars. Hardly a dozen life tables had been constructed before 1815 by various pioneers in demography and they exhibited no clear time trend (Dublin and Lotka 1936; Gille 1949). Second, there was little evidence in the first four official English life tables, covering the years 1831–80, of a downward trend in mortality.

By the third decade of the twentieth century, however, it became obvious that the new declines in British mortality rates were not just a cyclical phenomenon. Between 1871 and 1901 life expectation in Britain increased by 4 years. During the next three decades there was an additional gain of 16 years. Similar declines in mortality were recorded in other European nations.

The plunge in mortality rates during the early decades of the twentieth century delivered a major blow to the Malthusian theory of population. Improvements in mortality were supposed to be short lived because, under the conditions of population pressure against the food supply that Malthus specified, the elimination of deaths due to one disease would be replaced by those due to some other malady. Efforts to reconcile Malthusian doctrine with the observed mortality decline, to modify it, or to replace it produced a large new literature.

1. EXPLAINING THE SECULAR DECLINE IN MORTALITY

The drive to explain the secular decline in mortality pushed research in three directions. First, there was a concerted effort to develop time series of death rates that extended as far back in time as possible in order to determine just when the decline in mortality began. Second, the available data on mortality rates were analyzed in order to identify factors that might explain the decline as well as to establish patterns or "laws" that would allow predictions of the future course of mortality.

Third, a widespread effort was undertaken to determine the relationship between the food supply and mortality rates. There were several aspects to this effort. Perhaps the most important was the emergence of a science of nutrition that identified a series of diseases related to specific nutritional deficiencies and discovered the synergy between nutrition and infection

Fig. 1: The Secular Trends in Mortality Rates in England and France.

PART A. England: 1553 – 1975

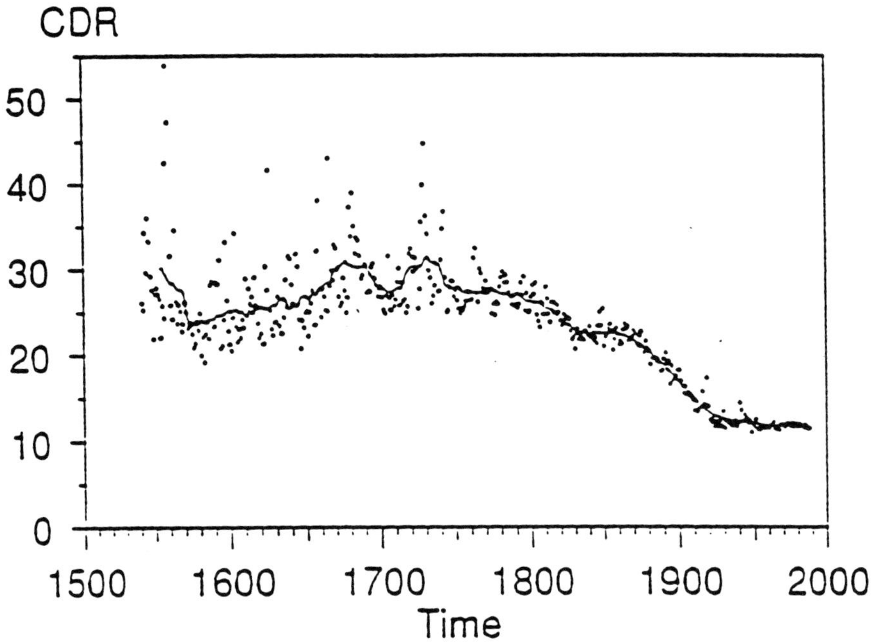

PART B. France: 1752 – 1974

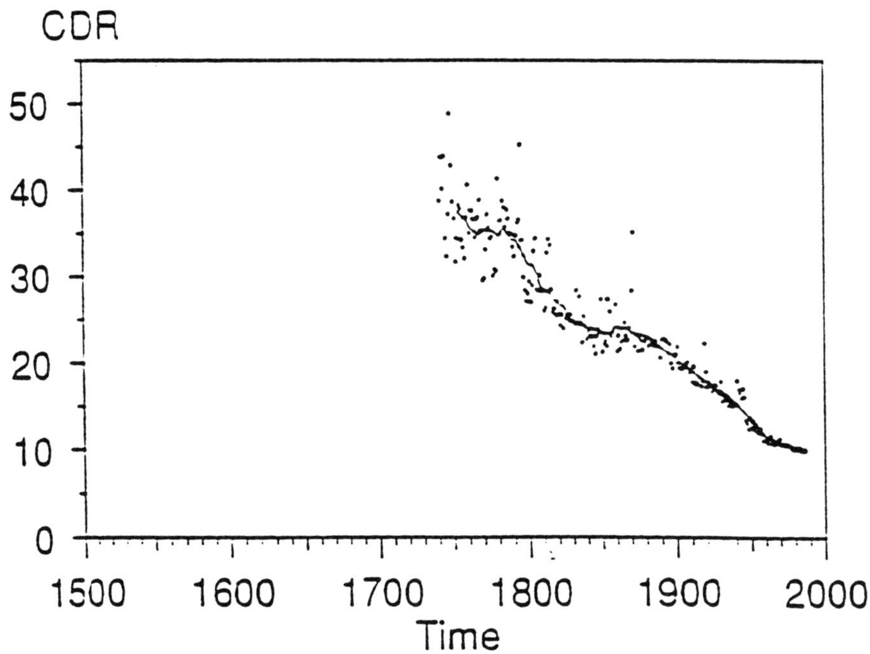

Note: Each diagram shows the scatter of annual death rates around a 25-year moving average. See Fogel and Floud 1994 for sources and procedures.

(Scrimshaw, Taylor and Gordon 1968). Another aspect was the emergence of the field of development economics after World War II as part of the campaign to close the yawning gap in income, health, and life expectancy between the industrialized nations and the "developing nations." Still another aspect was the combined effort of economic and demographic historians to study the role of mortality crises and their relationship to famines during the seventeenth and eighteenth centuries.

Prior to the 1960s, efforts to reconstruct the secular trend in European mortality were focused primarily on notable local communities and parishes. However, developments in statistical techniques and the remarkable reductions in computational costs during the 1960s and 1970s made it possible to draw and process large nationally representative samples. The results of these efforts, combined with official statistics after 1830 in France and after 1871 in England, are displayed in Figure 1. Analysis of the French and English series revealed that the secular decline in mortality took place in two waves. In the English case, the first wave began during the second quarter of the eighteenth century (18—II) and lasted through 19-I after which mortality rates stabilized for half a century. The decline resumed during 19-IV and continues through the present. The French case is similar except that the first wave of the decline in mortality began about half a century earlier in France and its rate of decline during the first wave was more rapid.

Perhaps the most surprising aspect of Figure 1 is the implication that the elimination of crisis mortality, whether related to famines or not, accounted for less than 10 percent of the secular decline in mortality rates (Wrigley and Schofield 1981; Lee 1981; Dupâquier 1989; Weir 1982 and 1989; Richards 1984; Galloway 1986; Fogel 1992b). Similar results were obtained by studies of official statistics for Sweden (Bengtsson and Ohlsson 1984, 1985; Galloway 1987; cf. Eckstein, Schultz, and Wolpin 1984; Perrenoud 1984 and 1991; Fridlizius 1984). By demonstrating that famines and famine mortality are a secondary issue in the escape from the high mortality rates of the early modern era, these studies shifted attention to the neglected issue of chronic malnutrition as the principal pathway through which malnutrition contributed to the high mortality rates of the past (cf. Sen 1981).

2. THE SYNERGY BETWEEN BIOMEDICAL AND ECONOMIC ANALYSES OF THE SECULAR TREND IN CHRONIC MALNUTRITION

Recently developed biomedical techniques, when integrated with economic techniques, make it possible to probe deeply into the extent of chronic malnutrition from the beginning of the eighteenth century in Europe and North America, to chart and explain the escape from such malnutrition, and to consider the impact of improved nutrition on the secular trend in health and life expectation, on labor productivity, and on economic growth. The combination of the economic and biomedical modes of analysis has been synergistic since it has yielded analytical insights that could not have been obtained merely by relying on the techniques of one of the disciplines.

Malnutrition can be caused either by an inadequate diet or by claims on that diet (including work and disease) so great as to produce malnutrition despite a nutrient intake that in other circumstances might be deemed adequate.[1] There can be little doubt that the high disease rates prevalent during the early modern era would have caused malnutrition even with diets otherwise adequate in calories, protein, and other critical nutrients. However, recent research indicates that, for many European nations before the middle of the nineteenth century, the national production of food was at such low levels that the poorer classes were bound to have been malnourished under any conceivable circumstance, and that the high disease rates of the period were not merely a cause of malnutrition but undoubtedly, to a considerable degree, a consequence of exceedingly poor diets.

2.1 Energy Cost Accounting and Secular Trends in Body Size

As a result of the work of agricultural historians we now have estimates of British agricultural production by half-century intervals going back to 1700. These provide the basis for national food balance sheets which indicate the secular trend in British caloric consumption (Chartres 1985; Holderness 1989; Allen 1994). Supplemented by household surveys of food purchases (Shammas 1984 and 1990; Oddy 1990; cf. Fogel 1987), these sources indicate that average daily caloric consumption in Britain c.1790 was about 2,060 kcal per capita or about 2,700 kcal per consuming unit (equivalent adult males). For France, Toutain (1971) has constructed estimates from national food balance sheets going back to the decade preceding the French Revolution. His estimates indicate that the daily per capita caloric consumption was 1,753 kcal during 1781–90 and 1,846 during 1803–12. Converted into calories per consuming unit, these figures become 2,290 and 2,410.

One implication of these estimates is that mature adults of the late eighteenth century must have been very small by current standards. Today the typical American male in his early thirties is about 177 cm (69.7 inches) tall and weighs about 78 kg (172 lbs) (USDHHS 1987). Such a male requires daily about 1,794 kcal for basal metabolism (the energy required to keep the body functioning while at rest) and a total of 2,279 kcal for baseline maintenance (the 1,794 kcal required for basal metabolism plus 485 kcal for digestion of food and vital hygiene) (Quenouille et al. 1951; FAO/UNU/WHO 1985). If either the British or the French had been that large during the eighteenth century, virtually all of the energy produced by their food supplies would have been required for maintenance and hardly any would have been available to sustain work. To have the energy necessary to produce the national products of these two countries c.1700, the typical adult male must have been quite short and very light.

This inference is supported by data on stature and weight which have been collected for European nations. Table 1 provides estimates of final

Table 1. Entimated Average Final Heights of Men Who Reached Maturity Between 1750 and 1875 in Six European Populations, by Quarter Centuries (cm)

	(1) Date of maturity by century and quarter	(2) Great Britain	(3) Norway	(4) Sweden	(5) France	(6) Denmark	(7) Hungary
1.	18–III	165.9	163.9	168.1	–	–	168.7
2.	18–IV	167.9	–	166.7	163.0	165.7	165.8
3.	19–I	168.0	–	166.7	164.3	165.4	163.9
4.	19–II	171.6	–	168.0	165.2	166.8	164.2
5.	19–III	169.3	168.5	165.6	165.6	165.3	–
6.	20–III	175.0	178.3	177.6	172.0	176.0	170.9

Sources: Fogel 1987. Table 7 for all columns except 5. *Col. 5;* Rows 3–5 were computed from Meerton 1989 as amended by Weir (1993) with 0.9 cm added to allow for additional growth between age 20 and manturity (Gould 1869, 104–105: cf Friedman 1982, 510, n. 14). The entry to row 2 is derived from a linear extrapolation of Meerton's data for 1815–1836 back to 1788, with 0.9 cm added for additional growth between age 20 and maturity. The entry in row 6 is from Fogel 1987, Table 7.

heights of adult males who reached maturity between 1750 and 1875. It shows that during the eighteenth and nineteenth centuries Europeans were severely stunted by modern standards (cf. line 6 of Table 1). Estimates of weights for European nations before 1860 are much more patchy. Those which are available, mostly inferential, suggest that c.1790 the average weight of English males in their thirties was about 61 kg (134 lbs), which is about 20 percent below current levels. The corresponding figure for French males c.1790 may have been only about 50 kg (about 110 lbs), which is about a third below current standards.

2.2 *Size Distributions of Calories*

The synergy between the economic and biomedical lines of analysis is apparent in the new insights obtained by switching from a reliance on the mean height, the mean weights, and the mean daily consumption of nutrients to the size distributions of these variables. Because of the limits of time, I focus here on the distributions of calories.[2]

Size distributions of caloric consumption are one of the most potent instruments in assessing the plausibility of proffered estimates of average diets. They not only bear on the implications of a given level of caloric consumption for morbidity and mortality rates, but they also indicate whether the calories available for work are consistent with the level of agricultural output and with the distribution of the labor force between agriculture and nonagriculture (Fogel and Floud 1994; Fogel 1991; cf. Wrigley 1987). Although national food-balance sheets, such as those constructed by Toutain (1971) for France over the period 1781–1952, provide mean values of per capita caloric consumption, they do not produce estimates of the size distribution of calories.[3]

Three factors make it possible to estimate the size distributions of calories from the patchy evidence available to historians. First, studies covering a wide range of countries indicate that distributions of calories are well described by the lognormal distribution. Second, the variation in the distribution of calories (as measured by the coefficient of variation [$s/\bar{X}$] or the Gini [G] ratio) is far more limited than the distribution of income. Third, when the mean of the distribution is known, the coefficient of variation (which together with the mean determines the distribution) can be estimated from information in either tail of the distribution. Fortunately, even in places and periods where little is known about ordinary people, there is a relative abundance of information about the rich. At the bottom end, it is demographic information, particularly the death rate, which rather tightly constrains the proportion of the population whose average daily consumption of calories could have been below BMR or baseline maintenance.

Table 2 shows the exceedingly low level of work capacity permitted by the food supply in France and England c.1790, even after allowing for the reduced requirements for maintenance because of small stature and body mass (cf. Freudenberger and Cummins 1976). In France the bottom 10 percent of the labor force lacked the energy for regular work and the next 10 percent had enough energy for less than 3 hours of light work daily (0.52 hours of heavy work). Although the English situation was somewhat better,

Table 2. A Comparison of the Probable French and English Distrubutions of the Daily Consumption of Kcals per Consuming Unit Toward the End of the Eighteenth Century

		A France c. 1785 $\bar{X}$ = 2.290 ($s/\bar{X}$) = 0.3		B England C. 1790 $\bar{X}$ = 2.700 ($s/\bar{X}$) = 0.3	
	Decile (1)	Daily kcal consumption (2)	Cumulative % (3)	Daily kcal consumption (4)	Cumulative % (5)
1.	Highest	3.672	100	4.329	100
2.	Ninth	2.981	84	3.514	84
3.	Eighth	2.676	71	3.155	71
4.	Seventh	2.457	59	2.897	59
5.	Sixth	2.276	48	2.684	48
6.	Fifth	2.114	38	2.492	38
7.	Fourth	1.958	29	2.309	29
8.	Third	1.798	21	2.120	21
9.	Second	1.614	13	1.903	13
10.	First	1.310	6	1.545	6

Sources: See Fogel (1993b), especially table 4 and the appendix.

the bottom 3 percent of its labor force lacked the energy for any work, but the balance of the bottom 20 percent had enough energy for about 6 hours of light work (1.09 hours of heavy work) each day.

Table 2 also points up the problem with the assumption that for *ancien régime* populations, a caloric intake that averaged 2,000 kcal per capita (2,600 per consuming unit) daily was adequate (Livi-Bacci 1990). That average level of consumption falls between the levels experienced by the French and the English c.1790. In populations experiencing such low levels of average consumption, the bottom 20 percent subsisted on such poor diets that they were effectively excluded from the labor force, with many of them lacking the energy even for a few hours of strolling. That appears to be the principal factor explaining why beggars constituted as much as a fifth of the populations of *ancien régimes* (Goubert 1973; Cipolla 1980; Laslett 1984). Even the majority of those in the top 80 percent of the caloric distribution were so stunted (height below U.S. standards) and wasted (weight below U.S. standards) that they were at substantially higher risk of incurring chronic health conditions and of premature mortality (see the next section).

3. WAALER CURVES AND SURFACES: A NEW ANALYTICAL TOOL

Extensive clinical and epidemiological studies over the past two decades have shown that height at given ages, weight at given ages, and weight-for-height (a body mass index, or BMI) are effective predictors of the risk of morbidity and mortality. Until recently most of the studies have focused on children under age 5, using one or more of the anthropometric indicators at these ages to assess risks of morbidity and mortality in early childhood, and it was at these ages that the relevance of anthropometric measures originally were established most firmly (Sommer and Lowenstein 1975; Chen, Chowdhury, and Huffman 1980; Billewicz and MacGregor 1982; Kielmann et al. 1983; Martorell 1985). During the last few years, however, a considerable body of evidence has accumulated suggesting that height at maturity is also an important predictor of the probability of dying and of developing chronic diseases at middle and late ages (Marmot, Shipley, and Rose 1984; Waaler 1984; John 1988; Costa 1993; Kim 1993). BMI has similar predictive properties (Heywood 1983; Waaler 1984; Martorell 1985; Payne 1992; Osmani 1992; cf. Srinivasan 1992).

Height and BMI measure different aspects of malnutrition and health. Height is a net rather than a gross measure of nutrition. Moreover, although changes in height during the growing years are sensitive to current levels of nutrition, mean final height reflects the accumulated past nutritional experience of individuals throughout their growing years, including the fetal period. It follows that when final heights are used to explain differences in adult mortality rates, they reveal the effect, not of adult levels of nutrition on adult mortality rates, but of nutritional levels during infancy, childhood, and adolescence on adult mortality rates. A weight-for-height index, on the other hand, reflects primarily the current nutritional status. It is also a net measure in the sense that BMI reflects the balance between current intakes and the claims on those intakes.

3.1 The Relationship Between Body Size and the Risk of Death at Middle and Late Ages

A number of recent studies have established the predictive power of height and BMI with respect to morbidity and mortality at later ages. The results of two of these studies are summarized in Figures 2 and 3. Part A of Figure 2 reproduces a diagram by Waaler (1984). It shows that short Norwegian men aged 40–59 at risk between 1963 and 1979 were much more likely to die than tall men. Indeed, the risk of mortality for men with heights of 165 cm (65.0 inches) was on average 71 percent greater than that of men who measure 182.5 cm (71.9 inches). Part B shows that height is also an important predictor of the relative likelihood that men aged 23–49 would be rejected from the Union Army during 1861–65 because of chronic diseases. Despite significant differences in ethnicities, environmental circumstances, the array and severity of diseases, and time, the functional relationship between height and relative risk are strikingly similar in the two cases.

Waaler (1984) has also studied the relationship in Norway between BMI and the risk of death in a sample of 1.7 million individuals. Curves summarizing his findings are shown in Figure 3 for both men and women. Although the observed values of the BMI (kg/m^2) ranged between 17 and 39, over 80 percent of the males over age 40 had BMI's within the range 21–29. Within the range 22–28, the curve is relatively flat, with the relative risk of mortality hovering close to 1.0. However, at BMIs of less than 22 and over 28, the risk of death rises quite sharply as the BMI moves away from its mean value. It will be noticed that the BMI curves are much more symmetrical than the height curves in Figure 2, which indicates that high BMIs are as risky as low ones.

Although Figures 2 and 3 are revealing, they are not sufficient to shed light on the debate over whether moderate stunting impairs health when weight-for-height is adequate, since Figure 2 is not controlled for weight and Figure 3 is only partially controlled for height (Fogel 1987; Fogel and Floud 1994). To get at the "small-but-healthy" issue one needs an iso-mortality surface that relates the risk of death to both height and weight simultaneously. Such a surface, presented in Figure 4, was fitted to Waaler's data by a procedure described elsewhere (Fogel 1993b). Transecting the iso-mortality map are lines which give the locus of each BMI between 16 and 34, and a curve giving the weights that minimize risk at each height.

Figure 4 shows that even when body weight is maintained at what Figure 3 indicates is an "ideal" level (BMI = 25), short men are at substantially greater risk of death than tall men. Thus, an adult male with a BMI of 25 who is 164 cm tall is at about 55 percent greater risk of death than a male at 183 cm who also has a BMI of 25. Figure 4 also shows that the "ideal" BMI (the BMI that minimizes the risk of death) varies with height. A BMI of 25 is

Fig. 2: Comparison of the Relationship between Body Height and Relative Risk in Two Populations.

PART A. Relative Mortality Risk among Norwegian Men Aged 40–59, between 1963 and 1979

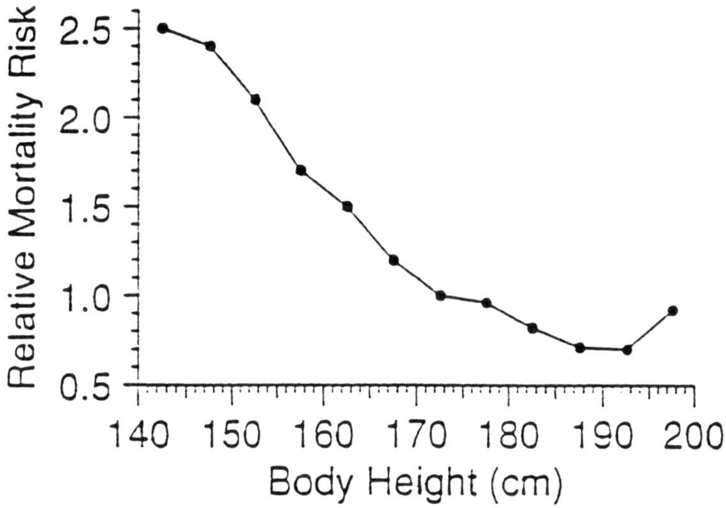

PART B. Relative Rejection Rates for Chronic Conditions in a Sample of 4,245 Men Aged 23–49, Examined for the Union Army

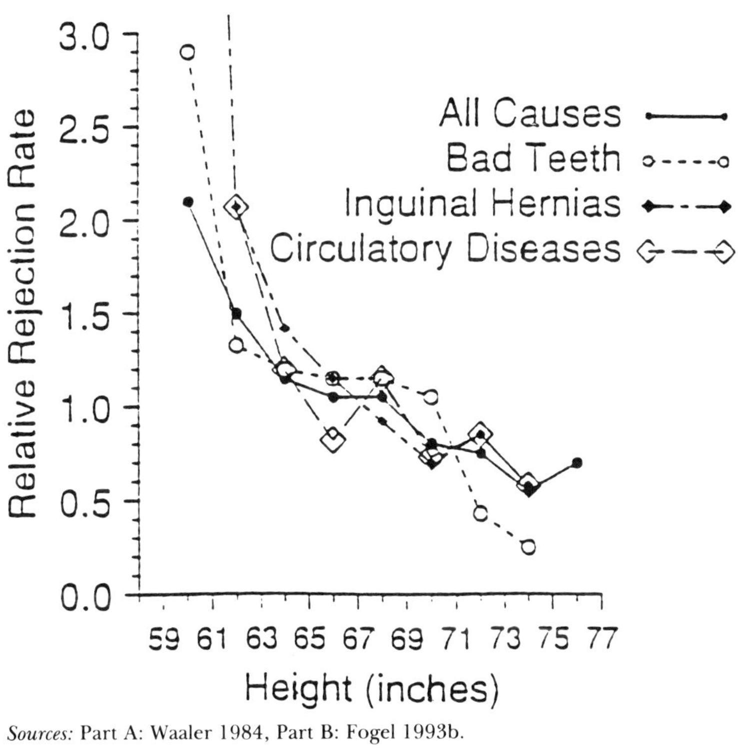

Sources: Part A: Waaler 1984, Part B: Fogel 1993b.

Fig. 3: Relationship between BMI and Prospective Risk among Norwegian Adults Aged 50 – 64 at Risk (1963 – 1979).

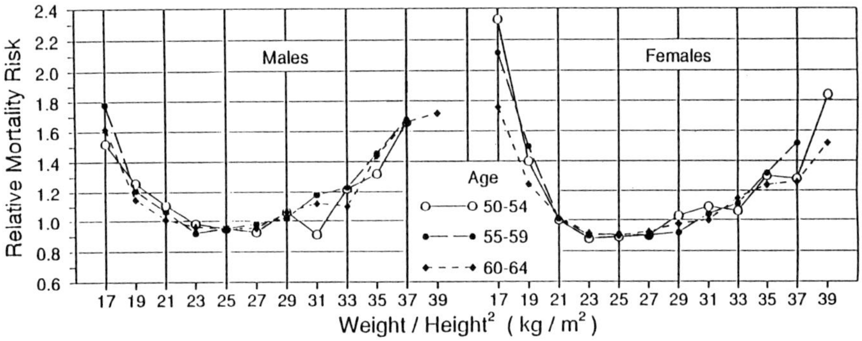

Source: Waaler 1984.

Fig. 4: Iso-Mortality Curves of Relative Risk for Height and Weight Among Norwegian Males Aged 50 – 64, With a Plot of the Estimated French Height and Weight at Four Dates.

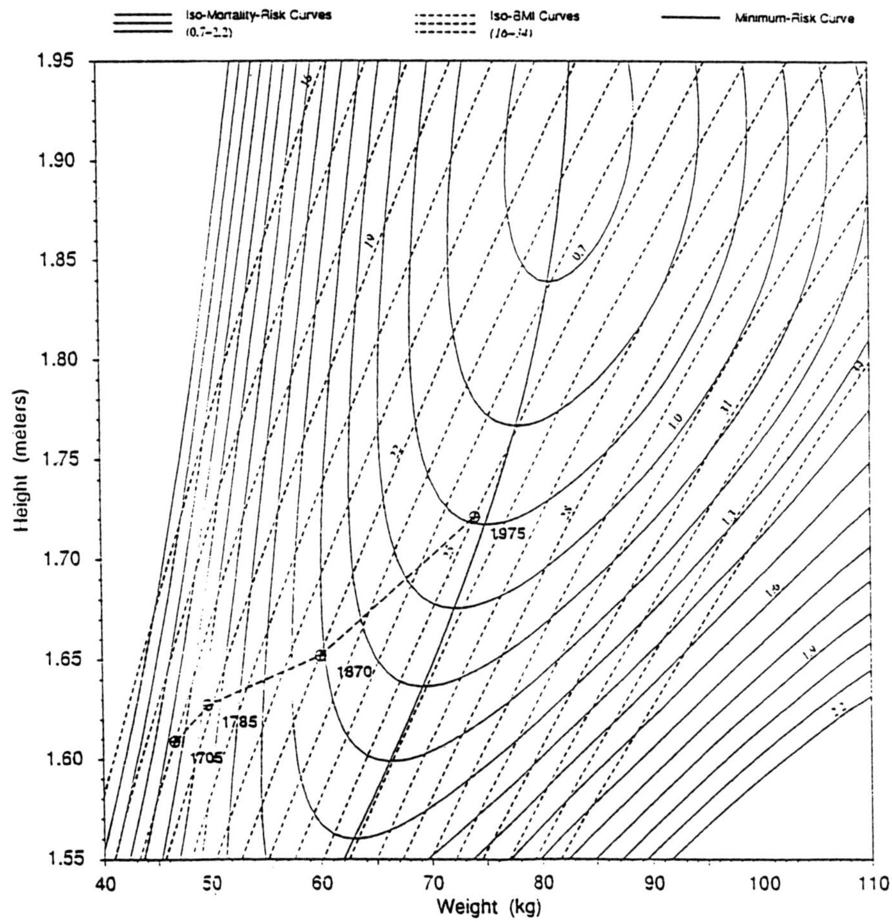

"ideal" for men in the neighborhood of 176 cm, but for tall men (greater than 183 cm) the "ideal" BMI is between 22 and 24, while for short men (under 168 cm) the "ideal" BMI is about 26.

3.2 Using Waaler Surfaces to Explain the Secular Decline in Mortality

Superimposed on Figure 4 are rough estimates of heights and weights in France at 4 dates. In 1705, the per capita food supply in France was lower than in Britain so that average body mass was probably even lower than in Britain. Circa 1705 the French probably achieved equilibrium with their food supply at an average height of about 161 cm and BMI of about 18. Over the next 270 years the food supply expanded with sufficient rapidity to permit both the height and the weight of adult males to increase. Figure 4 indicates that it was factors associated with the gain in BMI that accounted for most of the predicted reduction in the risk of mortality before 1870. After 1870, factors associated with the gain in height explain most of the predicted mortality decline. Figure 4 also implies that while these factors jointly explain about 90 percent of the actual decline in French mortality rates over the period between c.1785 and c.1870, they only explain about 50 percent of the actual decline in mortality rates during the past century. Increases in body size and the factors associated with it continued to have a major impact on the gains in life expectation among persons of relatively good nutritional status, but during the last century factors other than those related to height and BMI became increasingly important.

The analysis in this section points to the misleading nature of the concept of subsistence as Malthus originally used it and as it is still widely used today. Subsistence is not located at the edge of a nutritional cliff, beyond which lies demographic disaster. The evidence outlined in the paper implies that rather than one level of subsistence, there are numerous levels at which a population and a food supply can be in equilibrium, in the sense that they can be indefinitely sustained. However, some levels will have smaller people and higher "normal" (non-crisis) mortality than others.[4]

3.3 The Relevance of Waaler Surfaces for Predicting Trends in Chronic Diseases

Poor body builds increased vulnerability to diseases, not just contagious diseases, but chronic diseases as well. This point is implicit in Figure 2, which shows that chronic conditions were much more frequent among short young men in the 1860s than among tall men. Figure 5 shows that the same relationship between ill health and stature exists among the males covered by the U.S. National Health Interview Surveys (NHIS) for 1985–88. Stunting during developmental ages had a long reach and increased the likelihood that people would suffer from chronic diseases at middle and at late ages.

American males born during the second quarter of the nineteenth century were not only stunted by today's standards, but their BMIs at adult ages were about 15 percent lower than current U.S. levels (Fogel, Costa, and Kim 1993). The implication of the combined stunting and low BMI is

Fig. 5: The Relationship between Height and Relative Risk of Ill Health in NHIS Veterans Aged 40–59.

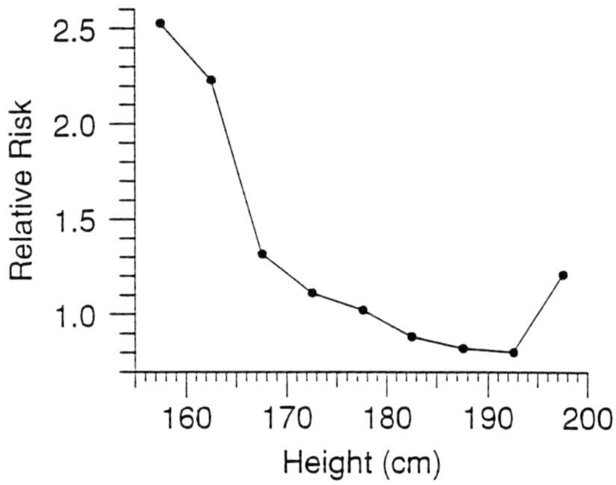

Source: Fogel, Costa, and Kim 1993.

brought out by Figure 6 which presents a Waaler surface for morbidity estimated by Kim (1993) from NHIS data for 1985–88.

The Waaler surface for risk from chronic conditions in Figure 6 is similar to, but not identical with, the Norwegian surface for mortality (see Figure 4). The iso-morbidity curves in ill health rise more steeply than the iso-mortality curves as one moves away in either direction from the optimal weight curve. Furthermore, the optimal weight curve in Figure 6 usually lies about one iso-BMI curve to the right of the optimal weight curve computed from the Norwegian mortality data. Thus, both the Norwegian mortality data and the U.S. health data indicate that for men in the neighborhood of 1.60–1.65 meters the optimal BMI is in the range of 25 to 27. This is above current levels recommended by FAO/WHO/UNU (1985), falling into the lower ranges of overweight in that standard.

Figure 6 also presents the coordinates in height and BMI of Union Army veterans who were 65 or over in 1910 and of veterans (mainly of World War II) who were the same ages during 1985–88. These coordinates predict a decline of about 35 percent in the prevalence of chronic disease among the two cohorts. About 61 percent of the predicted decline in ill health is due to factors associated with the increase in BMI and the balance is due to factors associated with increased stature.

The decline in the prevalence of chronic diseases predicted by Figure 6 is quite close to what actually occurred. Table 3 compares the prevalence of chronic diseases among Union Army men aged 65 and over in 1910 with two surveys of veterans of the same ages in the 1980s. That table indicates that heart disease was 2.9 times as prevalent, musculoskeletal and respiratory diseases were 1.6 times as prevalent, and digestive diseases were 4.7 times as prevalent among veterans aged 65 or over in 1910 as in 1985–88. During the 7.6 decades separating the two groups, the prevalence of heart disease among the elderly declined at a rate of 12.8 percent per decade,

Fig. 6: Health Improvement Predicted by NHIS 1985 – 1988 Health Surface.

All risks are measured relative to the average risk of morbidity (calculated over all heights and weights) among NHIS 1985 – 1988 white males aged 45 – 64.

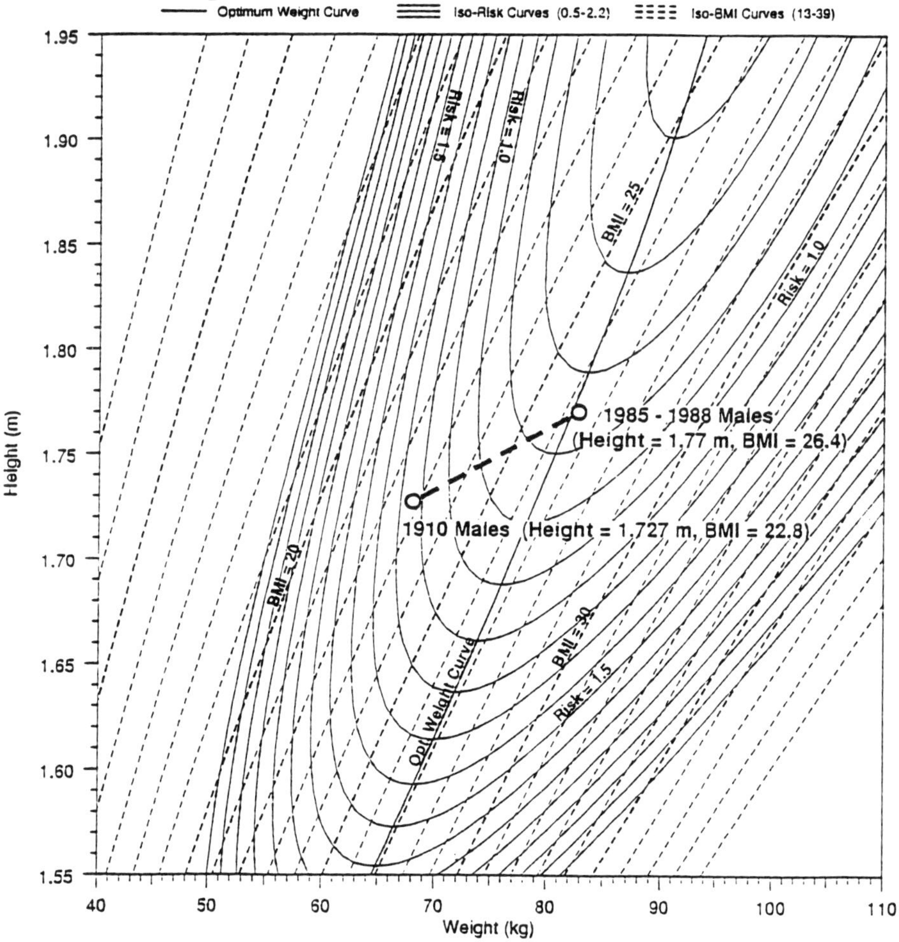

Source: Kim 1993.

while musculoskeletal and respiratory diseases each declined at a rate of 5.9 percent per decade.

Young adults born between 1822 and 1845 who survived the deadly infectious diseases of childhood and adolescence were not freer of degenerative diseases than persons of the same ages today, as some have suggested, but more afflicted. At ages 35 – 39 hernia rates, for example, were more than three times as prevalent in the 1860s as in the 1980s. Of special note is the much higher incidence of clubfoot in the 1860s – a birth anomaly which suggests that the uterus was far less safe for those awaiting birth than it is today.

Those who also survived diseases of middle age were more afflicted by degenerative chronic conditions at old age in the 1910s than in the 1980s.

Table 3. Comparison of the Prevalence of Chronic Conditions Among Union Army Veterans in 1910, Veterans in 1983 (Reporting whether they ever had specific chronic conditions), and Veterans in NHIS 1985–88 (Reporting whether they had specific chronic conditions during the preceding 12 months), Aged 65 and Above, Percentages

Disorder	1910 Union Army veterans[a]	1983 veterans[a]	Age-adjusted 1983 veterans[a]	NHIS 1985–88 veterans[a]
Musculoskeletal	67.7	47.9	47.2	42.5
Digestive	84.0	49.0	48.9	18.0
Hernia	34.5	27.3	26.7	6.6
Diarrhea	31.9	3.7	4.2	1.4
Genito-urinary	27.3	36.3	32.3	8.9
Central nervous, endocrine, Metabolic or blood	24.2	29.9	29.1	12.6
Circulatory[b]	90.1	42.9	39.9	40.0
Heart	76.0	38.5	39.9	26.6
Varicose veins	38.5	8.7	8.3	5.3
Hemorrhoids[c]	44.4			7.2
Respiratory	42.2	29.8	28.1	26.5

[a] Prevailing rates of Union Army veterans are based on examinations by physicians. Those for the 1980s are based on self reporting. Comparison of the NHIS rates with those obtained from physicians' examinations in NHANES II indicates that use of selfreported health conditions does not introduce a significant bias into the comparison. See the source for a more detailed discussion of possible biases and their magnitudes.

[b] Among veterans in 1983, the prevalence of all types of circulatory diseases will be underestimated because of underreporting of hemorrhoids.

[c] The variable indicating if the 1983 veteran ever had hemorrhoids is unreliable.

Sources: Fogel, Costa, and Kim 1993.

Nearly 74 percent of the elderly Union Army veterans suffered from three or more disabling chronic conditions, which is much higher than the rate among elderly veterans in 1983 (Fogel, Costa, and Kim 1993). It may be true that there were fewer genetically frail persons among those who survived to age 65 in 1910 than there are today. If so, that genetic advantage was apparently offset by a lifetime of socioeconomic and biomedical stress that left health in old age badly impaired and that sharply curtailed the life expectations of the elderly. During the 1910s the elderly died not from the infectious diseases that killed the great majority of their cohorts at relatively young ages but primarily from degenerative diseases which, at the two-digit level of the International Classification of Diseases, are similar to the distribution of causes of death during the 1980s, except that deaths from neoplasms were lower and deaths from tuberculosis were higher than in the 1980s.

The provisional findings thus suggest that chronic conditions were far more prevalent throughout the life-cycle for those who reached age 65 before World War I than is suggested by the theory of the epidemiological transition. Reliance on causes-of-death information to characterize the epidemiology of the past has led to a significant misrepresentation of the distribution of health conditions among the living. It has also promoted the view that the epidemiology of chronic diseases is more separate from that of contagious diseases than now appears to be the case.

4. Physiological Foundations for Waaler Surfaces and Curves

What is the basis for the predictive capacity of Waaler surfaces and curves? Part of the answer resides in the realm of human physiology, which concerns the functioning of the organs and the organ systems of the body. Variations in height and weight appear to be associated with variations in the chemical composition of the tissues that make up these organs, in the quality of the electrical transmission across membranes, and in the functioning of the endocrine system and other vital systems.

Research in this area is developing rapidly and some of the new findings are yet to be confirmed. The exact mechanisms by which malnutrition and trauma in utero or early childhood are transformed into organ dysfunctions are still unclear. What is agreed upon is that the basic structure of most organs are laid down early, and it is reasonable to infer that poorly developed organs may break down earlier than welldeveloped ones. The principal evidence so far is statistical and, despite agreement on certain specific dysfunctions, there is no generally accepted theory of cellular aging (cf. Tanner 1990 and 1993).

With these caveats in mind, recent research bearing on the connection between malnutrition and body size and the later onset of chronic diseases can conveniently be divided into three categories. The first category involves forms of malnutrition (including the ingestion of toxic substances) that cause permanent, promptly visible physiological damage, as is seen in the impairment of the nervous systems of fetuses due to excess consumption of alcohol or smoking by pregnant women. Alcohol, for example, induces growth retardation in fetuses and infants and causes atrial septal defect, microcephaly, and other birth anomalies which are collectively labeled Fetal Alcohol Syndrome or Fetal Alcohol Symptoms (Robbins, Cotran, Kumar 1984). It appears that protein calorie malnutrition (PCM) in infancy and early childhood can lead to a permanent impairment of central nervous system function (Scrimshaw and Gordon 1968; Martorell, Rivera, and Kaplowitz 1990; Chavez, Martinez, and Soberanes 1994; cf. Volpe 1987). Iodine deficiency in utero and moderate-to-severe iron deficiency during infancy also appear to cause permanent neurological damage (Lozoff, Jimenez, and Wolf 1991; Scrimshaw 1993).

Not all damage due to retarded development in utero or infancy caused by malnutrition shows up immediately. In a recent series of studies, D.J.P. Barker and his colleagues (Barker et al. 1989; Barker, Osmond, and Golding 1990; Barker 1991; Barker et al. 1992; Law et al. 1993; Phillips et al. 1993; Phipps et al. 1993) have reported that such conditions as coronary heart disease, hypertension, stroke, diabetes, and autoimmune thyroiditis begin in utero or in infancy, but do not become apparent until midadult or later ages. In these cases, individuals appear to be in good health, and function well in the interim. However, early onset of the degenerative diseases of old age appears to be linked to inadequate cellular development early in life. Some, but not all, such cases are associated with low birth weight. Some babies are born in the normal weight range but experience below average infant weight gains. In other instances, babies are small relative to the size of their placentas, short in relation to the size of their head, or long but thin (Barker 1993; cf. Tanner 1993).

Certain physiological dysfunctions incurred by persons suffering from malnutrition can, in principle, be reversed by improved dietary intake, but they often persist because the cause of the malnutrition persists. If the malnutrition persists long enough these conditions can become irreversible or fatal. This category of dysfunctions includes the degradation of tissue structure, especially in such vital organs as the lungs, the heart, and the gastrointestinal tract. In the case of the respiratory system, for example, there is not only decreased muscle mass and strength but also impaired ventilatory drive, biochemical changes in connective tissue, and electrolyte abnormalities. Malnutrition also has been related to the atrophy of the mucosal cells of the gut, the inhibition of wound healing, increased likelihood of traumatic shock and of sepsis, impaired functioning of the endocrine system, increased tendency to edema, electrical instability that can provoke acute arrhythmias, and degenerative joint diseases (Saba, Dillon, and Lanser 1983; Idiaquez 1988; McMahon and Bistrian 1990; Hill 1990; Fisler 1992; cf. Manton 1993).

Also relevant is the discovery of the relationship between birth weight and the probability of perinatal death. The curves in Figure 7 are "U" shaped, indicating that in each population babies significantly heavier than the optimal weight also incur high mortality risks. Moreover, the optimal birth weight in the two populations with small mothers was significantly lower than that of the U.S. population where mothers were relatively large. It appears that prior to high-technology interventions, the size of the mother's pelvis constrained the rate at which birth size (and perhaps the robustness of the vital organs of the baby) could have increased with the improvement in intrauterine nutrition. Babies at weights which optimized survival in a relatively tall population were at elevated risks of dying in populations with relatively short mothers, due to delivery distress. There was, in other words, an intergenerational constraint on the rate at which babies could escape from the effects of malnutrition as fetal nutrition improved (cf. Chandra 1975).

The recent physiological findings also cast new light on the first phase of the secular decline in mortality. Some investigators have called attention to changes in age-specific mortality rates that may indicate a shift in the balance between pathogens and their human hosts (Fridlizius 1984; Perrenoud 1984). Although the shift has been attributed to a decline in the virulence of pathogens, not enough evidence is in hand as yet to assess this

Fig. 7: Perinatal Death Rate by Birth Weight in Ghana, India, and U.S.A.

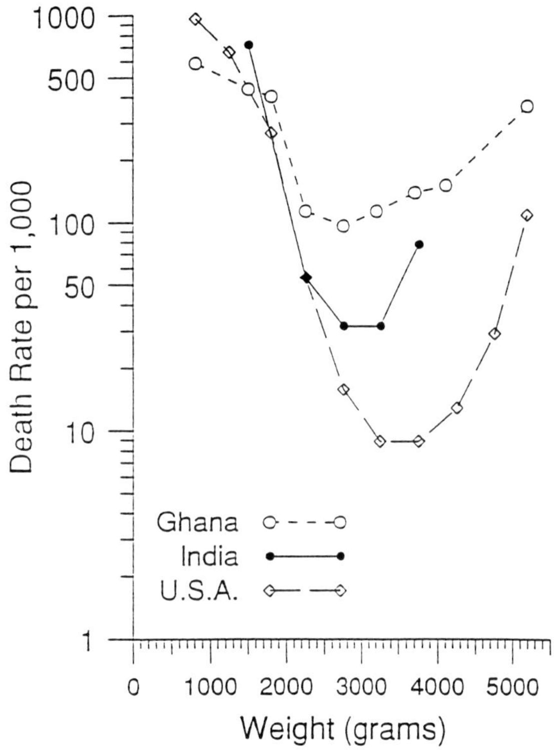

Source: Hytten and Leitch 1971.

possibility. However, the recent physiological research summarized in this section suggests a new pathway through which the balance between pathogens and human hosts may have turned in favor of the hosts. In addition to the improved operation of the immune system, there is the increased capacity of a vital organ to survive the attack of pathogens as a result of increased tissue resilience, including the improved operation of the nervous system. The process could have been synergistic since the improvement in the operation of the immune system might have interacted with the increased resilience of other vital organs.[5] The last possibility is consistent with the age-specific patterns of decline in mortality rates that have so far been uncovered for the eighteenth century.

5. SOME IMPLICATIONS FOR CURRENT POLICY

Malthus believed that malnutrition manifested itself in the exceptional—in periodic famines and in the excess mortality prevalent among the ultra-poor of his day who lived in misery and vice. He thought that persons near the middle of the social order, the sturdy agricultural laborer or the town artisan, were generally well fed, healthy, and lived normal life spans.

We now know, however, that famines accounted for less than 4 percent of the premature mortality of Malthus's age, and that the excess mortality of the ultra-poor (the bottom fifth of society) accounted for another sixth of premature mortality. About two-thirds of all premature mortality in Malthus's time came from the part of society that Malthus viewed as productive and healthy. Yet by current standards, even persons in the top half of the income distribution in Britain during the eighteenth century were stunted and wasted, suffered far more extensively from chronic diseases at young adult and middle ages than is true today, and died 30 years sooner than today.[6]

5.1 Implications for Poor Countries

The Malthusian legacy is embodied in such theses as "small-but-healthy" which holds that stunted or moderately wasted individuals may not be more vulnerable to ill health and mortality than those who conform to the U.S. standard. The paucity of life-cycle data sets in developing countries caused investigators to focus only on the early years of the life span, searching for interactions between natal or infant measures of size and measures of health and work capacity later in childhood. Such studies generally picked up the effects of only exceedingly severe stunting and wasting (more than 2 standard deviations below average), missing the impact of more moderate size effects, many of which do not show up until later in life (Seckler 1980; Sukhatme 1982; Lipton 1983; cf. West et al. 1990).

However, the information reported in this paper indicates that childhood stunting and wasting has a long reach, predicting chronic disease rates at young adult and later ages. The higher prevalence of disabling chronic diseases among adults in the developing nations has escaped attention because the relevant information on such conditions is not generally collected. But the long reach of childhood malnutrition in rich countries, both now and when they were much poorer than they are today, suggests that a similar interconnection also exists in developing countries.

Chronic diseases are not the only way that chronic malnutrition reduces the productivity of the labor force. When the mean amounts of calories are as low as they are in the poor nations of the world, labor force participation rates and measures of labor productivity are bound to be low, especially when the hours of labor are adjusted for the intensity of labor (see Fogel 1991; cf. Dasgupta 1993). Elsewhere (Fogel 1991), I have estimated that when the labor input is adjusted for intensity (measured by calories), improved gross nutrition accounts for roughly 30 percent of the growth of per capita income in Britain between 1790 and 1980.

5.2 Implications for Rich Countries

Between 1850 and 1950, U.S. life expectation at birth increased from about 40 to 68 years. Then for the next two decades further progress in longevity came to a virtual halt. During and following this interregnum investigators who reviewed the progress in mortality over the preceding century tended toward a consensus on three propositions: (1) The century-long decline in mortality rates was unique and could not be repeated because virtually all of the gains made through the elimination of death from contagious diseases below age 60 had been made. (2) Deaths, now concentrated at older ages, were due to degenerative diseases that were unrelated to the contagious diseases that they superseded. The degenerative diseases were caused by accelerated organ losses that were part of the natural process of aging. (3) There was an upper limit to life expectation that was genetically determined. One influential paper put that limit at 85 ± 7 years (Fries 1980, cf. Fries 1989).

More recent studies, responding to the renewed decline in mortality, which this time is concentrated at ages 65 and over, have uncovered evidence that militates against the notion of a genetically fixed life span or, if it is fixed, suggests that the upper limit is well above 85. Vaupel's study of Danish twins indicates that genetic factors account for only about 30 percent of the variance in age of death (Vaupel 1991a). His study of Swedish males who lived to age 90 indicates that the death rate at that age has declined at a rate of about 1 percent per annum since 1950, a finding that is contradictory to the rectangularization of the survivorship curve (Vaupel 1991b; cf. Thatcher 1992; Vaupel and Lundstrom 1994; Kannisto et al. 1994). Two recent studies of insect populations (Carey et al. 1992; Curtsinger et al. 1992) indicated that variation in environmental conditions had a much larger effect on the life span than genetic factors and revealed no pattern suggestive of a fixed upper limit. Collectively, these studies do not rule out genetic factors but suggest something much less rigid than the genetic programming of absolute life spans. An emerging theory combines genetic susceptibility of various organs with cumulative insults as a result of exposure to risk.

Recent studies also indicate that age-specific rates of chronic conditions above age 65 are generally falling. According to Manton, Corder, and Stallard (1993) the rate of disability among the elderly in the U. S. declined by 4.7 percent between 1982 and 1989. Put on a decade basis, this rate of decline is quite similar to the long-term rates of decline between 1910 and 1985–88 in chronic conditions among elderly veterans (Fogel, Costa, and Kim 1993). The finding is consistent with the growing body of evidence (reported in section 3 and 4 above) indicating that chronic diseases at later ages are, to a considerable degree, the result of exposure to infectious diseases, malnutrition, and other types of biomedical and socioeconomic stress early in life. It is also consistent with the predicted decline of about 6 percent per decade in chronic diseases based on the Waaler surface in ill health displayed in Figure 6 (cf. Blair et al. 1989; Manton, Stallard, and Singer 1992; Manton and Soldo 1992).

Much current research is now focused on explaining the decline in chronic conditions. Part of the emerging explanation is a change in life styles, particularly reduced smoking, improved nutrition, and increased exercise, which appear to be involved in reducing the prevalence of coronary heart disease and respiratory diseases. Another part of the explanation is the increasing effectiveness of medical intervention. This point is strikingly demonstrated by comparing the second and last columns of the line on hernias in Table 3, above. Prior to World War II, hernias, once they occurred, were generally permanent and often exceedingly painful conditions. However, by the 1980s about three-quarters of all veterans who ever had hernias were cured of them. Similar progress over the seven decades is indicated by the line on genito-urinary conditions. Other areas where medical intervention has been highly effective include control of hypertension and reduction in the incidence of stroke, surgical removal of osteoarthritis, replacement of knee and hip joints, curing of cataracts, and chemotherapies that reduce the incidence of osteoporosis and heart disease (Manton, Corder, and Stallard 1993).

The success in medical interventions combined with rising incomes has naturally led to a huge increase in the demand for medical services. Econometric estimates suggest a long-run income elasticity in the demand for medical services across OECD nations in the neighborhood of 1.5 and indicate that 90 percent of the variance in medical expenditures across OECD countries is explained by variations in income (Moore, Newman, and Fheili 1992). The rapidly growing level of demand, combined with the egalitarian policy of providing medical care at highly subsidized prices, has created the crisis in health care costs that is now such a focus of public policy debates across OECD nations, with various combinations of price and governmental rationing under consideration (*Economist* 1990; Newhouse 1992; Schwartz and Aaron 1991, Schieber, Poullier, and Greenwald 1993).

Whatever the eventual outcome of these policy debates, it is clear that we are in a much different world than that of Malthus. Instead of debating whether to provide food to paupers who might otherwise die, we are now debating how to distribute services that have proved successful in raising the quality of life of the aged and in extending life expectation. And we are now struggling with entirely new ethical issues such as whether it is right to restrict medical services that extend life of a low quality (Shuttleworth 1990; Wolfe 1986; Pellegrino 1993).

Growing opportunity to improve health at young ages, to reduce the incidence of chronic diseases at late ages, and to cure or alleviate the disabilities associated with chronic diseases raises two other post-Malthusian population issues. One is the impact of improved health on population size. A recent paper by Ahlburg and Vaupel (1990) pointed out that if mortality rates at older ages continue to decline at 2 percent per annum, the U.S. elderly population of 2050 would be 36 million larger than forecast by the Census Bureau (cf. Preston 1993). That possibility poses policy issues with respect to health care costs (because total medical costs may rise sharply even if cure rates continue to improve) and to pension costs (because the number of persons eligible for benefits under present proposed rules and of projected levels of compensation will become so large that outpayments will exceed planned reserves).

Some policymakers have sought to meet the pension problem by delaying retirement. Such schemes are based on the proposition that improved health will make it possible for more people to work past age 65. However, the recent findings on the secular improvement in health at older ages make it clear that worsening health is not the explanation for the steep decline since 1890 in labor force participation rates of males over 65. As Costa (1993) has reported, the U.S. decline in participation rates of the elderly over the past century is largely explained by the secular rise in income and a decline in the income elasticity of the demand for retirement. It is also related to the vast increase in the supply and the quality of leisure-time activities for the laboring classes.

In Malthus's time, and down to the opening of this century, leisure was in very short supply in the OECD countries and, as Veblen pointed out (1934), it was conspicuously consumed by a small upper class. The typical person labored over 60 hours per week for wages and many had chores at home which consumed an additional 10 or 12 hours (Kuznets 1952; Fogel 1993a; Olson 1992; cf. Atack and Bateman 1992). Aside from sleep, eating, and hygiene, such workers usually had barely 2 hours a day for leisure. Although opera, theater, and ballet were available, they were too expensive to be consumed ordinarily by the laboring classes.

Over the twentieth century, hours of work have fallen by nearly half for typical workers. Ironically, those in the top decile of the income distribution have not shared much in this gain of leisure since the highly paid professionals and businessmen who populate the top decile work closer to the nineteenth-century standard of 3,200 hours per year than the current working-class standard of about 1,800 hours. There has also been a vast increase in the supply of leisure-time activities—movies, radio, television, amusement parks, participant and spectator sports, travel—and a decline in the relative price of such activities. Many firms cater especially to the tastes of the elderly, offering reduced prices and special opportunities. As a result, the typical worker spends two-thirds as much time in leisure activities as in work and looks forward to retirement (Fogel 1992a and 1993a).

Given the growing and income-inelastic demand for leisure that characterizes the post-Malthusian milieu of the OECD nations, it remains to be seen to what extent the demand for leisure and retirement can be throttled. Policymakers may encounter as much resistance to efforts to reduce the implicit subsidies for leisure as they have had recently in raising the taxes on work.

6. SOME IMPLICATIONS FOR THE THEORY AND MEASUREMENT OF ECONOMIC GROWTH

Recent findings in the biomedical area call attention to what may be called the thermodynamic and physiological factors in economic growth. Although largely neglected by theorists of both the "old" and the "new" growth economics, these factors can easily be incorporated into standard growth models. Viewed in the human capital context, both factors may be thought of as labor enhancing technological changes that were brought about by developments in the agricultural, public health, medical services, and household sectors. They may also be thought of as adjustments for the mismeasurement of the labor input, when labor is measured only in person-hours.

I referred to the thermodynamic factor indirectly in section 5.1, when I indicated that about 30 percent of the British growth rate over the past 200 years was attributable to improvements in gross nutrition. That computation was based on the first law of thermodynamics, which holds that energy output cannot exceed energy input. Since that law applies as much to human engines as to mechanical ones, it is possible to use energycost-accounting techniques to estimate the increase in the energy available for work over the past two centuries. In the British case that increase had two effects. It raised the laborforce participation rate by bringing into the labor force the bottom 20 percent of consuming units in 1790 who had, on average, only enough energy for a few hours of strolling. Moreover, for those in the labor force, the intensity of work per hour has increased because the number of calories available for work increased. This change in the intensity of effort, by itself, appears to have accounted for about 20 percent of the long-term growth rate.

The contention that the British intensity of effort increased over time may seem dubious since the work day, week, and year (measured in hours) declined significantly over the past two centuries. However, the British (and other Europeans) could not have worked at the same average intensity *per hour* in 1790 as they do today, since that would have required a considerably larger supply of dietary energy per capita than was actually available. Increases in the intensity of labor *per hour* was also a factor in the American case, where food supplies were far more abundant than in Europe. Even if it is assumed that the daily number of calories available for work was the same in the U.S. in 1860 as today, the intensity of work per hour would have been well below today's levels, since the average number of hours worked in 1860 was about 1.75 times as great as today. During the mid-nineteenth century only slaves on southern gang-system plantations appear to have worked at levels of intensity per hour approaching current standards (cf. Fogel 1991 and 1993a; Olson 1992; Fogel and Engerman 1992).

The physiological factor pertains to the efficiency with which the human engine converts energy input into work output. Nutritionists, physiologists and development economists have contributed to the extensive literature on this topic. Since some important issues are still unresolved, a firm assessment of the physiological contribution to economic growth is not yet possible. However, some aspects of the contribution can be indicated.

Changes in health, in the composition of diet, and in clothing and shelter can significantly affect the efficiency with which ingested energy is converted into work output.[7] Reductions in the incidence of infectious diseases increase the proportion of ingested energy that is available for work both because of savings in the energy required to mobilize the immune system and because the capacity of the gut to absorb nutrients is improved, especially as a consequence of a reduction in diarrheal diseases. Thermodynamic efficiency has also increased because of changes in the composition of the diet, including the shift from grains and other foods with high fiber content to sugar and meats. These dietary changes raised the proportion of ingested energy that can be metabolized (increased the average value of the "Atwater factors," to use the language of nutritionists). Improvements in clothing and shelter have also increased thermodynamic efficiency by reducing the amount of energy lost through radiation.

Individuals who are stunted but otherwise healthy at maturity will be at an increased risk of incurring chronic diseases and of dying prematurely. To evaluate the significance of changes in the rate of deterioration of the capacity to work over the life cycle, one needs to calculate the effect of changes in stature and weight on the discounted present value of the difference between earnings and maintenance over the life-cycle (cf. Dasgupta 1993). A procedure for estimating this effect is set forth in the notes, and illustrative estimates of the key variables are provided.[8] The exercise indicates that the discounted revenues would have increased by about 37 percent. This last figure, combined with a guess on the effect of the shifting of Atwater factors, suggests that the average efficiency of the human engine in Britain increased by about 53 percent between 1790 and 1980. The combined effect of the increase in dietary energy available for work, and of the increased human efficiency in transforming dietary energy into work output, appears to account for about 50 percent of the British economic growth since 1790.[9]

Focusing on the thermodynamic and physiological aspects of economic growth calls attention to the long lags that frequently occur between the time that certain investments are made and the time that their benefits occur. Much of the gain in thermodynamic efficiency that occurred in Britain and other OECD countries between 1910 and 1980 was due to a series of investments made as much as a century earlier. Failure to take account of these extremely long lags between investments and payoffs leads to puzzling paradoxes. During the Depression Decade of the 1930s, for example, the U.S. unemployment rate was never less than 16 percent; for half the period unemployment ranged between 20 and 25 percent. Yet life expectation between 1929 and 1939 increased by 4 years and the heights of men reaching maturity during this period increased by 1.6 cm (U.S. Bureau of the Census 1975; Karpinos 1958).

The resolution of the paradox turns, I believe, on the huge social investments made between 1870 and 1930 and whose payoffs were not counted as part of national income during the 1920s and 1930s even though they produced a large stream of benefits during these decades. I refer, of course, to the social investment in biomedical research (which included the establishment and expansion of modern teaching and research hospitals) whose largest payoffs came well after the investment was made. Also included in this category are such public health investments as the construction of facilities to improve the supply of water, the cleaning up of the milk supply, the draining of swamps, the development of effective systems of quarantines, and the cleaning up of the slums.

* * *

Keynes said: "In the long run we are all dead." That was an appropriate point to make during the interwar period, which included the severe inflations of the 1920s and the worst depression in history during the 1930s. Urgent, forceful action was needed to regain control of the money supply, to take care of the millions of unemployed, and to prevent the collapse of the democracies.

We live in another era. The major issues of economic policy in OECD nations today cannot be understood from a purely short-run perspective. The crisis in medical care, the pension crisis, and the challenges of globalization are governed by long-run processes that policymakers need to understand. As I have tried to point out in this lecture, we have not yet completed the escape from hunger and premature death that began nearly three centuries ago. Chronic diseases and death are still occurring prematurely even in the rich countries. If the reforms of health care and pension programs now being considered by policymakers are to be successful, they must be consistent with the long-term physiological changes governing the decline in chronic diseases and the increase in longevity. Long-term forecasts that do not take account of the dynamics of these changes over the past century, and of the socioeconomic, biomedical, and other environmental improvements that made them possible, are liable to be far off the mark.

At the outset of this lecture I stressed the need for economists to take account of long-run dynamic processes through a study of history. Uncovering what actually happened in the past requires an enormous investment in time and effort. Fortunately for theorists, that burden is borne primarily by economic historians. Theorists only need to spend the time necessary to comprehend what the historians have discovered. A superficial knowledge of the work of economic historians is at least as dangerous as a superficial knowledge of theory.

NOTES

1. Before proceeding with the discussion of chronic malnutrition it is necessary to clarify a terminological confusion that has misled some investigators: That is the distinction between the term "diet" or food intake (which represents gross nutrition) and the term "malnutrition" (which represents net nutrition—the nutrients available to sustain cellular growth). I will not dwell on this distinction here but will only emphasize that when I mean gross nutrition I will use the term "*diet*" and that such other terms as "*malnutrition,*" "*undernutrition,*" "*net nutrition,*" and "*nutritional status*" are meant to designate the balance between the nutrient intake (diet) and the claims on that intake. See Fogel and Floud (1994) for a further elaboration of this distinction.
2. See the appendix to Floud and Fogel 1994 for the estimated distributions of height, weight and the body mass index (BMI) in France c.1790.
3. In principle, it is possible to construct size distributions of calories from household consumption surveys. Inasmuch as most of these surveys during the nineteenth century were focused on the lower classes, in order to make use of them it is necessary to know from what centiles of either the national caloric or the national income distribution the surveyed households were drawn.
4. Moreover, with a given population and technology, changes in the allocation of labor between agriculture and other sectors may lead to changes in body size and mortality. In an *ancien régime* economy the lower the share of the labor force that is in agriculture, *cet. par.*, the lower the share of caloric production that can be devoted to baseline maintenance. The reasoning behind this statement is as follows: Assume that one worker in agriculture feeds himself plus three persons outside of agriculture. Hence, a movement of one percent of agricultural workers to nonagriculture would reduce the per capita availability of food to the increased nonagricultural sector by about 1.33 percent. If baseline maintenance accounts for 75 percent of caloric consumption and if per capita calories reserved for work remain constant in the nonagricultural sector, calories available for baseline maintenance in that sector would decline by about 1.8 percent (assuming that within the agricultural sector per capita production and consumption is unchanged).
5. Such possible synergies call into question the proposition that, because an individual appears to be currently well fed, malnutrition does not affect the outcome of diseases such as influenza, smallpox or typhoid (cf. Duncan, Scott, and Duncan 1993). Individuals may be more likely to succumb to such infections, even if they are currently well fed, because past malnutrition, either in utero or subsequently, has degraded vital organs (cf. Scrimshaw, Taylor, and Gordon 1968).
6. Premature mortality is defined here as death rates higher than the 1980 death rates when standardized for the 1700 age structure (cf. Fogel 1986 and 1992b). Estimates of the overall death rate c.1790 are from Wrigley and Schofield (1981). Estimates of the relative death rates by deciles of the caloric consumption distribution were based on the estimated average heights and BMI in these deciles and on the relative mortality risks that they imply, as indicated in Figure 4. For further details on the computations see the appendix in Fogel and Floud 1994 and Table A2 in Fogel 1993b.
7. The discussion in this paragraph draws on Dasgupta 1993 and the sources cited there.
8. The discounted present value of the age-earnings profile for n years beginning with the age at which earnings peak is given by:

$$P_x = E_x \int_0^n e^{-(\mu+\phi+r)t}\, dt \qquad (1)$$

where μ is the rate of decline in the survivorship function (the l_x curve of the life table), ϕ is the rate of decline in annual net earnings after age x; r is the discount rate (which, for convenience, is set at six percent), x is the age at which earnings peak, E_x is net earnings at that age, n is the average number of years that elapsed between x and the average age at which a living male ceased to be in the labor force regularly (which, for convenience, will be taken to be equal to 35), and P_x is the discounted present value of the net earnings stream.

The value of μ for 1790 was computed from Wrigley and Schofield (1981), taking the average of their e_0 for 1786–1795 (which is 36.63) and interpolating between levels 8 and 9 in their family of English life tables to obtain the proper l_x curve for c.1790. The value of μ over ages 35–70 in that schedule is 0.0289.

The projected shift in the l_x curve was based on the Waaler surface in Table A1, Fogel 1993b. Using 1.68m and 61kg for 1790, and 1.76m and 76kg for 1980, yields a predicted decline of 31 percent in the mortality rate. The corresponding l_x schedule was obtained from Princeton model North tables at male level 14, using $0.69({}_{35}m_{35})$ as the basis for the fit. The value of μ between ages 35–70 in that l_x schedule is -0.0202.

The changes in E_x associated with changes in height and weight were estimated from an equation reported by Robert A. Margo and Richard H. Steckel (1982). The data they used pertained to slaves seized as booty of war by the Union Army in 1863. The traders who related the value of slaves to their height and weight appear to have focused only on the differences in the location (not the slope) of the age-earnings profile, showing no apparent awareness of the relationship of stature and BMI to mortality and chronic diseases (cf. Fogel 1992c). The Margo-Steckel equation is:

$$\text{(2)} \quad \begin{aligned} \ln V = \underset{(1.47)}{2.73} + \underset{(0.92)}{0.032S} + \underset{(2.22)}{0.17A} - \underset{(-2.23)}{0.005A^2} + \underset{(2.10)}{0.000046A^3} + \underset{(2.16)}{0.053H} \\ + \underset{(1.79)}{0.019W} - \underset{(-1.73)}{0.00027(H \cdot W)};\ N = 523;\ \bar{R}^2 = 0.20; \end{aligned}$$

where V is the value of a slave, S is a dummy for skin color, A is age, H is height (in inches), and W is weight (in lbs). T- statistics are in parentheses. For 1790, I used 66.1 inches and 134 lbs. For 1980, I used 69.3 inches and 167 lbs. These figures indicate that E_x increased by about 7 percent as a result of changes associated with body size.

The value of ϕ for 1790 between ages 35 and 70 was computed from data reported in Fogel and Engerman 1974. These data indicate that net earnings at age 70 were about 17 percent of peak earnings, which was attained at age 35.

With the foregoing information and an initial assumption that ϕ remained constant, the increase in P_x can be computed from the data shown in equations (3) and (4):

$$\text{(3)} \qquad P_{x,1790} = \frac{E_x\,[1 - e^{-(0.0289+0.0494+0.06)35}]}{0.1383} = 7.17\,E_x$$

$$\text{(4)} \qquad P_{x,p} = \frac{1.07\,E_x\,[1 - e^{-(0.0202+0.0494+0.06)35}]}{0.1296} = 8.17\,E_x$$

where $P_{x,1790}$ is the present value of the 1790 earnings profile and $P_{x,p}$ is the present value of the profile projected from the changes in height and BMI. Equations (3) and (4) imply that P_x increased by about 14 percent [(8.17 ÷ 7.17) − 1 = 0.14].

It is now necessary to take account of the effect of changes in body size on the rate of decline in the net earnings function (the value of ϕ). If it is assumed that net earnings at age 70 rose from 17 to 40 percent of peak-age earnings as a result of physiological improvements, P_x increases by 37 percent. However, even the last figure is probably too low since it does not take account of the secular shift in the peak of the age-earnings profile from the mid-thirties to the mid-forties. Moreover, studies of the profiles of manual workers in recent times suggest that net earnings now decline much more slowly after the peak than in past times (cf. Fogel and Engerman 1974; Jablonski, Rosenblum, and Kunze 1988; Murphy and Welch 1990).

9. The following procedure was used to arrive at this estimate: Bringing the bottom 20 percent of the caloric distribution of c.1790 into the labor force increased the labor force participation rate by 25 percent. Among those in the labor force the average number of calories available for work increased by 56 percent between c.1790 and 1980. Hence, the total increase in output per capita as a result of the increased availability of calories for work was 95 percent ($1.25 \times 1.56 = 1.95$). Dasgupta's (1993) discussion suggests that reductions in diarrheal and other diseases combined with a shift in the compositon of the diet increased the Atwater factors by about 12 percent. Since the exercise based on the equation in note 8 implies that the reduction in chronic diseases and premature mortality increased thermodynamic efficiency by 37 percent, the combined increase in thermodynamic efficiency is about 53 percent ($1.12 \times 1.37 = 1.53$). In combination, then, increased calories available for work and the increased thermodynamic efficiency increased per capita income between c.1790 and 1980 by 198 percent ($1.95 \times 1.53 = 2.98$) or by 0.58 percent per annum ($2.98^{(1/190)} - 1 = 0.0058$), which is about half of the annual British growth rate ($0.58 \div 1.15 = 0.50$). For further details, including discussion of possible upward and downward biases in this computation, see Fogel 1987 and Fogel and Floud 1994.

REFERENCES

Ahlburg, D. A., and J. W. Vaupel. 1990. Alternative projections of the U.S. population. *Demography* 27: 639–52.

Allen, R. C. 1994. Agriculture during the Industrial Revolution, 1700–1850. In *The economic history of Britain since 1700*, 2d ed., edited by R. Floud, and D. McCloskey, Cambridge: Cambridge University Press, forthcoming.

Atack, J., and F. Bateman. 1992. How long was the workday in 1880? *Journal of Economic History* 52: 129–60.

Barker, D. J. P. 1991. The intrauterine environment and adult cardiovascular disease. In *The childhood environment and adult disease*, Ciba Foundation Symposium 156, 3–16. Chichester, UK: John Wiley & Sons.

– – –. 1993. Fetal origins of coronary heart disease. *British Heart Journal* 69: 195–96.

Barker, D. J. P., C. Osmond, and J. Golding. 1990. Height and mortality in the counties of England and Wales. *Annals of Human Biology* 17: 1–6.

Barker, D. J. P., et al. 1989. Growth in utero, blood pressure in childhood and adult life, and mortality from cardiovascular disease. *British Medical Journal* 298: 564–67.

Barker, D. J. P., et al. 1992. Relation of fetal and infant growth to plasma fibrinogen and factor VII concentrations in adult life. *British Medical Journal* 304: 148–52.

Bengtsson, T., and R. Ohlsson. 1984. Population and economic fluctuations in Sweden 1749–1914. In *Pre-industrial population change*, edited by T. Bengtsson, G. Fridlizius, and R. Ohlsson, 277–97. Stockholm: Almquist and Wiksell.

– – –. 1985. Age-specific mortality and short-term changes in the standard of living: Sweden, 1751–1859. *European Journal of Population* 1: 309–26.

Billewicz, W. Z., and I. A. MacGregor. 1982. A birth to maturity longitudinal study of heights and weights in two West African (Gambian) villages, 1951–1975. *Annals of Human Biology* 9: 309–20.

Blair, S. N., et al. 1989. Physical fitness and all-cause mortality: A prospective study of healthy men and women. *JAMA* 262: 2395–2401.

Carey, J. R., et al. 1992. Slowing of mortality rates at older ages in large medfly cohorts. *Science* 258: 457–61.

Chandra, R. K. 1975. Antibody formation in first and second generation offspring of nutritionally deprived rats. *Science* 190: 289–90.

Chartres, J. A. 1985. The marketing of agricultural produce. In *The agrarian history of England and Wales*, vol. 5: *1640–1750*, pt. 2: *Agrarian change*, edited by J. Thirsk, 406–502. Cambridge: Cambridge University Press.

Chavez, A., C. Martinez, and B. Soberanes. 1994. The effect of malnutrition on human development. In *Longitudinal community based studies of the impact of early malnutrition on child health and development*, edited by N. S. Scrimshaw. Boston: INFDC, in press.

Chen, L., A. K. M. Chowdhury, and S. L. Huffman. 1980. Anthropometric assessment of energy-protein malnutrition and subsequent risk of mortality among preschool aged children. *American Journal of Clinical Nutrition* 33: 1836–45.

Cipolla, C. M. 1980. *Before the Industrial Revolution: European society and economy, 1000–1700*. New York: W. W. Norton.

Costa, D. L. 1993. Health, income, and retirement: Evidence from nineteenth century America. Ph.D. diss., University of Chicago.

Curtsinger, J. W., et al. 1992. Demography of genotypes: Failure of the limited lifespan paradigm in *Drosphila melanogaster*. *Science* 258: 461–63.

Dasgupta, P. 1993. *An inquiry into well-being and destitution*. Oxford: Clarendon Press.

Dublin, L. I., and A. J. Lotka. 1936. *Length of life: A study of the life table*. New York: Ronald Press Co.

Duncan, S. R., S. Scott, and C. J. Duncan. 1993. The dynamics of smallpox epidemics in Britain, 1550–1800. *Demography* 30: 405–23.

Dupâquier, J. 1989. Demographic crises and subsistence crises in France, 1650–1725. In *Famine, disease and the social order in early modern society*, edited by J. Walter, and R. Schofield, 189–99. Cambridge: Cambridge University Press.

Eckstein, Z., T. P. Schultz, and K. I. Wolpin. 1984. Short-run fluctuations in fertility and mortality in pre-industrial Sweden. *European Economic Review* 26: 297–317.

Economist. 1990. Squeezing in the next five billion. 20 January, 19–20, 22.

FAO/WHO/UNU. 1985. Energy and protein requirements. Report of a joint FAO/WHO/UNU expert consultation. Technical Report Series no. 724. Geneva: World Health Organization.

Fisler, J. S. 1992. Cardiac effects of starvation and semistarvation diets: Safety and mechanisms of action. *American Journal of Clinical Nutrition* 56: 230S-34S.

Fogel, R. W. 1986. Nutrition and the decline in mortality since 1700: Some preliminary findings. In *Long-term factors in American economic growth*, edited by S. L. Engerman, and R. E. Gallman, 439–555. Chicago: University of Chicago Press (for NBER).

– – –. 1987. Biomedical approaches to the estimation and interpretation of secular trends in equity, morbidity, mortality, and labor productivity in Europe, 1750–1980. Typescript, University of Chicago.

– – –. 1991. New findings on secular trends in nutrition and mortality: Some implications for population theory. Typescript, University of Chicago.

– – –. 1992c. The body mass index of adult male slaves in the U.S. c.1863 and its bearing on mortality rates. In *Without consent or contract*, vol. 2: *Evidence and methods*, edited by R. W. Fogel, R. A. Galantine, and R. L Manning, 311–18. New York: W. W. Norton.

— — —. 1992a. Egalitarianism: The economic revolution of the twentieth century. The 1992 Simon Kuznets Memorial Lectures presented at Yale University (April 22–24). Typescript, University of Chicago.

— — —. 1992b. Second thoughts on the European escape from hunger: Famines, chronic malnutrition, and mortality. In *Nutrition and poverty*, edited by S. R. Osmani, 243–86. Oxford: Clarendon Press.

— — —. 1993a. A comparison of biomedical and economic meausres of egalitariansim: Some implications of secular trends for current policy. Paper presented at the Workshop on Economic Theories of Inequality, Stanford University (March 11–13). Typescript, University of Chicago.

— — —. 1993b. New sources and new techniques for the study of secular trends in nutritional status, health, mortality, and the process of aging. *Historical Methods* 26: 5–43.

Fogel, R. W., D. L. Costa, and J. M. Kim. 1993. Secular trends in the distribution of chronic conditions and disabilities at young adult and late ages, 1860–1988: Some preliminary findings. Paper presented at the NBER Summer Institute, Economics of Aging Program (July 26–28). Typescript, University of Chicago.

Fogel, R. W., and S. L. Engerman. 1974. *Time on the cross: The economics of American slavery*, 2 vols. Boston: Little, Brown & Co.

— — —. 1992. The slave diet on large plantations in 1860. In *Without consent or contract*, vol. 2: *Evidence and methods*, edited by R. W. Fogel, R. A. Galantine, and R. L Manning, 291–304. New York: W. W. Norton.

Fogel, R. W., and R. Floud. 1994. Nutrition and mortality in France, Britain, and the United States. Typescript, University of Chicago.

Freudenberger, H., and G. Cummins. 1976. Health, work, and leisure before the Industrial Revolution. *Explorations in Economic History* 13: 1–12.

Fridlizius, G. 1984. The mortality decline in the first phase of the demographic transition: Swedish experiences. In *Pre-industrial population change*, edited by T. Bengtsson, G. Fridlizius, and R. Ohlsson, 71–114. Stockholm: Almquist and Wiksell.

Friedman, G. C. 1982. The heights of slaves in Trinidad. *Social Science History* 6: 482–515.

Fries, J. F. 1980. Aging, natural death, and the compression of morbidity. *New England Journal of Medicine* 303: 130–36.

— — —. 1989. The compression of morbidity: Near or far? *Milbank Quarterly* 67: 208–32.

Galloway, P. 1986. Differentials in demographic responses to annual price variations in pre-revolutionary France: A comparison of rich and poor areas in Rouen, 1681–1787. *European Journal of Population* 2: 269–305.

— — —. 1987. Population, prices and weather in preindustrial Europe. Ph.D. diss., University of California, Berkeley.

Gille, H. 1949/50. The demographic history of northern European countries in the eighteenth century. *Population Studies* 3: 3–70.

Goubert, P. 1973. *The ancien régime*, translated by S. Cox. New York: Harper Torchbooks.

Gould, B. A. 1869. *Investigations in the military and anthropological statistics of American soldiers*. New York: Hurd and Houghton.

Heywood, P. F. 1983. Growth and nutrition in Papua New Guinea. *Journal of Human Evolution* 12: 131–43.

Hill, G. L. 1990. Some implications of body composition research for modern clinical management. *Infusionstherapie* 17(suppl. 3): 79–80.

Holderness, B. A. 1989. Prices, productivity, and output. In *The agrarian history of England and Wales*, vol. 6: *1750–1850*, edited by G. E. Mingay, 84–189. Cambridge: Cambridge University Press.

Hytten, F. E., and I. Leitch. 1971. *The physiology of human preganancy*, 2d ed. Oxford: Blackwell Scientific.

Idiaquez, J. 1988. Nutritional status and autonomic nervous system function. *Functional Neurology* 3: 205–9.

Jablonski, M., L. Rosenblum, and K. Kunze. 1988. Productivity, age, and labor composition changes in the U. S. *Monthly Labor Review* 111(9): 34–38.

John, A. M. 1988. *The plantation slaves of Trinidad, 1783–1816: A mathematical and demographic inquiry*. Cambridge: Cambridge University Press.

Kannisto, V., et al. 1994. Reductions in mortality at advanced ages. *Population and Development Review*, forthcoming.

Karpinos, B. D. 1958. Height and weight of selective service registrants processed for military service during WW II. *Human Biology* 30: 292–321.

Keynes, J. M. [1923] 1971. *Collected writings of John Maynard Keynes*, vol. 4: *A tract on monetary reform*. London: Macmillan, St. Martin's Press (for the Royal Economic Society.

Kielmann, A. A., et al. 1983. *Child and maternal health services in rural India: The Narangwal experiment*. Vol. 1: *Integrated nutrition and health*. Baltimore: Johns Hopkins University Press for The World Bank.

Kim, J. M. 1993. Economic and biomedical implications of Waaler surfaces: A new perspective on height, weight, morbidity, and mortality. Typescript, University of Chicago.

Kuznets, S. 1941. Statistics and economic history. *Journal of Economic History* 1: 26–41.

– – –. 1952. Long-term changes in the national income of the United States of America since 1870. In *Income and wealth of the United States: Trends and structure*, edited by S. Kuznets, International Association for Research in Income and Wealth, Income and Wealth Series 2, 2–241. Baltimore: The Johns Hopkins Press.

Laslett, P. [1965] 1984. *The world we have lost: England before the industrial age*. 3rd ed. New York: Scribner's.

Law, C. M., et al. 1993. Initiation of hypertension in utero and its amplification throughout life. *British Medical Journal* 306: 24–27.

Lee, R. 1981. Short-term variation: Vital rates, prices, and weather. In E. A. Wrigley and R. S. Schofield, *The population history of England, 1541–1871: A reconstruction*, 356–401. Cambridge: Harvard University Press.

Lipton, M. 1983. Poverty, undernutrition and hunger. World Bank Staff Working Papers no. 597. Washington, D.C.: World Bank.

Livi-Bacci, M. 1990. *Population and nutrition: An essay on European demographic history*. New York: Cambridge University Press.

Lozoff, B., E. Jimenez, and A. W. Wolf. 1991. Long term developmental outcome of infants with iron deficiency. *New England Journal of Medicine* 325: 687–95.

McMahon, M. M., and B. R. Bistrian. 1990. The physiology of nutritional assessment and therapy in protein-calorie malnutrition. *Disease-a-Month* 36: 373–417.

Manton, K. G. 1993. Biomedical research and changing concepts of disease and aging: Implications for long-term forecasts for elderly populations. In *Forecasting the health of elderly populations*, edited by K. G. Manton, B. H. Singer, and R. M. Suzman, 319–65. New York: Springer-Verlag.

Manton, K. G., L. S. Corder, and E. Stallard. 1993. Estimates of change in chronic disability and institutional incidence and prevalence rates in the U.S. elderly population from the 1982, 1984, and 1989 National Long-Term Care Survey. Photocopy, Durham, NC, Duke University, Center for Demographic Studies.

Manton, K. G., and B. J. Soldo. 1992. Disability and mortality among the oldest old: Implications for current and future health and long-term care service needs. In *The oldest old*, edited by R. M. Suzman, K. G. Manton, and D. P. Willis, 199–250. New York & Oxford: Oxford University Press.

Manton, K. G., E. Stallard, and B. Singer. 1992. Projecting the future size and health status of the U. S. elderly population. *International Journal of Forecasting* 8: 433–58.

Margo, R. A., and R. H. Steckel. 1982. The heights of American slaves: New evidence on slave nutrition and health. *Social Science History* 6: 516–38.

Marmot, M. G., M. J. Shipley, and G. Rose. 1984. Inequalities in death–specific explanations of a general pattern? *Lancet* 8384 (May 5): 1003–6.

Martorell, R. 1985. Child growth retardation: A discussion of its causes and its relationship to health. In *Nutritional adaptation in man*, edited by K. Blaxter, and J. C. Waterlow, 13–29. London and Paris: John Libby.

Martorell, R., J. Rivera, and H. Kaplowitz. 1990. Consequences of stunting in early childhood for adult body size in rural Guatemala. *Annales Nestlé* 48: 85–92.

Meerton, M. A. von. 1989. Croissance économique en France et accroissement des française: Une analyse "Villermetrique". Typescript, Leuven, Center voor Economische Studiën.

Moore, W. J., R. J. Newman, and M. Fheili. 1992. Measuring the relationship between income and NHEs. *Health Care Financing Review* 14: 133–39.

Murphy, K. M., and Welch, F. 1990. Empirical age-earnings profiles. *Journal of Labor Economics* 8: 202–29.

Newhouse, J. P. 1992. Medical care costs: How much welfare loss? *Journal of Economic Perspectives* 6(3): 3–21.

Oddy, D. J. 1990. Food, drink and nutrition. In *The Cambridge social history of Britain 1750–1950*, vol. 2: *People and their environment*, edited by F. M. L. Thompson, 251–78. New York: Cambridge University Press.

Olson, J. F. 1992. Clock time versus real time: A comparison of the lengths of the northern and southern agricultural years. In *Without consent or contract*, vol. 3: *Markets and production: Technical papers volume 1*, edited by R. W. Fogel, and S. L. Engerman, 216–40. New York: W. W. Norton.

Osmani, S. R. 1992. On some controversies in the measurement of undernutrition. In *Nutrition and poverty*, edited by S. R. Osmani, 121–64. Oxford: Clarendon Press.

Payne, P. 1992. Undernutrition: Measurement and implications. In *Nutrition and povery*, edited by S. R. Osmani, Oxford: Clarendon Press.

Pellegrino, E. D. 1993. The metamorphosis of medical ethics: A 30-year retrospective. *JAMA* 269: 1158–62.

Perrenoud, A. 1984. The mortality decline in a long-term perspective. In *Pre-industrial population change*, edited by T. Bengtsson, G. Fridlizius, and R. Ohlsson, 41–69. Stockholm: Almquist and Wiksell.

– – –. 1991. The attenuation of mortality crises and the decline of mortality. In *The decline of mortality in Europe*, edited by R. Schofield, D. Reher, and A. Bideau, 18–37. Oxford: Clarendon Press.

Phillips, D. I. W., et al. 1993. Fetal growth and autoimmune thyroid disease. *Quarterly Journal of Medicine* 86: 247–53.

Phipps, K., et al. 1993. Fetal growth and impaired glucose tolerance in men and women. *Diabetologia* 36: 225–28.

Preston, S. H. 1993. Demographic changes in the United States, 1970–2050. In *Demography and retirement: The twenty-first century*, edited by A. M. Rappaport and S. J. Schieber, 19–48. Westport, CT: Praeger.

Quenouille, M. H., et al. 1951. Statistical studies of recorded energy expenditure in Man. Technical Communication no. 17. Aberdeenshire, Scotland: Commonwealth Bureau of Animal Nutrition.

Richards, T. 1984. Weather, nutrition and the economy: The analysis of short run fluctuations in births, deaths and marriages, France 1740–1909. In *Pre-industrial population change*, edited by T. Bengtsson, G. Fridlizius, and R. Ohlsson, 357–89. Stockholm: Almquist and Wiksell International.

Robbins, S. L., R. S. Cotran, and V. Kumar. 1984. *Pathologic basis of disease*. 3d ed. Philadelphia: W. B. Saunders.

Saba, T. M., B. C. Dillon, and M. E. Lanser. 1983. Fibronectin and phagocytic host defense: Relationship to nutritional support. *Journal of Parenteral and Enteral Nutrition* 7: 62–68.

Schieber, G. J., J.-P. Poullier, and L. M. Greenwald. 1993. Health care systems in twenty-four countries. *Health Affairs* 10(3): 22–38.

Schwartz, W. B., and H. J. Aaron. 1991. Must we ration health care? *Best's Review*. January, 37–41.

Scrimshaw, N. S. 1993. Malnutrition, brain development, learning and behavior. The Twentieth Kamla Puri Sabharwal Memorial Lecture presented at Lady Irwin College, New Delhi (November 23). Typescript.

Scrimshaw, N. S., and J. E. Gordon, eds. 1968. *Malnutrition, learning and behavior*. Cambridge: MIT Press.

Scrimshaw, N. S., C. E. Taylor, and J. E. Gordon. 1968. *Interactions of nutrition and infection*. Geneva: World Health Organization.

Seckler, D. 1980. Malnutrition: An intellectual odyssey. *Western Journal of Agricultural Economics* 5: 219–27.

Sen, A. 1981. *Poverty and famines: An essay on entitlement and deprivation*. Oxford: Clarendon Press.

Shammas, C. 1984. The eighteenth-century English diet and economic change. *Explorations in Economic History* 21: 254–69.

— — —. 1990. *The pre-industrial consumer in England and America*. Oxford: Clarendon Press.

Shuttleworth, J. S. 1990. Ethical issues in long-term care. *Journal of the Medical Association of Georgia* 79: 843–45.

Sommer, A., and M. S. Lowenstein. 1975. Nutritional status and mortality: A prospective validation of the QUAC stick. *American Journal of Clinical Nutrition* 28: 287–92.

Srinivasan, T. N. 1992. Undernutrition: Concepts, measurement, and policy implications. In *Nutrition and poverty*, edited by S. R. Osmani, 97–120. Oxford: Clarendon Press.

Sukhatme, P. V. 1982. Poverty and malnutrition. In *Newer concepts in nutrition and their implications for policy*, edited by P. V. Sukhatme, 11–63. Pune, India: Maharashtra Association for the Cultivation of Science Research Institute.

Tanner, J. M. 1990. *Foetus into man: Physical growth from conception to maturity*, rev. ed. Cambridge: Harvard University Press.

— — —. 1993. Review of D. J. P. Barker's *Fetal and infant origins of adult disease*. *Annals of Human Biology* 20: 508–509.

Thatcher, A. R. 1992. Trends in numbers and mortality at high ages in England and Wales. *Population Studies* 46: 411–26.

Toutain, J. 1971. La consommation alimentaire en France de 1789 à 1964. *Economies et Sociétés, Cahiers de l'ISEA* 5(11): 1909–2049.

U. S. Bureau of Statistics. 1975. *Historical statistics of the United States, colonial times to 1970*. Washington, D.C.: GPO.

U. S. Department of Health and Human Services. 1987. Anthropometric reference data and prevalence of overweight. Vital and Health Statistics, Series 11 no. 238. Washington, D.C.: GPO.

Vaupel, J. W. 1991a. The impact of population aging on health and health care costs: Uncertainties and new evidence about life expectancy. Unpublished manuscript, Center for Health and Social Policy, Odense University, Denmark.

— — —. 1991b. Prospects for a longer life expectancy. Paper presented to the annual meeting of the Population Association of America, Washington, D.C. (March 21–23).

Vaupel, J. W., and H. Lundström. 1994. Prospects for longer life expectancy. In *Economics of aging*, edited by David Wise. Chicago: University of Chicago Press (for NBER), forthcoming.

Veblen, T. [1899] 1934. *The theory of the leisure class: An economic study of institutions.* New York: Modern Library.

Volpe, J. J. 1987. Hypoxic-ischemic encephalopathy—Clinical aspects. In *Neurology of the newborn*, 2d ed., 236—79. Philadelphia: W. B. Saunders.

Waaler, H. T. 1984. Height, weight and mortality: The Norwegian experience. *Acta Medica Scandinavica* suppl. 679: 1—51.

Weir, D. R. 1982. Fertility transition in rural France, 1740—1829. Ph.D. diss., Stanford University.

— — —. 1989. Markets and mortality in France, 1600—1789. In *Famine, disease and the social order in early modern society*, edited by J. Walter, and R. Schofield, 201—34. Cambridge: Cambridge University Press.

— — —. 1993. Parental consumption decisions and child health during the early French fertility decline, 1790—1914. *Journal of Economic History* 53: 259—74.

West, P., et al. 1990. Social class and health in youth: Findings from The West of Scotland Twenty-07 Study. *Social Science and Medicine* 30: 665—73.

Wolfe, B. L. 1986. Health status and medical expenditures: Is there a link? *Social Science and Medicine* 22: 993—99.

Wrigley, E. A. 1987. Urban growth and agricultural change: England and the continent in the early modern period. In *Peoples, cities and wealth: The transformation of traditional society*, 157—93. Oxford: Basil Blackwell.

Wrigley, E. A., and R. S. Schofield. 1981. *The population history of England, 1541—1871: A reconstruction.* Cambridge: Harvard University Press.

Young, V. R., and N. S. Scrimshaw. 1971. The physiology of starvation. *Scientific American* 225(October): 14—21.

Douglass C North

DOUGLASS C. NORTH

I was born in Cambridge, Massachusetts – not because my family had any connection with higher education, but because my father was a manager at the Metropolitan Life Insurance Company in a nearby town and Cambridge was the nearest hospital – in 1920. In the ensuing years we moved a number of times as a result of my father's business. First Connecticut and then, when he became head of the Metropolitan's Canadian office, Ottawa. Because my mother believed in education broadly construed, we also lived in Europe and I went to school at the Lycee Jacquard in Lausanne, Switzerland, in 1929–30. My brother and sister are both older than I am and were born before my father went off to World War I.

I went to elementary school in Ottawa, and then to a private secondary school. When we moved back to the United States in 1933, I went to private schools in New York City and on Long Island, and then completed my high school education at the Choate School in Wallingford, Connecticut. While I was there I became deeply interested in photography, and indeed the most noteworthy event in my early life was winning first, third, fourth and seventh prizes in an international competition for college and high school students.

Our family life was certainly not intellectual. My father had not even completed high school when he started as an office boy working for the Metropolitan Life Insurance Company, and I am not sure that my mother completed high school. Nevertheless, she was an exciting person, intelligent, intellectually curious, and she played an important part in my intellectual development. My aunt and uncle were, and in the case of my aunt (Adelaide North) still is, a powerful influence. They introduced me to classical music and my aunt continues to be, to this day, a very special person in my life.

When it came time to go to college I had been accepted for Harvard when my father was offered the position of head of the Metropolitan Life Insurance Company office on the west coast, and we moved to San Francisco. Because I did not want to be that far from home, I decided to go instead to the University of California at Berkeley. While I was there my life was completely changed by becoming a convinced Marxist and engaging in a variety of student liberal activities. I was opposed to World War II, and indeed on June 22, 1941 when Hitler invaded the Soviet Union I suddenly found myself the lone supporter of peace since everybody else had, because of their communist beliefs, shifted over to become supporters of the war. My record at the University of California as an undergraduate was mediocre to say the best. I had only slightly better than a "C" average, although I did have a triple major in political science, philosophy, and economics. I had hoped to go to law school, but the war started, and because of the strong feeling that I did not want to kill anybody, I joined the Merchant Marine when I graduated from Berkeley. We had been to sea only a short time when the Captain called me up on the bridge and asked me if I could learn to navigate since most of the officers had had only rudimentary educations, and we needed to get from San Francisco to Australia. I became navigator and enjoyed it very much. We made repeated trips from San Francisco to Australia, and then to the front lines in New Guinea and the Solomon Islands.

What the war did was give me the opportunity of three years of continuous reading, and it was in the course of reading that I became convinced that I should become an economist. Then the last year of the war I taught celo-navigation at the Maritime Service Officers' School in Alameda, California; I took up photography again and had a difficult decision as to whether to become a photographer or go into economics. In the summer of 1941 I had worked with Dorothea Lange, head of the photographic division of the Farm Security Administration, travelling with and photographing migrants through the Central Valley of California. Now Dorothea tried to persuade me to become a photographer. Her husband, Paul Taylor, who was in the economics department at the University of California, tried to persuade me to become an economist. He won.

I went back to graduate school with the clear intention that what I wanted to do with my life was to improve societies, and the way to do that was to find out what made economies work the way they did or fail to work. I believed that once we had an understanding of what determined the performance of economies through time, we could then improve their performance. I have never lost sight of that objective.

I cannot say that I learned much formal economics as a graduate student in Berkeley. My most influential professors were Robert Brady; Leo Rogin, a Marxist and a very influential teacher of history of economic thought; and M. M. Knight (Frank Knight's brother) who certainly was agnostic, to say the least, about theory, but who had a wonderful knowledge of the facts and background in economic history. He became my mentor and my thesis advisor at Berkeley. But while I learned by rote most of the theory I was supposed to know, I did not acquire a real understanding of theory. It was not until I got my first job, at the University of Washington in Seattle, and began playing chess with Don Gordon, a brilliant young theorist, that I learned economic theory. In the three years of playing chess every day from noon to two, I may have beaten Don at chess, but he taught me economics; more important he taught me how to reason like an economist, and that skill is still perhaps the most important set of tools that I have acquired.

I had written my dissertation on the history of life insurance in the United States and had had a Social Science Research Council Fellowship to go to the East Coast and do the spade work. That turned out to be a very productive year. I not only sat in on Robert Merton's seminars in sociology at Columbia, but also became deeply involved in the Entrepreneurial school of Arthur Cole at Harvard. The result was that Joseph Schumpeter had a strong influence upon me. My early work and publications centered around expanding on the analysis of life insurance in my dissertation and its relationship to investment banking.

I next turned to developing an analytical framework to look at regional economic growth and this led to my first article in the Journal of Political Economy, entitled "Location Theory and Regional Economic Growth." That work eventually led me to developing a staple theory of economic growth.

I was very fortunate that at a meeting of the Economic History Association I come to know Solomon Fabricant, who was then director of research at the National Bureau of Economic Research; and in 1956–57 I was invited to spend the year at the Bureau as a research associate. That was an enormously important year in my life. I not only became acquainted with most of the leading economists who passed through the bureau, but spent one day a week in Baltimore with Simon Kuznets and did the empirical work that led to my early major quantitative study of the balance of payments of the United States from 1790 to 1860.

I married for the first time in 1944. During my graduate training my wife taught school, providing our major source of support. We had three sons, Douglass, Christopher, and Malcolm, born between 1951 and 1957. After the boys were in school my wife became a successful politician in the Washington State legislature.

Between my year at the National Bureau and 1966–67, when I went off to Geneva as a Ford Faculty Fellow, I did my major work in American economic history, which led to my first book, The Economic Growth of the United States from 1790 to 1860. It was a straightforward analysis of how markets work in the context of an export staple model of growth.

By this time (1960) there was a substantial stirring to try to change and transform economic history. The year that I was at NBER, the Bureau and the Economic History Association had the first joint quantitative program on the growth of the American economy, a conference that was held at Williamstown, Massachusetts, in the late spring of 1957. This meeting was really the beginning of the new economic history, but the program coalesced when Jon Hughes and Lance Davis, two former students of mine who had become faculty members at Purdue, called the first conference of economic historians interested in trying to develop and apply economic theory and quantitative methods to history. The first meeting was held in February of 1960. This program was highly successful and the reception that it received amongst economists was certainly enthusiastic. Economics departments very quickly became interested in having new economic historians, or, as we came to call ourselves, cliometricians (Clio being the muse of history). Therefore, as I developed a graduate program jointly with my colleague Morris David Morris at the University of Washington we attracted some of the best students to do work in economic history, and during the

1960s and early 70s the job market was very responsive and our students were easily placed throughout the country.

In 1966–67 I decided that I should switch from American to European economic history, and therefore, when I received the above-mentioned grant to live in Geneva for a year, I decided to re-tool. Re-tooling turned out to change my life radically, since I quickly became convinced that the tools of neo-classical economic theory were not up to the task of explaining the kind of fundamental societal change that had characterized European economies from medieval times onward. We needed new tools, but they simply did not exist. It was in the long search for a framework that would provide new tools of analysis that my interest and concern with the new institutional economics evolved. The result was two initial books, one with Lance Davis, *Institutional Change and American Economic Growth,* and the other with Robert Thomas, *The Rise of the Western World: A New Economic History.*

Both books were early tentative attempts to develop some tools of institutional analysis and apply them to economic history. Both were still predicated on neo-classical economic theory, and there were too many loose ends that did not make sense: such as the notion that institutions were efficient (however defined). Perhaps more serious, it was not possible to explain long-run poor economic performance in a neo-classical framework. So I began to explore what was wrong. Individual beliefs were obviously important to the choices people make, and only the extreme myopia of economists prevented them from understanding that ideas, ideologies, and prejudices mattered. Once you recognize that, you are forced to examine the rationality postulate critically.

The long road towards developing a new analytical framework involved taking all of these considerations seriously: to develop a view of institutions that would account for why institutions produced results that in the long-run did not manage to produce economic growth; develop a model of political economy in order to be able to handle and explain the underlying source of institutions. Finally, one had to come to grips with why people had the ideologies and ideas that determined the choices they made.

In Structure and Change in Economic History (1981) I abandoned the notion that institutions were efficient and attempted to explain why "inefficient" rules would tend to exist and be perpetuated. This was tied to a very simple and still neo-classical theory of the state which could explain why the state could produce rules that did not encourage economic growth. I was still dissatisfied with our understanding of the political process, and indeed searched for colleagues who were interested in developing political-economic models. This led me to leave the University of Washington in 1983 after being there for 33 years, and to move to Washington University in St. Louis where there was an exciting group of young political scientists and economists who were attempting to develop new models of political economy. This proved to be a felicitous move. I created the Center in Political Economy, which continues to be a creative research center.

The development of a political-economic framework to explore long-run institutional change occupied me during all of the 1980s and led to the publication of *Institutions, Institutional Change and Economic Performance* in 1990. In that book I began to puzzle seriously about the rationality postulate. It is clear that we had to have an explanation for why people make the choices they do; why ideologies such as communism or Muslim fundamentalism can shape the choices people make and direct the way economies evolve through long periods of time. One simply cannot get at ideologies without digging deeply into cognitive science in attempting to understand the way in which the mind acquires learning and makes choices. Since 1990, my research has been directed toward dealing with this issue. I still have a long way to go, but I believe that an understanding of how people make choices; under what conditions the rationality postulate is a useful tool; and how individuals make choices under conditions of uncertainty and ambiguity are fundamental questions that we must address in order to make further progress in the social sciences.

In 1972 I married again, to Elisabeth Case; she continues to be wife, companion, critic and editor: a partner in the projects and programs that we undertake.

I would be remiss if I left the impression that my life has been totally preoccupied with scholarly research. True, it has been the fundamental focus of my life, but it has been intermingled with a variety of activities that have complemented that central preoccupation and enriched my life. I continue to be a photographer; I have enjoyed fishing and hunting with a close friend; and have owned two ranches, first in northern California and then in the state of Washington. I learned to fly an airplane, and had my own airplane during the 1960s. I have always taken seriously good food and wine. In addition, music has continued to be an important part of my life.

My wife and I now live in the summers in northern Michigan in an environment which is wonderfully conducive to research, and where most of my work in the last 15 years has been done. I work on research all morning. In the afternoons I hike with my dog, play tennis or go swimming. In the evening, as we are only 16 miles from the National Music Camp at Interlochen, we may listen to music two or three nights a week. It is a wonderful place for that mixture of research and leisure which has made my life such a rich experience.

ECONOMIC PERFORMANCE THROUGH TIME

Nobel Lecture, December 9, 1993

by

Douglass C. North

Washington University, Eliot Hall 205, St Louis, MO 63130-4899, USA*

I

Economic history is about the performance of economies through time. The objective of research in the field is not only to shed new light on the economic past but also to contribute to economic theory by providing an analytical framework that will enable us to understand economic change. A theory of economic dynamics comparable in precision to general equilibrium theory would be the ideal tool of analysis. In the absence of such a theory we can describe the characteristics of past economies, examine the performance of economies at various times, and engage in comparative static analysis; but missing is an analytical understanding of the way economies evolve through time.

A theory of economic dynamics is also crucial for the field of economic development. There is no mystery why the field of development has failed to develop during the five decades since the end of the second World War. Neo-classical theory is simply an inappropriate tool to analyze and prescribe policies that will induce development. It is concerned with the operation of markets, not with how markets develop. How can one prescribe policies when one doesn't understand how economies develop? The very methods employed by neo-classical economists have dictated the subject matter and militated against such a development. That theory in the pristine form that gave it mathematical precision and elegance modeled a frictionless and static world. When applied to economic history and development it focused on technological development and more recently human capital investment, but ignored the incentive structure embodied in institutions that determined the extent of societal investment in those factors. In the analysis of economic performance through time it contained two erroneous assumptions: one that institutions do not matter and two that time does not matter.

* I am indebted to Robert Bates, Lee and Alexandra Benham, Avner Greif, Margaret Levi, Randy Nielsen, John Nye, Jean-Laurent Rosenthal, Norman Schofield, and Barry Weingast for their comments on an earlier draft and to Elisabeth Case for editing this essay.

This essay is about institutions and time. It does not provide a theory of economic dynamics comparable to general equilibrium theory. We do not have such a theory.[1] Rather it provides the initial scaffolding of an analytical framework capable of increasing our understanding of the historical evolution of economies and a necessarily crude guide to policy in the ongoing task of improving the economic performance of economies. The analytical framework is a modification of neo-classical theory. What it retains is the fundamental assumption of scarcity and hence competition and the analytical tools of micro-economic theory. What it modifies is the rationality assumption. What it adds is the dimension of time.

Institutions form the incentive structure of a society and the political and economic institutions, in consequence, are the underlying determinant of economic performance. Time as it relates to economic and societal change is the dimension in which the learning process of human beings shapes the way institutions evolve. That is, the beliefs that individuals, groups, and societies hold which determine choices are a consequence of learning through time—not just the span of an individual's life or of a generation of a society but the learning embodied in individuals, groups, and societies that is cumulative through time and passed on intergenerationally by the culture of a society.

The next two sections of this essay summarize the work I, and others, have done on the nature of institutions and the way they affect economic performance (II) and then characterize the nature of institutional change (III).[2] The remaining four sections describe a cognitive science approach to human learning (IV); provide an institutional/cognitive approach to economic history (V); indicate the implications of this approach for improving our understanding of the past (VI); and finally suggest implications for current development policies (VII).

II

Institutions are the humanly devised constraints that structure human interaction. They are made up of formal constraints (rules, laws, constitutions), informal constraints (norms of behavior, conventions, and self imposed codes of conduct), and their enforcement characteristics. Together they define the incentive structure of societies and specifically economies.

Institutions and the technology employed determine the transaction and transformation costs that add up to the costs of production. It was Ronald Coase (1960) who made the crucial connection beween institutions, transaction costs, and neo-classical theory. The neo-classical result of efficient markets only obtains when it is costless to transact. Only under the conditions of costless bargaining will the actors reach the solution that maximizes aggregate income regardless of the institutional arrangements. When it is costly to transact then institutions matter. And it is costly to transact. Wallis and North (1986) demonstrated in an empirical study that 45 percent of U.S. GNP was devoted to the transaction sector in 1970. Efficient markets are created in the real world when competition is strong enough via arbitrage and efficient information feedback to approximate the Coase zero transaction cost conditions and the parties can realize the gains from trade inherent in the neo-classical argument.

But the informational and institutional requirements necessary to achieve such efficient markets are stringent. Players must not only have objectives but know the correct way to achieve them. But how do the players know the correct way to achieve their objectives? The instrumental rationality answer is that even though the actors may initially have diverse and erroneous models, the informational feedback process and arbitraging actors will correct initially incorrect models, punish deviant behavior and lead surviving players to correct models.

An even more stringent implicit requirement of the discipline-of-the-competitive-market model is that when there are significant transaction costs, the consequent institutions of the market will be designed to induce the actors to acquire the essential information that will lead them to correct their models. The implication is not only that institutions are designed to achieve efficient outcomes but that they can be ignored in economic analysis because they play no independent role in economic performance.

These are stringent requirements that are realized only very exceptionally. Individuals typically act on incomplete information and with subjectively derived models that are frequently erroneous; the information feedback is typically insufficient to correct these subjective models. Institutions are not necessarily or even usually created to be socially efficient; rather they, or at least the formal rules, are created to serve the interests of those with the bargaining power to create new rules. In a world of zero transaction costs, bargaining strength does not affect the efficiency of outcomes; but in a world of positive transaction costs it does.

It is exceptional to find economic markets that approximate the conditions necessary for efficiency. It is impossible to find political markets that do. The reason is straightforward. Transaction costs are the costs of specifying what is being exchanged and of enforcing the consequent agreements. In economic markets what is being specified (measured) is the valuable attributes—the physical and property rights dimensions—of goods and services or the performance of agents. While measurement can frequently be costly, there are some standard criteria: the physical dimensions have objective characteristics (size, weight, color, etc.) and the property rights dimensions are defined in legal terms. Competition also plays a critical role in reducing enforcement costs. The judicial system provides coercive enforcement. Still, economic markets in the past and present are typically imperfect and beset by high transaction costs.

Measuring and enforcing agreements in political markets is far more difficult. What is being exchanged (between constituents and legislators in a democracy) is promises for votes. The voter has little incentive to become informed because the likelihood that one's vote matters is infinitesimal; further the complexity of the issues produces genuine uncertainty. Enforcement of political agreements is beset by difficulties. Competition is far less effective than in economic markets. For a variety of simple, easy-to-measure and important-to-constituent-well-being policies, constituents may be well informed, but beyond such straightforward policy issues ideological stereotyping takes over and (as I shall argue below in section IV) shapes the consequent performance of economies.[3] It is the polity that defines and enforces property rights and in consequence it is not surprising that efficient economic markets are so exceptional.

III

It is the interaction between institutions and organizations that shapes the institutional evolution of an economy. If institutions are the rules of the game, organizations and their entrepreneurs are the players.

Organizations are made up of groups of individuals bound together by some common purpose to achieve certain objectives. Organizations include political bodies (political parties, the Senate, a city council, regulatory bodies), economic bodies (firms, trade unions, family farms, cooperatives), social bodies (churches, clubs, athletic associations), educational bodies (schools, universities, vocational training centers).

The organizations that come into existence will reflect the opportunities provided by the institutional matrix. That is, if the institutional framework rewards piracy then piratical organizations will come into existence; and if the institutional framework rewards productive activities then organizations—firms—will come into existence to engage in productive activities.

Economic change is a ubiquitous, ongoing, incremental process that is a consequence of the choices individual actors and entrepreneurs of organizations are making every day. While the vast majority of these decisions are routine (Nelson and Winter, 1982) some involve altering existing "contracts" between individuals and organizations. Sometimes that recontracting can be accomplished within the existing structure of property rights and political rules; but sometimes new contracting forms require an alteration in the rules. Equally, norms of behavior that guide exchanges will gradually be modified or wither away. In both instances, institutions are being altered.

Modifications occur because individuals perceive that they could do better by restructuring exchanges (political or economic). The source of the changed perceptions may be exogenous to the economy—for instance a change in the price or quality of a competitive product in another economy that alters perceptions of entrepreneurs in the given economy about profitable opportunities. But the most fundamental long run source of change is learning by individuals and entrepreneurs of organizations.

While idle curiosity will result in learning, the rate of learning will reflect the intensity of competition amongst organizations. Competition, reflecting ubiquitous scarcity, induces organizations to engage in learning to survive. The degree of competition can and does vary. The greater the degree of monopoly power the lower the incentive to learn.

The speed of economic change is a function of the rate of learning but the direction of that change is a function of the expected pay-offs to acquiring different kinds of knowledge. The mental models that the players develop shape perceptions about the pay-offs.

IV

It is necessary to dismantle the rationality assumption underlying economic theory in order to approach constructively the nature of human learning. History demonstrates that ideas, ideologies, myths, dogmas, and prejudices matter; and an understanding of the way they evolve is necessary for further progress in developing a framework to understand societal change. The rational choice framework assumes that individuals know what is in their self interest and act accordingly. That may be correct for individuals making choices in the highly developed markets of modern economies[4] but it is patently false in making choices under conditions of uncertainty—the conditions that have characterized the political and economic choices that shaped (and continue to shape) historical change.

Herbert Simon has stated the issues succinctly:

> If... we accept the proposition that both the knowledge and the computational power of the decisionmaker are severely limited, then we must distinguish between the real world and the actor's perception of it and reasoning about it. That is to say we must construct a theory (and test it empirically) of the process of decision. Our theory must include not only the reasoning processes but also the processes that generated the actor's subjective representation of the decision problem, his or her frame. (Simon, 1986, pp. S210–11)

The analytical framework we must build, must originate in an understanding of how human learning takes place. We have a way to go before we can construct such a theory but cognitive science has made immense strides in recent years—enough strides to suggest a tentative approach that can help us understand decision making under uncertainty.[5]

Learning entails developing a structure by which to interpret the varied signals received by the senses. The initial architecture of the structure is genetic but the subsequent scaffolding is a result of the experiences of the individual. The experiences can be classified into two kinds—those from the physical environment and those from the socio-cultural linguistic environment. The structures consist of categories—classifications that gradually evolve from earliest childhood to organize our perceptions and keep track of our memory of analytic results and experiences. Building on these classifications, we form mental models to explain and interpret the environment—typically in ways relevant to some goal. Both the categories and the mental models will evolve, reflecting the feedback derived from new experiences: feedback that sometimes strengthens our initial categories and models or may lead to modifications—in short, learning. Thus, the mental models may be continually redefined with new experiences, including contact with others' ideas.

At this juncture the learning process of human beings diverges from that of other animals (such as the sea slug—a favorite research subject of cognitive scientists) and particularly diverges from the computer analogy that dominated early studies of artificial intelligence. The mind appears to order and reorder the mental models from their special purpose origins to successively more abstract form so that they become available to process other information. The term used by Clark and Karmiloff-Smith (1993) is representational redescription. The capacity to generalize from the particular to the general and to use analogy is a part of this redescription process. It is this capacity that is the source not only of creative thinking but also of the ideologies and belief systems that underlie the choices humans make.[6]

A common cultural heritage provides a means of reducing the divergence in the mental models that people in a society have, and constitutes the means for the intergenerational transfer of unifying perceptions. In premodern societies cultural learning provided a means of internal communication; it also provided shared explanations for phenomena outside the immediate experiences of the members of society in the form of religions, myths and dogmas. Such belief structures are not, however, confined to primitive societies but are an essential part of modern societies as well.

Belief structures get transformed into societal and economic structures by institutions—both formal rules and informal norms of behavior. The relationship between mental models and institutions is an intimate one. Mental models are the internal representations that individual cognitive sytems create to interpret the environment; institutions are the external (to the mind) mechanisms individuals create to structure and order the environment.

V

There is no guarantee that the beliefs and institutions that evolve through time will produce economic growth. Let me pose the issue that time presents us by a brief institutional/cognitive story of long-run economic/political change.

As tribes evolved in different physical environments they developed different languages and, with different experiences, different mental models to explain the world around them. The languages and mental models formed the informal constraints that defined the institutional framework of the tribe and were passed down intergenerationally as customs, taboos, and myths that provided cultural continuity.[7]

With growing specialization and division of labor the tribes evolved into polities and economies; the diversity of experience and learning produced increasingly different societies and civilizations with different degrees of success in solving the fundamental economic problem of scarcity. The reason is that as the complexity of the environment increased as human beings became increasingly interdependent, more complex institutional structures were necessary to capture the potential gains from trade. Such evolution requires that the society develop institutions that will permit anonymous, impersonal exchange across time and space. To the extent that the culture and local experiences had produced diverse institutions and belief systems with respect to the gains from such cooperation, the likelihood of creating the necessary institutions to capture the gains from trade of more complex contracting varied. In fact most societies throughout history got "stuck" in an institutional matrix that did not evolve into the impersonal exchange essential to capturing the productivity gains that came from the specialization and division of labor that have produced the Wealth of Nations.

The key to the foregoing story is the kind of learning that the individuals in a society acquired through time. Time in this context entails not only current experiences and learning but also the cumulative experience of past generations that is embodied in culture. Collective learning—a term used by Hayek—consists of those experiences that have passed the slow test of time and are embodied in our language, institutions, technology, and ways of doing things. It is "the transmission in time of our accumulated stock of knowledge" (Hayek 1960: 27). It is culture that provides the key to path dependence—a term used to describe the powerful influence of the past on the present and future. The current learning of any generation takes place within the context of the perceptions derived from collective learning. Learning then is an incremental process filtered by the culture of a society which determines the perceived pay-offs, but there is no guarantee that the cumulative past experience of a society will necessarily fit them to solve new problems. Societies that get "stuck" embody belief systems and institutions that fail to confront and solve new problems of societal complexity.

We need to understand a great deal more about the cumulative learning of a society. The learning process appears to be a function of 1) the way in which a given belief structure filters the information derived from experiences; and 2) the different experiences confronting individuals and societies at different times. The perceived rate of return (private) may be high to military technology (in medieval Europe), to the pursuit and refinement of religious dogma (Rome during and after Constantine) or to the research for an accurate chronometer to determine longitude at sea (for which a substantial reward was offered during the age of exploration).

The incentives to acquire pure knowledge, the essential underpinning of modern economic growth, are affected by monetary rewards and punishments; they are also fundamentally influenced by a society's tolerance of creative developments, as a long list of creative individuals from Galileo to Darwin could attest. While there is a substantial literature on the origins and development of science, very little of it deals with the links between institutional structure, belief systems and the incentives and disincentives to acquire pure knowledge. A major factor in the development of Western Europe was the gradual perception of the utility of research in pure science.

Incentives embodied in belief systems as expressed in institutions determine economic performance through time, and however we wish to define economic performance the historical record is clear. Throughout most of history and for most societies in the past and present, economic performance has been anything but satisfactory. Human beings have, by trial and error, learned how to make economies perform better; but not only has this learning taken ten millenia (since the first economic revolution)—it has still escaped the grasp of almost half of the world's population. Moreover the radical improvement in economic performance, even when narrowly defined as material well-being, is a modern phenomenon of the last few centuries and confined until the last few decades to a small part of the world. Explaining the pace and direction of economic change throughout history presents a major puzzle.

Let us represent the human experience to date as a 24 hour clock in which the beginning consists of the time (apparently in Africa between 4 and 5 million years ago) when humans became separate from other primates. Then the beginning of so-called civilization occurs with the development of agriculture and permanent settlement in about 8000 B.C. in the Fertile Crescent—in the last three or four minutes of the clock. For the other twenty three hours and fifty six or seven minutes, humans remained hunters and gatherers and while population grew it did so at a very slow pace.

Now if we make a new 24 hour clock for the time of civilization—the ten thousand years from development of agriculture to the present—the pace of change appears to be very slow for the first 12 hours although our archeological knowledge is very limited. Historical demographers speculate that the rate of population growth may have doubled as compared to the previous era but still was very slow. The pace of change accelerates in the past five thousand years with the rise and then decline of economies and civilizations. Population may have grown from about three hundred million at the time of Christ to about eight hundred million by 1750—a substantial acceleration as compared to earlier rates of growth. The last 250 years—just 35 minutes on our new 24 hour clock—are the era of modern economic growth accompanied by a population explosion that now puts world population in excess of five billion.

If we focus now on the last 250 years we see that growth was largely restricted to Western Europe and the overseas extensions of Britain for 200 of those 250 years.

Not only has the pace varied over the ages; the change has not been unidirectional. That is not simply a consequence of the decline of individual civilizations; there have been periods of apparent secular stagnation—the most recent being the long hiatus between the end of the Roman Empire in the west and the revival of Western Europe approximately five hundred years later.

VI

What can an institutional/cognitive approach contribute to improving our understanding of the economic past? First of all it should make sense out of the very uneven pattern of economic performance described in the previous section. There is nothing automatic about the evolving of conditions that will permit low cost transacting in the impersonal markets that are essential to productive economies. Game theory characterizes the issue. Individuals will usually find it worthwhile cooperating with others in exchange when the play is repeated, when they possess complete information about the other player's past performance, and when there are small numbers of players. Cooperation is difficult to sustain when the game is not repeated (or there is an endgame), when information about the other players is lacking, and when there are large numbers of players. Creating the institutions that will alter the benefit/cost ratios in favor of cooperation in impersonal exchange is a complex process because it not only entails the creation of economic institutions but requires that they be undergirded by appropriate political institutions.

We are just beginning to explore the nature of this historical process. The remarkable development of Western Europe from relative backwardness in the tenth century to world economic hegemony by the eighteenth century is a story of a gradually evolving belief system in the context of competition among fragmented political/economic units producing economic institutions and political structure that produced modern economic growth.[8] And even within Western Europe there were successes (The Netherlands and England) and failures (Spain and Portugal) reflecting diverse external environmental experiences.[9]

Second, institutional/cognitive analysis should explain path dependence, one of the remarkable regularities of history. Why do economies once on a path of growth or stagnation tend to persist? Pioneering work on this subject is beginning to give us insights into the sources of path dependence (Arthur, 1989 and David, 1985). But there is much that we still do not know. The rationality assumption of neo-classical theory would suggest that political entrepreneurs of stagnating economies could simply alter the rules and change the direction of failed economies. It is not that rulers have been unaware of poor performance. Rather the difficulty of turning economies around is a function of the nature of political markets and, underlying that, the belief systems of the actors. The long decline of Spain, for example, from the glories of the Habsburg Empire of the sixteenth century to its sorry state under Franco in the twentieth century was characterized by endless self appraisals and frequently bizarre proposed solutions.[10]

Third, this approach will contribute to our understanding of the complex interplay between institutions, technology, and demography in the overall process of economic change. A complete theory of economic performance would entail such an integrated approach to economic history. We certainly have not put all the pieces together yet. For example, Robert Fogel's path breaking work on demographic theory[11] and its historical implications for reevaluating past economic performance has yet to be fully integrated with institutional analysis. The same is true for technological change. The important contributions of Nathan Rosenberg (1976) and Joel Mokyr (1990), exploring the impetus for and consequences of technological change have ongoing implications which need to be integrated with institutional analysis. An essay by Wallis and North (forthcoming) is a beginning at integrating technological and institutional analysis. But a major task of economic history is to integrate these separate strands of research.

VII

We cannot account for the rise and decline of the Soviet Union and world communism with the tools of neo-classical analysis, but we should with an institutional/cognitive approach to contemporary problems of development. To do so—and to provide an analytical framework to understand economic change—we must take into account the following implications of this approach:

1. It is the admixture of formal rules, informal norms, and enforcement characteristics that shapes economic performance. While the rules may be changed overnight, the informal norms usually change only gradually. Since it is the norms that provide "legitimacy" to a set of rules, revolutionary change is never as revolutionary as its supporters desire and performance will be different than anticipated. And economies that adopt the formal rules of another economy will have very different performance characteristics than the first economy because of different informal norms and enforcement. The implication is that transferring the formal political and economic rules of successful western market economies to Third World and eastern European economies is not a sufficient condition for good economic performance. Privatization is not a panacea for solving poor economic performance.

2. Polities significantly shape economic performance because they define and enforce the economic rules. Therefore, an essential part of development policy is the creation of polities that will create and enforce efficient property rights. However, we know very little about how to create such polities because the new political economy (the new institutional economics applied to politics) has been largely focused on the United States and developed polities. A pressing research need is to model Third World and eastern European polities. However, the foregoing analysis does have some implications:

a. Political institutions will be stable only if undergirded by organizations with a stake in their perpetuation.

b. Both institutions and belief systems must change for successful reform since it is the mental models of the actors that will shape choices.

c. Developing norms of behavior that will support and legitimize new rules is a lengthy process and in the absence of such reinforcing mechanisms polities will tend to be unstable.

d. While economic growth can occur in the short run with autocratic regimes, long run economic growth entails the development of the rule of law.

e. Informal constraints (norms, conventions and codes of conduct) favorable to growth can sometimes produce economic growth even with unstable or adverse political rules. The key is the degree to which such adverse rules are enforced.

3. It is adaptive rather than allocative efficiency which is the key to long run growth. Successful political/economic systems have evolved flexible institutional structures that can survive the shocks and changes that are a part of successful evolution. But these systems have been a product of long gestation. We do not know how to create adaptive efficiency in the short run.

We have just set out on the long road to achieving an understanding of economic performance through time. The ongoing research embodying new hypotheses confronting historical evidence not only will create an analytical framework enabling us to understand economic change through time; in the process it will enrich economic theory enabling it to deal effectively with a wide range of contemporary issues currently beyond its ken. The promise is there. The recognition of that promise by the Nobel Committee should be the essential spur to move us on down that road.

NOTES

1. In fact such a theory is unlikely. I refer the reader to Frank Hahn's prediction about the future of economic theory (Hahn, 1991).
2. These two sections briefly summarize material contained in North (1990a).
3. See the author's "A Transaction Cost Theory of Politics" for a transaction cost approach to the relative inefficiency of political markets (North, 1990b).
4. However, see the anomalies even here in the studies by Kahneman, Tversky and others (Hogarth and Reder, 1986).
5. See Holland et al. (1986) for an excellent introduction to the cognitive science literature.
6. Ideologies are shared frameworks of mental models that groups of individuals possess that provide both an interpretation of the environment and a prescription as to how that environment should be ordered.
7. Ronald Heiner (1983) in a path-breaking article not only made the connection between the mental capacities of humans and the external environment but suggested the implications for arresting economic progress.
8. See North and Thomas (1973), Jones (1981), Rosenberg and Birdzell (1986) for accounts of this growth.
9. See North (1990a) Part III for a brief discussion of the contrasting paths of The Netherlands and England on the one hand and Spain on the other.
10. DeVries (1976) has a description of the bizarre remedies proposed by a Royal Commission to reverse Spain's decline (p.28).
11. See Fogel's accompanying Nobel lecture.

REFERENCES

Arthur, Brian, (1989) "Competing Technologies, Increasing Returns, and Lockin by Historical Events", *Economic Journal 99* (March): 116–131.

Clark, Andy, and Annette Karmiloff-Smith, (forthcoming) "The Cognizer's Innards: A Psychological and Philosophical Perspective on the Development of Thought," *Mind and Language.*

Coase, Ronald, (1960) "The Problem of Social Cost," *Journal of Law and Economics* 3(1): 1–44.

David, Paul A., (1985) "Clio and the Economics of QWERTY," *American Economic Review* 75 (May): 332–37.

De Vries, Jan, (1976) *The Economy of Europe in an Age of Crises, 1600–1750,* Cambridge and New York: Cambridge University Press.

Hahn, Frank, (1991) "The Next Hundred Years," *The Economic Journal* 101 (Jan.): 47–50.

Hayek, Friedrich A., (1960) *The Constitution of Liberty,* Chicago: The University of Chicago Press.

Hogarth, Robin M., and Melvin W. Reder (eds.), (1986) *Rational Choice,* Chicago and London: The University of Chicago Press.

Heiner, Ronald (1983) "The Origins of Predictable Behavior," *American Economic Review* 75: 560–95.

Holland, John H., Keith J. Holyoak, Richard E. Nisbett and Paul R. Thagard, (1986) *Induction: Processes of Inference, Learning, and Discovery,* Cambridge: M.I.T. Press.

Jones, E.L., (1981) *The European Miracle,* Cambridge: Cambridge University Press.

Mokyr, Joel, (1990) *The Lever of Riches,* New York and Oxford: Oxford University Press.

Nelson, Richard, and Sidney G. Winter, (1982) *An Evolutionary Theory of Economic Change.* Cambridge: Harvard University Press.

North, Douglass C., (1990a) *Institutions, Institutional Change, and Economic Performance,* New York: Cambridge University Press.

North, Douglass C., (1990b) "A Transactions Cost Theory of Politics" *Journal of Theoretical Politics* 2 (4): 355–67.

North, Douglass C., and Robert P. Thomas, (1973) *The Rise of the Western World: A New Economic History,* Cambridge: Cambridge University Press.

Rosenberg, Nathan, (1976) *Perspectives on Technology,* Cambridge: Cambridge University Press.

Rosenberg, Nathan, and L.E. Birdzell, (1986) *How the West Grew Rich: The Economic Transformation of the Industrial World,* New York: Basic Books.

Simon, Herbert, (1986) "Rationality in Psychology and Economics," in Hogarth, Robin M., and Melvin W. Reder (eds.), *Rational Choice,* Chicago and London: The University of Chicago Press.

Tversky, Amos, and Daniel Kahneman, (1986) "Rational Choice and the Framing of Decisions" in Hogarth, Robin M., and Melvin M. Reder (eds.), *Rational Choice,* Chicago and London: The University of Chicago Press.

Wallis, John J., and Douglass C. North, (1986) "Measuring the Transaction Sector in the American Economy," in S.L. Engerman and R.E. Gallman, (eds.), *Long Term Factors in American Economic Growth,* Chicago: University of Chicago Press.

Wallis, John J., and Douglass C. North, (forthcoming) "Institutional Change and Technical Change in American Economic Growth: A Transactions Costs Approach, *Journal of Institutional and Theoretical Economics.*

ECONOMIC SCIENCES 1994

JOHN C. HARSANYI, JOHN F. NASH and REINHARD SELTEN

for their pioneering analysis of equilibria in the theory of non-cooperative games

THE SVERIGES RIKSBANK (BANK OF SWEDEN) PRIZE IN ECONOMIC SCIENCES IN MEMORY OF ALFRED NOBEL

Speech by Professor Karl-Göran Mäler of the Royal Swedish Academy of Sciences.
Translation from the Swedish text.

Your Majesties, Your Royal Highnesses, Ladies and Gentlemen,

Many situations in society, from everyday life to high-level politics, are characterized by what economists call strategic interactions. When there is strategic interaction, the outcome for one agent depends not only on what that agent does, but also very largely on how other agents act or react. A firm that decreases its price to attract more customers will not succeed in this strategy if the other major firms in the market use the same strategy. Whether a political party will be successful in attracting more votes by proposing lower taxes or increased spending will depend on the proposals from other parties. The success of a central bank which is trying to fight inflation by maintaining a fixed exchange rate depends – as we know – on decisions on fiscal policy, and also on reactions in markets for labor and commodities.

A simple economic example of strategic interaction is where two firms are competing with identical products on the same market. If one firm increases its production, this will make the market price fall and therefore reduce profits for the other firm. The other firm will obviously try to counteract this, for example by increasing its production and so maintaining its market share but at the cost of further reduction in market price. The first company must therefore anticipate this countermove and possible further countermoves when it makes its decision to increase production. Can we predict how the parties will choose their strategies in situations like this?

As early as the 1830s, the French economist Auguste Cournot had studied the probable outcome when two firms compete in the same market. Many economists and social scientists subsequently tried to analyze the outcome in other specific forms of strategic interaction. However, prior to the birth of game theory, there was no toolbox that gave scholars access to a general but rigorous method of analyzing different forms of strategic interaction. The situation is totally different now. Scientific journals and advanced textbooks are filled with analyses that build on game theory, as it has been developed by this year's Laureates in economics, John Nash, John Harsanyi and Reinhard Selten.

Non-cooperative game theory deals with situations where the parties cannot make binding agreements. Even in very complicated games, with many parties and many available strategies, it will be possible to describe the outcome in terms of a so-called Nash equilibrium – so named after one of the Laureates. John Nash has shown that there is at least one stable outcome, that is an outcome such that no player can improve his own outcome by choosing a different strategy when all players have correct expectations of each other's strategy. Even if each party acts in an individually rational way, the Nash equilibrium shows that strategic interaction can quite often cause collective irrationality: trade wars or excessive emission of pollutants that threaten the global environment are examples in the international sphere. One should also add that the Nash equilibrium has been important within evolutionary ecology – to describe natural selection as a strategic interaction within and between species.

In many games, the players lack complete information about each other's objective. If the government, for example, wants to deregulate a firm but does not know the cost situation in the firm, while the firm's management has this knowledge, we have a game with incomplete information. In three articles published toward the end of the 1960s, John Harsanyi showed how equilibrium analysis could be extended to handle this difficulty, which game theorists up to that time had regarded as insurmountable. Harsanyi's approach has laid an analytical basis for several lively research areas including information economics which starts from the fact that different decision makers, in a market or within an organization, often have access to different information. These areas cover a broad range of issues, from contracts between shareholders and a company's management to institutions in developing countries.

One problem connected with the concept of Nash equilibrium is that there may be several equilibria in non-cooperative games. It may thus be difficult – both for the players and an outside analyst – to predict the outcome. Reinhard Selten has, through his "perfection" concepts, laid the foundations for the research program that has tried to exclude improbable or unreasonable equilibria. Certain Nash equilibria can, in fact, be such that they are based on threats or promises intended to make other players choose certain strategies. These threats and promises are often empty because it is not in the player's interest to carry them out if a situation arises in which he has threatened to carry them out. By excluding such empty threats and promises Selten could make stronger predictions about the outcome in the form of so-called perfect equilibria.

Selten's contributions have had great importance for analysis of the dynamics of strategic interaction, for example between firms trying to reach dominant positions on the market, or between private agents and a government that tries to implement a particular economic policy.

Professor John Harsanyi, the analysis of games with incomplete information is due to you, and it has been of great importance for the economics of information.

Dr John Nash, your analysis of equilibria in non-cooperative games, and all your other contributions to game theory, have had a profound effect on the way economic theory has developed in the last two decades.
Professor Reinhard Selten, your notion of perfection in the equilibrium analysis has substantially extended the use of non-cooperative game theory.

It is an honour and a privilege for me to convey to all of you, on behalf of the Royal Swedish Academy of Sciences, our warmest congratulations. I now ask you to receive your prizes from the hands of his Majesty the King.

John C. Harsanyi

JOHN C. HARSANYI

I was born in Budapest, Hungary, on May 29, 1920. The high school my parents chose for me was the Lutheran Gymnasium in Budapest, one of the best schools in Hungary, with such distinguished alumni as John von Neumann and Eugene Wigner. I was very happy in this school and received a superb education. In 1937, the year I graduated from it, I won the First Prize in Mathematics at the Hungary-wide annual competition for high school students.

My parents owned a pharmacy in Budapest, which gave us a comfortable living. As I was their only child, they wanted me to become a pharmacist. But my own preference would have been to study philosophy and mathematics. Yet, in 1937 when I actually had to decide my field of study, I chose pharmacy in accordance with my parents' wishes. I did so because Hitler was in power in Germany, and his influence was steadily increasing also in Hungary. I knew that as a pharmacy student I would obtain military deferment. As I was of Jewish origin, this meant that I would not have to serve in a forced-labor unit of the Hungarian army.

As a result, I did have military deferment until the German army occupied Hungary in March 1944. Then I did have to serve in a labor unit from May to November 1944.

In that November the Nazi authorities finally decided to deport my labor unit from Budapest to an Austrian concentration camp, where most of my comrades eventually perished. But I was lucky enough to make my escape from the railway station in Budapest, just before our train left for Austria. Then a Jesuit father I had known gave me refuge in the cellar of their monastery.

In 1946 I re-enrolled at the University of Budapest in order to obtain a Ph.D. in philosophy with minors in sociology and in psychology. As I got credit for my prior studies in pharmacy, I did get my Ph.D. in June 1947, after only one more year of course work and after writing a dissertation in philosophy.

From September 1947 to June 1948 I served as a junior faculty member at the University Institute of Sociology. There I met Anne Klauber, a psychology student who attended a course I was teaching and who later became my wife. But in June 1948, I had to resign from the Institute because the political situation no longer permitted them to employ an outspoken anti-Marxist as I had been.

Yet Anne did go on with her studies. But she was continually harassed by her Communist classmates to break up with me because of my political views, but she did not. This made her realize, before I did, that Hungary was becoming a completely Stalinist country, and that the only sensible course of action for us was to leave Hungary.

Actually we did so only in April 1950. We had to cross the Hungarian border illegally over a marshy terrain, which was less well guarded than other border areas. But even so, we were very lucky not to be stopped or shot at by the Hungarian border guards.

After waiting in Austria for our Australian landing permits for several months, we actually reached Sydney, Australia, on December 30, 1950. On January 2, 1951, Anne and I got married. Her unfailing emotional support and her practical good sense have always been a great help to me.

As my English was not very good and as my Hungarian university degrees were not recognized in Australia, during most of our first three years there I had to do factory work. But in the evening I took economics courses at the University of Sydney. (I changed over from sociology to economics because I found the conceptual and mathematical elegance of economic theory very attractive.) I was given some credit for my Hungarian university courses so that I had to do only two years of further course work and had to write an M.A. thesis in economics in order to get an M.A. I did receive the degree late in 1953.

Early in 1954 I was appointed Lecturer in Economics at the University of Queensland in Brisbane. Then, in 1956, I was awarded a Rockefeller Fellowship, enabling me and Anne to spend two years at Stanford University, where I got a Ph.D. in economics, whereas Anne got an M.A. in psychology. I had the good fortune of having Ken Arrow as advisor and as dissertation supervisor. I benefitted very much from discussing many finer points of economic theory with him. But I also benefitted substantially by following his advice to spend a sizable part of my Stanford time studying mathematics and statistics. These studies proved very useful in my later work in game theory.

In 1958 Anne and I returned to Australia, where I got a very attractive research position at the Australian National University in Canberra. But soon I felt very isolated because at that time game theory was virtually unknown in Australia. I turned to Ken Arrow for help. With his and Jim Tobin's help, I was appointed Professor of Economics at Wayne State University in Detroit. Then, in 1964, I became at first Visiting Professor and then Professor at the Business School of the University of California in Berkeley. Later my appointment was extended also to the Department of Economics. Our only child Tom was born in Berkeley.

In the early 1950s I published papers on the use of von Neumann-Morgenstern utility functions in welfare economics and in ethics and on the welfare economics of variable tastes.

My interest in game-theoretic problems in a narrower sense was first aroused by John Nash's four brilliant papers, published in the period 1950 – 53, on cooperative and on noncooperative games, on two-person bargaining games and on mutually optimal threat strategies in such games, and on what we now call Nash equilibria.

In 1956 I showed the mathematical equivalence of Zeuthen's and of Nash's bargaining models and stated algebraic criteria for optimal threat strategies.

In 1963 I extended the Shapely value to games without transferable utility and showed that my new solution concept was a generalization both of the Shapley value and of Nash's bargaining solution with variable threats.

In a three-part paper published in 1967 and 1968, I showed how to convert a game with incomplete information into one with complete yet imperfect information, so as to make it acessible to game-theoretic analysis.

In 1973 I showed that "almost all" mixed-strategy Nash equilibria can be reinterpreted as pure-strategy strict equilibria of a suitably chosen game with randomly fluctuating payoff functions.

I also published a number of papers on utilitarian ethics.

I published four books. One of them, *Rational Behavior and Bargaining Equilibrium in Games and Social Situations* (1977), was an attempt to unify game theory by extending the use of bargaining models from cooperative games also to noncooperative games. Two books, *Essays on Ethics, Social Behavior, and Scientific Explanation* (1976) and *Papers in Game Theory* (1982), were collections of some of my journal articles. Finally, *A General Theory of Equilibrium Selection in Games* (1988) was joint work with Reinhard Selten. Its title indicates its content.

Let me add that in 1993 and 1994 I wrote two, as yet unpublished papers, proposing a *new theory* of equilibrium selection. My 1993 paper does so for games with *complete* information, while my 1994 paper does so for games with *incomplete* information. My new theory is based on our 1988 theory but is a much simpler theory and is in my view an intuitively more attractive one.

I am a member of the National Academy of Sciences, and a Fellow of the American Academy of Arts and Sciences and of the Econometric Society, as well as a Distinguished Fellow of the American Economic Association. In 1965 – 66 I was a Fellow of the Center for Advanced Study in the Behavioral Sciences at Stanford. I have an honorary degree of Doctor of Science from Northwestern University. After my retirement from my university, Reinhard Selten edited a volume in my honor with the help of H. W. Brock. It has the title Rational Interaction.

VITA

Name:	John C. (Charles) Harsanyi.
Date and Place of Birth:	May 29, 1920. Budapest, Hungary.
Citizenship:	U.S. citizen.
Countries of Residence:	Hungary 1920 – 50. Australia, 1950 – 56 and 1958 – 61. United States, 1956 – 58 and 1961 – .
Family Status:	Married – one child.
Present Position:	Flood Research Professor in Business Administration, Emeritus, and Professor of Economics, Emeritus, University of California, Berkeley.
Past Positions:	University Assistant, University of Budapest, Hungary, 1947 – 48. Lecturer in Economics, University of Queensland, Brisbane, Australia, 1954 – 56. Research Associate, Cowles Foundation at Yale University, 1957. Visiting Assistant Professor, Stanford University, 1958. Senior Fellow, Australian National University, Canberra, Australia, 1959 – 61. Professor of Economics, Wayne State University, 1961 – 63. Professor, University of California, Berkeley, 1964 – 90.
Degrees:	Dr. Phil., University of Budapest, Hungary, 1947. M. A., Sydney University, Australia, 1953. Ph. D., Stanford University, 1959.
Fields of Interest:	Game theory, decision theory, mathematical economics, the use of rational-choice models in political science and in sociology, utilitarian ethics, the philosophy of science.
Publications:	See list attached.
Honors and Awards:	First Prize in Mathematics, *National Competition of Hungarian High School Students*, 1937.

14. *Some probabilities.*

I shall assume that, *before any other moves are made* in game G*, some lottery L will choose one particular *appropriate set a* to be the *active set* $\bar{a}$ of the game. The n types in this set $\bar{a}$ will be called *active types* whereas all types *not* in $\bar{a}$ will be called *inactive types.*

I shall assume that the *probability* that a *particular* appropriate set a_h will be chosen by lottery L to be the active set $\bar{a}$ of the game is

$$Pr(\bar{a} = a_h) = r_h \text{ for } h = 1,\ldots,H. \tag{14}$$

Of course, all these H probabilities r_h will be *nonnegative* and will add up to *unity.* Obviously, they will correspond to the H probabilities p_{km} [defined by (3)] we used in the two-person case.

Suppose that a particular type t_i^k of some player i has been chosen by lottery L to be an *active type* in the game. Then, under our assumptions, he *will know* that he is type t_i^k and *will know* also that he now has the status of an *active type.* In other words, t_i^k will know that

$$t_i^k \in \bar{a}. \tag{15}$$

Yet, the statement $t_i^k \in \bar{a}$ implies the statement

$$\bar{a} \in \mathrm{A}_i^k \tag{16}$$

and conversely, because A_i^k contains exactly those appropriate sets that have type t_i^k as their *member.* Thus, we can write

$$(t_i^k \in \bar{a}) \leftrightarrow (\bar{a} \in \mathrm{A}_i^k). \tag{17}$$

We have already concluded that if type t_i^k has the status of an *active type* then he will know (15). We can now add that in this case he will know also (16) and (17). On the other hand, he can also easily compute that the *probability* for lottery L to choose an active set $\bar{a}$ belonging to the family A_i^k is

$$Pr(\bar{a} \in \mathrm{A}_i^k) = \sum_{h \in B_i^k} r_h. \tag{18}$$

In view of statements (15) to (18), how should this type t_i^k assess the *probability* that the active set $\bar{a}$ chosen by lottery L is actually a *particular* appropriate set a_h? Clearly, he should assess this probability as being the *conditional* probability

$$\pi_i^k(h) = Pr(\bar{a} = a_h | t_I k \in \bar{a} \tag{19}$$

Yet, in view of (17) and (18), we can write

$$\begin{aligned} Pr(\bar{a} = a_h | t_i^k \in \bar{a}) &= Pr(\bar{a} = a_h | \bar{a} \in A_i^k) = \\ = Pr(\bar{a} = a_h / Pr(\bar{a} \in A_i^k) &= r_h / \sum_{h \in B_i^k} r_h . \end{aligned} \tag{20}$$

Consequently, by (19) and (20) the required *conditional* probability is

$$\pi_i^k(h) = r_h / \sum_{h \in B_i^k} r_h . \tag{21}$$

15. *Strategy profiles.*
Suppose that the K_i types $t_i^1,\ldots,t_i^k,\ldots,t_i^{K_i}$ of player i *would* use the strategies $s_i^1,\ldots,s_i^k,\ldots,s_i^{K_i}$ (pure or mixed) in case they *were* chosen by lottery L to be *active types* in the game. (Under our assumptions, *inactive types* do not actively participate in the game and, therefore, do *not* choose any strategies.) Then I shall write

$$s_i^* = (s_i^1,\ldots,s_i^k,\ldots,s_i^{K_i}) \text{ for } i = 1,\ldots,n \tag{22}$$

to denote the *strategy profile*[8] of the K_i *types* of player i.

Let

$$s^* = (s_i^*,\ldots,s_n^*) \tag{23}$$

be the ordered set we obtain if we first list all K_1 strategies in s_1^*, then all K_2 strategies in s_2^*,..., then all K_1 strategies in s_i^*,..., and finally all K_n strategies in s_n^*. Obviously, s^* will be a *strategy profile* of *all* types in the game. In view of (10), s^* will contain Z different strategies.

Finally, let $s^*(h)$ denote the *strategy profile* of the n types belonging to a *particular* appropriate set a_h for $h = 1,\ldots,H$.

16. *The conditional payoff functions.*
Let a_h be an appropriate set defined as

$$a_h = (t_1^{k_1},\ldots,t_i^{k_i},\ldots,t_n^{k_n}). \tag{24}$$

The *characteristic vector* $c(h)$ for a_h will be defined as the n-vector

$$c(h) = (k_1,\ldots,k_i,\ldots,k_n). \tag{25}$$

Suppose that this set a_h has been chosen by lottery L to be the *active set* $\bar{a}$ of the game, and that some particular type t_i^k of player i has been chosen by lottery L to be an *active type*. This of course means that t_i^k must be a *member* of this set a_h, which can be the case only if type t_i^k is identical to type $t_i^{k_i}$ listed in (24), which implies that we must have $k=k_i$.

Yet, if all these requirements are met, then this set a_h and this type t_i^k together will satisfy all the statements (14) to (21).

As we saw in section 6, the payoff v_i^k of any active type t_i^k will depend both

1. On the *strategies* used by the *n active types* in the game, and
2. On the *identities* of these active types.

This means, however, that t_i^k's payoff v_i^k will depend on the *strategy profile* $s^*(h)$ defined in the last paragraph of section 15, and on the *characteristic vector* $c(h)$ defined by (25).

Thus, we can write

$$v_i^k = V_i^k(s^*(h), c(h)) \text{ if } t_i^k \in \bar{a} = a_h. \tag{26}$$

The payoff functions V_i^k $(i=1,\ldots,n; k=1,\ldots K_i)$ I shall call *conditional* payoff functions. *Firstly*, any given type will obtain the payoff v_i^k defined by (26) *only* if he will be chosen by lottery L to be an *active type* in the game. (This is what the condition $t_i^k \in \bar{a}$ in (26) refers to.)

Secondly, even if t_i^k *is* chosen to be an active type, (26) makes his payoff v_i^k *dependent* on the set a_h chosen by lottery L to be an active set $\bar{a}$ of the game.

17. *Semi-conditional payoff functions.*

By reasoning similar to that we used in section 12, one can show that the quantity any active type t_i^k will try to maximize will *not* be his *payoff* v_i^k defined by (26). Rather, it will be his *expected payoff*, i.e., the *expected value* u_i^k of his payoff v_i^k.

We can define u_i^k as

$$u_i^k = U_i^k(s^*) = \sum_{h=1}^{H} \pi_i^k(h)\, V_i^k(s^*(h), c(h)) \text{ if } t_i^k \in \bar{a}. \tag{27}$$

These payoff functions U_i^k $(i=1,\ldots,n; k=1,\ldots,K_i)$ I shall call *semi-conditional*. I shall do so because they are subject to the *first* condition to which the payoff functions V_i^k are subject but *not* to the *second*. That is to say, any given type t_i^k will obtain the *expected payoff* u_i^k defined by (27) *only if* he is an *active type* of the game. But, if he is, then his expected payoff u_i^k will *not* depend on which particular appropriate set a_h has been chosen by lottery L to be the active set $\bar{a}$ of the game.

It is true also in the *n*-person case that if an I-game is reinterpreted in accordance with our *probabilistic model* then it will be converted into a *C-game* G*.

Moreover, this C-game G*, under its *type-centered* interpretation, can be regarded as a Z-person game whose "players" are the Z different types in the game. As the payoff function of each type t_i^k we can use his *semi-conditional* payoff function U_i^k.

Using these payoff functions U_i^k, it will be easy to define the *Nash equilibria* (Nash, 1951) of this Z-person game, and to choose one of them as its *solution* on the basis of a suitable theory of equilibrium selection.

1 See Harsanyi, 1967 – 68 (pp. 167 – 168).

2 The subjective probability distributions of various orders discussed in this section all are probability distributions over function spaces, whose proper mathematical definition poses some well – known technical difficulties. Yet, as Aumann (1963 and 1964) has shown, these difficulties can be overcome. But even so, the above model of higher and higher-order subjective probability distributions remains a hopelessly cumbersome model for analysis of I-games.

3 Let $\pi_1^k(m)$ for $m = 1,\ldots,M$ be the *probability* that some type t_1^k of player 1 assigns to the assumption that the Russian side will be represented by type t_2^m in the game. According to Bayesian theory, the M probabilities $\pi_1^k(1)$, $\pi_1^k(2),\ldots\pi_1^k(m),\ldots,\pi_1^k(M)$ will *fully characterize* the *expectations* that this type t_1^k entertains about the characteristics of player 2 in the game. On the other hand, as we shall see, the *probabilistic model* we shall propose for the game will imply that these *probabilities* $\pi_1^k(m)$ must be equal to certain *conditional probabilities* so that

$$\pi_1^k(m) = Pr\,(t_2^m | t_1^k) \text{ for } m = 1,\ldots,M.$$

A similar relationship will obtain between the K *[probabilities* $\pi_2^m(k)$ entertained by any given type t_2^m of player 2 and the *conditional probabilities* $Pr\,(t_1^k | t_2^m)$ for $k = 1,\ldots,K$.

4 *Personal moves* are moves the various *players* have chosen to make. *Chance moves* are moves made by some *chance mechanism,* such as a roulette wheel. Yet, moves made by some players yet decided by chance, such as throwing a coin, or a shuffling of cards, can also count as chance moves.

5 Cf. footnote 3 to section 4 above.

6 Using player-centered language, in Harsanyi (1967 – 68, p. 180), I called the M-tuple s_2^* and the K-tuple s_1^* (see below), the *normalized strategies* of player 2 and player 1, respectively.

7 As defined by John Nash in Nash (1951). But he actually called them *equilibrium points.*

8 In Harsanyi, 1967 – 68, I called a strategy combination such as S_i^* the *normalized strategy* of player i (cf. Footnote 6 to section 12 above).

REFERENCES

Aumann, Robert J. 1963. "On Choosing a Function at Random." In Fred B. Wright (ed.), *Symposium on Ergodic Theory,* 1 – 20. New Orleans: Academic Press.

Aumann, Robert J. 1964. "Mixed and Behavior Strategies in Infinite Extensive Games." In M. Dresher, L.S. Shapley, and A.W. Tucker (eds.), *Advances in Game Theory,* 627 – 650. Princeton: Princeton University Press.

Fudenberg, Drew, and Tirole, Jean. 1991. *Game Theory.* Cambridge. MA: Cambridge University Press.

Harsanyi, John C. 1967 – 68. "Games with Incomplete Information Played by Bayesian Players." *Management Science* 14, 159 – 182, 320 – 334, and 486 – 502.

Nash, John F. 1951. "Noncooperative Games." *Annals of Mathematics* 54, 289 – 295.

von Neumann, John, and Morgenstern, Oskar. 1944, 1947. *Theory of Games and Economic Behavior.* Princeton: Princeton University Press.

SELECTED LIST OF PUBLICATIONS

A. BOOKS:
Essays on Ethics, Social Behavior, and Scientific Explanation. With Foreword by Kenneth J. Arrow. Dordrecht, Holland: D. Reidel, 1976. xvi + 262 pp.
Rational Behavior and Bargaining Equilibrium in Games and Social Situations. Cambridge, England: Cambridge University Press, 1977. x + 314 pp.
Papers in Game Theory. Dordrecht, Holland: D. Reidel, 1982. xii + 258 pp.
A General Theory of Equilibrium Selection in Games (joint work with Reinhard Selten). With Foreword by Robert Aumann. Cambridge, MA: MIT Press, 1988. xiv + 378.

B. SELECTED JOURNAL ARTICLES:
"Cardinal Utility in Welfare Economics and in the Theory of Risk-taking," Journal of Political Economy, 61 (1953), 434 – 435.
"Welfare Economics of Variable Tastes," Review of Economic Studies, 21 (1953 – 54), 204 – 213.
"Cardinal Welfare, Individualistic Ethics, and Interpersonal Comparisons of Utility," Journal of Political Economy, 63 (1955), 309 – 321.
"Approaches to the Bargaining Problem Before and After the Theory of Games: A Critical Discussion of Zeuthen's Hicks's and Nash's Theories," Econometrica, 24 (1956), 144 – 157.
"Ethics in Terms of Hypothetical Imperatives," Mind, 67 (1958), 305 – 316.
"Measurement of Social Power, Opportunity Costs, and the Theory of Two-Person Bargaining Games," Bahavioral Science, 7 (1962), 67 – 80.
"Measurement of Social Power in n-Person Reciprocal Power Situations," Behavioral Science, 7 (1962), 81 – 91.
"A Simplified Bargaining Model for the n-Person Cooperative Game," International Economic Review, 4 (1963), 194 – 220.
"A Bargaining Model for Social Status in Informal Groups and Formal Organizations," Behavioral Science, 11 (1966), 357 – 369.
"Games with Incomplete Information Played by 'Bayesian' Players," Parts I to III, Management Science, 14 (1967 – 68), pp. 159 – 182, 320 – 334, and 486 – 502.
"Rational-Choice Models of Political Behavior vs. Functionalist and Conformist Theories," World Politics, 21 (1969), 513 – 538.
"Games with Randomly Disturbed Payoffs: A New Rationale for Mixed Strategy Equilibrium Points," International Journal of Game Theory, 2 (1973), 1 – 23.
"Oddness of the Number of Equilibrium Points: A New Proof," International Journal of Game Theory, 2 (1973), 235 – 250.
"An Equilibrium-Point Interpretation of Stable Sets and a Proposed Alternative Definition," Management Science, 20 (1974), 1472 – 1495.
"Can the Maximin Principle Serve as a Basis for Morality? A Critique of John Rawls's Theory," American Political Science Review, 69 (1975), 594 – 606.
"Nonlinear Social Welfare Functions: Do Welfare Economists Have a Special Exemption from Bayesian Rationality?" Theory and Decision, 6 (1975), 311 – 332.
"The Tracing Procedure: A Bayesian Approach to Defining a Solution for n-Person Noncooperative Games, International Journal of Game Theory, 4 (1975), 61 – 94.
"Rule Utilitarianism and Decision Theory," Erkenntnis, 11 (1977), 25 – 53.
"Advances in Understanding Rational Behavior." In R. E. Butts and J. Hintikka (eds.), Proceedings of the Fifth International Congress of Logic, Methodology and Philosophy of Science, Part II. Dordrecht, Holland: D. Reidel, 1977, 315 – 343.
"Rationality, Reasons, Hypothetical Imperatives, and Morality," in Hal Berghel et al., Wittgenstein, the Vienna Circle, and Critical Rationalism. Vienna, Austria: Verlag Hoelder – Pichler – Tempsky, 1979, 463 – 475.
"Bayesian Decision Theory, Rule Utilitarianism, and Arrow's Impossibility Theorem," Theory and Decision, 11 (1979), 289 – 317.
"Mathematics, the Empirical Facts, and Logical Necessity," Erkenntnis, 19 (1983), 167 – 192.

"Bayesian Decision Theory, Subjective and Objective Probabilities, and Acceptance of Empirical Hypotheses," Synthese, 57 (1983), 341 – 365.
"Acceptance of Empirical Statements: A Bayesian Theory Without Cognitive Utilities," Theory and Decision, 18 (1985), 1 – 30.
"Rule Utilitarianism, Equality, and Justice," Social Philosophy and Policy, 2 (1985), 115 – 127.
"Does Reason Tell Us What Moral Code to Follow, and Indeed, to Follow Any Moral Code at All?" Ethics, 96 (1985), 42 – 55.
"Utilitarian Morality in a World of Very Half-Hearted Altruists." In W. P. Heller et al. (eds.), Social Choice and Public Decision Making: Essays in Honor of K. J. Arrow, Vol. I Cambridge, England: Cambridge University Press, 1986, pp. 57 – 73.
"Von Neumann-Morgenstern Utilities, Risk Taking, and Welfare." In G. R. Feiwel (ed.), Arrow and the Ascent of Modern Economic Theory. New York: New York University Press, 1987, pp. 545 – 558.
"Assessing Other People's Utilities," in B. E. Munier (ed.), Risk, Decision, and Rationality. Dordrecht, Holland: D. Reidel, 1988, pp. 127 – 138.
"Problems with Act Utilitarianism and Malevolent Preferences." A Critique of Richard Hare's Theory. In D. Seanor and N. Fotion (eds.), Hare and Critics. Oxford, England: Clarendon Press, 1988, pp. 89 – 99.
"Equality, Responsibility, and Justice As Seen from a Utilitarian Perspective," Theory and Decision, 31 (1991), 141 – 158.
"Game and Decision Theoretic Models in Ethics." In R. J. Aumann and S. Hart (eds.), Handbook of Game Theory, Vol. 1. Amsterdam, The Netherlands: Elsevier (North-Holland), 1992; Chapter 19.

John Forbes Nash, Jr.

JOHN F. NASH, JR.

My beginning as a legally recognized individual occurred on June 13, 1928 in Bluefield, West Virginia in the Bluefield Sanatarium, a hospital that no longer exists. Of course I can't consciously remember anything from the first two or three years of my life after birth. (And also one suspects, psychologically, that the earliest memories have become "memories of memories" and are comparable to traditional folk tales passed on by tellers and listeners from generation to generation.) But facts are available when direct memory fails for many circumstances.

My father, for whom I was named, was an electrical engineer and had come to Bluefield to work for the electrical utility company there which was and is the Appalachian Electric Power Company. He was a veteran of WW1 and had served in France as a lieutenant in the supply services and consequently had not been in actual front lines combat in the war. He was originally from Texas and had obtained his B. S. degree in electrical engineering from Texas Agricultural and Mechanical (Texas A. and M.).

My mother, originally Margaret Virginia Martin, but called Virginia, was herself also born in Bluefield. She had studied at the University of West Virginia and was a school teacher before her marriage, teaching English and sometimes Latin. But my mother's later life was considerably affected by a partial loss of hearing resulting from a scarlet fever infection that came at the time when she was a student at WVU.

Her parents had come as a couple to Bluefield from their original homes in western North Carolina. Her father, Dr. James Everett Martin, had prepared as a physician at the University of Maryland in Baltimore and came to Bluefield, which was then expanding rapidly in population, to start up his practice. But in his later years Dr. Martin became more of a real estate investor and left actual medical practice. I never saw my grandfather because he had died before I was born but I have good memories of my grandmother and of how she could play the piano at the old house which was located rather centrally in Bluefield.

A sister, Martha, was born about two and a half years later than me on November 16, 1930.

I went to the standard schools in Bluefield but also to a kindergarten before starting in the elementary school level. And my parents provided an encyclopedia, Compton's Pictured Encyclopedia, that I learned at lot from by reading it as a child. And also there were other books available from either our house or the house of the grandparents that were of educational value.

Bluefield, a small city in a comparatively remote geographical location in the Appalachians, was not a community of scholars or of high technology. It was a center of businessmen, lawyers, etc. that owed its existence to the railroad and the rich nearby coal fields of West Virginia and western Virginia. So, from the intellectual viewpoint, it offered the sort of challenge that one had to learn from the world's knowledge rather than from the knowledge of the immediate community.

By the time I was a student in high school I was reading the classic "Men of Mathematics" by E. T. Bell and I remember succeeding in proving the classic Fermat theorem about an integer multiplied by itself p times where p is a prime.

I also did electrical and chemistry experiments at that time. At first, when asked in school to prepare an essay about my career, I prepared one about a career as an electrical engineer like my father. Later, when I actually entered Carnegie Tech. in Pittsburgh I entered as a student with the major of chemical engineering.

Regarding the circumstances of my studies at Carnegie (now Carnegie-Mellon U.), I was lucky to be there on a full scholarship, called the George Westinghouse Scholarship. But after one semester as a chem. eng. student I reacted negatively to the regimentation of courses such as mechanical drawing and shifted to chemistry instead. But again, after continuing in chemistry for a while I encountered difficulties with quantitative analysis where it was not a matter of how well one could think and understand or learn facts but of how well one could handle a pipette and perform a titration in the laboratory. Also the mathematics faculty were encouraging me to shift into mathematics as my major and explaining to me that it was not almost impossible to make a good career in America as a mathematician. So I shifted again and became officially a student of mathematics. And in the end I had learned and progressed so much in mathematics that they gave me an M. S. in addition to my B. S. when I graduated.

I should mention that during my last year in the Bluefield schools that my parents had arranged for me to take supplementary math. courses at Bluefield College which was then a 2-year institution operated by Southern Baptists. I didn't get official advanced standing at Carnegie because of my extra studies but I had advanced knowledge and ability and didn't need to learn much from the first math. courses at Carnegie.

When I graduated I remember that I had been offered fellowships to enter as a graduate student at either Harvard or Princeton. But the Princeton fellowship was somewhat more generous since I had not actually won the Putnam competition and also Princeton seemed more interested in getting me to come there. Prof. A. W. Tucker wrote a letter to me encouraging me to come to Princeton and from the family point of view it seemed attractive that geographically Princeton was much nearer to Bluefield. Thus Princeton became the choice for my graduate study location.

But while I was still at Carnegie I took one elective course in "International

Economics" and as a result of that exposure to economic ideas and problems arrived at the idea that led to the paper "The Bargaining Problem" which was later published in Econometrica. And it was this idea which in turn, when I was a graduate student at Princeton, led to my interest in the game theory studies there which had been stimulated by the work of von Neumann and Morgenstern.

As a graduate student I studied mathematics fairly broadly and I was fortunate enough, besides developing the idea which led to "Non-Cooperative Games", also to make a nice discovery relating to manifolds and real algebraic varieties. So I was prepared actually for the possibility that the game theory work would not be regarded as acceptable as a thesis in the mathematics department and then that I could realize the objective of a Ph. D. thesis with the other results.

But in the event the game theory ideas, which deviated somewhat from the "line" (as if of "political party lines") of von Neumann and Morgenstern's book, were accepted as a thesis for a mathematics Ph. D. and it was later, while I was an instructor at M.I.T., that I wrote up "Real Algebraic Manifolds" and sent it in for publication.

I went to M.I.T. in the summer of 1951 as a "C.L.E. Moore Instructor". I had been an instructor at Princeton for one year after obtaining my degree in 1950. It seemed desirable more for personal and social reasons than academic ones to accept the higher-paying instructorship at M.I.T.

I was on the mathematics faculty at M.I.T. from 1951 through until I resigned in the spring of 1959. During academic 1956 – 1957 I had an Alfred P. Sloan grant and chose to spend the year as a (temporary) member of the Institute for Advanced Study in Princeton.

During this period of time I managed to solve a classical unsolved problem relating to differential geometry which was also of some interest in relation to the geometric questions arising in general relativity. This was the problem to prove the isometric embeddability of abstract Riemannian manifolds in flat (or "Euclidean") spaces. But this problem, although classical, was not much talked about as an outstanding problem. It was not like, for example, the 4-color conjecture.

So as it happened, as soon as I heard in conversation at M.I.T. about the question of the embeddability being open I began to study it. The first break led to a curious result about the embeddability being realizable in surprisingly low-dimensional ambient spaces provided that one would accept that the embedding would have only limited smoothness. And later, with "heavy analysis", the problem was solved in terms of embeddings with a more proper degree of smoothness.

While I was on my "Sloan sabbatical" at the IAS in Princeton I studied another problem involving partial differential equations which I had learned of as a problem that was unsolved beyond the case of 2 dimensions. Here, although I did succeed in solving the problem, I ran into some bad luck since, without my being sufficiently informed on what other people were doing in the area, it happened that I was working in parallel with Ennio de Giorgi of Pisa, Italy. And de Giorgi was first actually to achieve the ascent of the summit (of the figuratively described problem) at least for the particularly interesting case of "elliptic equations".

It seems conceivable that if either de Giorgi or Nash had failed in the attack on this problem (of a priori estimates of Hölder continuity) then that the lone climber reaching the peak would have been recognized with mathematics' Fields medal (which has traditionally been restricted to persons less than 40 years old).

Now I must arrive at the time of my change from scientific rationality of thinking into the delusional thinking characteristic of persons who are psychiatrically diagnosed as "schizophrenic" or "paranoid schizophrenic". But I will not really attempt to describe this long period of time but rather avoid embarrassment by simply omitting to give the details of truly personal type.

While I was on the academic sabbatical of 1956 – 1957 I also entered into marriage. Alicia had graduated as a physics major from M.I.T. where we had met and she had a job in the New York City area in 1956 – 1957. She had been born in El Salvador but came at an early age to the U.S. and she and her parents had long been U.S. citizens, her father being an M. D. and ultimately employed at a hospital operated by the federal government in Maryland.

The mental disturbances originated in the early months of 1959 at a time when Alicia happened to be pregnant. And as a consequence I resigned my position as a faculty member at M.I.T. and ultimately after spending 50 days under "observation" at the McLean Hospital, travelled to Europe and attempted to gain status there as a refugee.

I later spent times of the order of five to eight months in hospitals in New Jersey, always on an involuntary basis and always attempting a legal argument for release.

And it did happen that when I had been long enough hospitalized that I would finally renounce my delusional hypotheses and revert to thinking of myself as a human of more conventional circumstances and return to mathematical research. In these interludes of, as it were, enforced rationality, I did succeed in doing some respectable mathematical research. Thus there came about the research for "Le Problème de Cauchy pour les Équations Différentielles d'un Fluide Générale"; the idea that Prof. Hironaka called "the Nash blowing-up transformation"; and those of "Arc Structure of Singularities" and "Analyticity of Solutions of Implicit Function Problems with Analytic Data".

But after my return to the dream-like delusional hypotheses in the later 60's I became a person of delusionally influenced thinking but of relatively moderate behavior and thus tended to avoid hospitalization and the direct attention of psychiatrists.

Thus further time passed. Then gradually I began to intellectually reject some of the delusionally influenced lines of thinking which had been characteristic of my orientation. This began, most recognizably, with the rejection of politically-oriented thinking as essentially a hopeless waste of intellectual effort.

So at the present time I seem to be thinking rationally again in the style that is characteristic of scientists. However this is not entirely a matter of joy as if someone returned from physical disability to good physical health. One aspect of this is that rationality of thought imposes a limit on a person's concept of his relation to the cosmos. For example, a non-Zoroastrian could think of Zarathustra as simply a madman who led millions of naive followers to adopt a cult of ritual fire worship. But without his "madness" Zarathustra would necessarily have been only another of the millions or billions of human indivuduals who have lived and then been forgotten.

Statistically, it would seem improbable that any mathematician or scientist, at the age of 66, would be able through continued research efforts to add much to his or her previous achievements. However I am still making the effort and it is conceivable that with the gap period of about 25 years of partially deluded thinking providing a sort of vacation my situation may be atypical. Thus I have hopes of being able to achieve something of value through my current studies or with any new ideas that come in the future.

THE WORK OF JOHN NASH IN GAME THEORY

Nobel Seminar, December 8, 1994

(The document that follows is edited version of a seminar devoted to the contributions to game theory of John Nash. The participants, in the order of their appearance, were:

HAROLD W. KUHN
Department of Mathematics, Princeton University, Princeton, NJ 08544, USA

JOHN C. HARSANYI
The Walter A. Haas School of Business, University of California at Berkeley, Berkeley, CA 94720, USA

REINHARD SELTEN
Department of Economics, University of Bonn, Adenauerallee 24 – 42, D-53113 Bonn, Germany

JÖRGEN W. WEIBULL
Department of Economics, Stockholm University, S-10691 Stockholm, Sweden

ERIC VAN DAMME
Center for Economic Research, Tilburg University, 5037 AB Tilburg, The Netherlands

JOHN F. NASH, JR
Department of Mathematics, Princeton University, Princeton, NJ 08544, USA

PETER HAMMERSTEIN, Max-Plank-Institute für Verhaltens Physiologie, 82319 Seewiesen, Germany, is the co-author of the intervention of Professor Selten.
A unified bibliography for the seminar is provided at the end.)

KUHN

It gives me great pleasure to chair this seminar on the importance of Nash's work on the occasion of the first Nobel award that recognizes the central importance of game theory in current economic theory. I shall be joined by two colleagues whom I've known for over thirty years, John Harsanyi and Reinhard Selten, two new friends, Jörgen Weibull and Eric van Damme, and John Nash, whom I've known since we were graduate students together in Princeton forty-six years ago.

The timing of these awards has historical significance, since this year is the fiftieth anniversary of the publication of "The Theory of Games and Economic Behavior" [52] by the Princeton University Press. Although von

Neumann had laid the mathematical foundation of the theory of games in his paper entitled "Zur Theorie der Gesellshaftsspiele" [51], published in the Mathematische Annalen in 1928, it was largely through the collaboration of von Neumann and Morgenstern that economists learned of this new tool for analyzing economic problems.

Some of you may have read Morgenstern's own account [33] of this collaboration. There is a new historical study [29] by Robert Leonard of the University of Quebec at Montreal that points out that "understandably, but regrettably, Morgenstern's reminiscence sacrifices some of the historical complexity of the run up to 1944." Leonard's study gives most of the credit for the creation of game theory to von Neumann who had written essentially all of the mathematical manuscript nine months before Morgenstern ever saw it. Nevertheless, had von Neumann and Morgenstern never met, it seems unlikely that we would be here today celebrating the central rôle of the theory of games in economics.

This leads to a natural question which has been asked repeatedly by journalists in the last two months: "Why did it take fifty years for these new ideas to be recognized?" To give a partial answer to this question, we must look more closely at the developments in the late forties and early fifties. A crucial fact is that von Neumann's theory was too highly mathematical for economists. Therefore, the theory of games was developed almost exclusively by mathematicians during this period. To describe the spirit of the time, allow me to quote from Robert J. Aumann's magnificent article [3] on game theory in the New Palgrave Dictionary "The period of the late 40's and early 50's was a period of excitement in game theory. The discipline had broken out of its cocoon and was testing its wings. Giants walked the earth. At Princeton, John Nash laid the groundwork for the general non-cooperative theory and for cooperative bargaining theory. Lloyd Shapley defined the value for coalitional games, initiated the theory of stochastic games, coinvented the core with D.B. Gillies, and together with John Milnor developed the first game models with a continuum of players. Harold Kuhn reformulated the extensive form of a game, and worked on behavior strategies and perfect recall. Al Tucker discovered the Prisoner's Dilemma, and supported a number of young game theorists through the Office of Naval Research."

HARSANYI

When did Tucker discover the Prisoner's Dilemma?

KUHN

Al Tucker was on leave at Stanford in the Spring of 1950 and, because of the shortage of offices, he was housed in the Psychology Department. One day a psychologist knocked on his door and asked what he was doing. Tucker replied: "I'm working on game theory.", and the psychologist asked if he would give a seminar on his work. For that seminar, Al Tucker invented the Prisoner's Dilemma as an example of game theory, Nash equilibria, and the attendant paradoxes of non-socially-desirable equilibria. A truly seminal example, it inspired dozens of research papers and several entire books.

It is important to recognize that the results that I have enumerated did not respond to some suggestion of von Neumann, nor did they follow work that he had outlined or proposed; rather they were revolutionary new ideas that ran counter to von Neumann's theory. In almost every instance, it was a repair of some inadequacy of the theory as outlined by von Neumann and Morgenstern, and indeed in the case of Nash's cooperative and general non-cooperative theory, von Neumann and Morgenstern criticized it publicly on several occasions. In the case of the extensive form, von Neumann claimed that it was impossible to give a practical geometric extensive form. All of the results that Aumann cited were obtained by members of the Mathematics Department at Princeton University. At the same time, the RAND Corporation, funded by the US Air Force, which was to be for many years the other major center of game-theoretic research, had just opened its doors in Santa Monica.

This suggests a second part of our answer to the question: "Why did it take so long for economists to recognize game theory as crucial to their field?" It is a historical fact that initially the main financial support for research in this area came from military agencies in the United States. Quoting Aumann again, "The major applications were to tactical military problems: defense from missiles, Colonel Blotto assignment problems, fighter-fighter duels, etc. Later the emphasis shifted to deterrence and cold war strategy with contributions by political scientists like Herman Kahn, Kissinger, and Schelling."

In any event, it was into this environment at Princeton of research ferment that the twenty-year old John Nash came in September of 1948. He came to the Mathematics Department with a one sentence letter of recommendation from R.L. Duffin of Carnegie Institute of Technology. This letter said, simply: "This man is a genius." As his thesis advisor, Professor A.W. Tucker was to write several years later: "At times I have thought this recommendation was extravagant, but the longer I've known Nash the more I am inclined to agree that Duffin was right." If we do the arithmetic of subtracting the date of Nash's arrival in Princeton, which was September 1948, from the date of submission by Solomon Lefschetz to the Proceedings of the National Academy of Sciences of the main result of Nash's thesis, November 1949, we find the results for which he is being honored this week were obtained in his first fourteen months of graduate study. It is a fine goal to set before the graduate students who are in the audience today. We shall return to the thesis later.

Although the speed with which Nash obtained these results is surprising, equally surprising and certainly less widely known is that Nash had already completed an important piece of work on bargaining while still an undergraduate at the Carnegie Institute of Technology. This work, a paper for an elective course in international economics, possibly the only formal course in economics he has ever had, was done in complete ignorance of the work of von Neumann and Morgenstern. In short, when he did this work he didn't know that game theory existed. This result, which is a model of theoretical elegance, posits four reasonable requirements or axioms: (1), that any solution should be invariant under positive linear affine transformations of the utility functions, (2), that the solution should be efficient in the sense of Pareto optimality, (3), that irrelevant alternatives should not change the outcome of the solution, and (4), that bargaining problems with symmetric outcome sets should have symmetric solutions. If these four reasonable conditions are satisfied then there is a unique solution, namely, the outcome that maximizes the product of the players' utilities. There is evidence in the published form of this paper, [37], that, before it appeared in Econometrica in 1950, he had met von Neumann and Morgenstern. This evidence is a reference to Cournot, Bowley, Tintner, and Fellner. It is almost certain that these were added at the suggestion of Morgenstern, because I don't think John has even read these papers as of now.

If it is clear that Nash had not read those writers, it is equally clear that this paper was written by a teenager. The evidence is that the objects in the example to be bargained over are a bat, a ball, a toy, and a knife. No amount of urging by his colleagues, or by the editor of Econometrica, persuaded John to change this example.

I should now like to discuss the thesis itself and show you some sections of John's work from the actual document. We already know that the main result, the definition of a Nash equilibrium, and a proof of existence had been completed prior to November 1949, the date of submission by Lefschetz to the National Academy of Sciences. The thesis itself was completed and submitted after the persistent urging and counsel of Professor Tucker. John always wanted to add more material, and Tucker had the wisdom to say "get the result out early." It was submitted and accepted by the Mathematics Department in May of 1950.

The formal rules at Princeton require that the thesis must be read by two professors, who prepare a report evaluating the work. In this case, the readers were Tucker and the statistician, John Tukey; the evaluation was written by Tucker himself. He wrote, "This is a highly original and important contribution to the Theory of Games. It develops notions and properties of "non-cooperative games," finite n-person games which are very interesting in themselves and which may open up many hitherto untouched problems that lie beyond the zero-sum two-person case. Both in conception and in execution this thesis is entirely the author's own."

In my discussion of the thesis itself, I shall try not to duplicate observations that will be made by later speakers. Some overlap is inevitable. For example, the abstract begins boldly: "This paper introduces the concept of a non-cooperative game and develops methods for the mathematical analysis of such games." Take careful note, there had been no general theory of non-cooperative games before this thesis. Although he was using the same strategic form as had been developed by von Neumann, the theory which occupies fully half of the von Neumann and Morgenstern book deals with cooperative theory envisaging coalitions, side-payments, and binding agreements. In addition, they proposed as a solution concept a notion we now call a "stable set", which need not exist for every game. By contrast, Nash proved by page 6 of his thesis that every n-person finite non-cooperative game has at least one (Nash) equilibrium point. This is a profile of mixed strategies, one for each player, which is such that no player can improve his payoff by changing his mixed strategy unilaterally.

The entire thesis is 27 pages of typescript, very generously double-spaced. Frankly, I have always considered the most important sections to be the first 6 pages summarized above and the last pages (from page 21 to 26) on motivation, interpretation, and applications. For many years, I have accused John of padding the thesis in the middle section (15 pages in all).

The two interpretations which form the essential motivation of work to be described by later speakers occur in the last pages of the thesis. On page 21, we find: "We shall now take up the mass action interpretation of equilibrium points." This interpretation will be discussed in detail by Selten and Weibull. The second interpretation is found on page 23, where we read: "We now sketch another interpretation ... investigating the question: what would be a "rational" prediction of the behavior to be expected of rational playing the game in question." This interpretation will be discussed by van Damme. It is important to recognize that, although these very influential interpretations are explicitly in the thesis, they appear in no other publication by Nash.

To conclude my introduction to this seminar, I shall quote Aumann [3] again:

> "[The Nash] equilibrium is without doubt the single game theoretic solution concept that is most frequently applied in economics. Economic applications include oligopoly, entry and exit, market equilibrium, search, location, bargaining, product quality, auctions, insurance, principal-agent [problems], higher education, discrimination, public goods, what have you. On the political front, applications include voting, arms control and inspection, as well as most international political models (deterrence, etc.). Biological applications all deal with forms of strategic equilibrium; they suggest an interpretation of equilibrium quite different from the usual overt rationalism. We cannot even begin to survey all of this literature here."

It is now my pleasure to introduce an economist whom I have known since we were co-directors of a Summer Institute on Bargaining and Conflict in Princeton in 1962: John Harsanyi.

HARSANYI

In the short period of 1950 – 53, John Nash published four brilliant papers ([35], [37], [38], [39]), in which he made at least *three* fundamentally important contributions to game theory:

(1) He introduced the distinction between *cooperative* and *non-cooperative* games. The former are games in which the players can make *enforceable* agreements and can also make *irrevocable* threats to other players. That is to say, they can fully *commit* themselves to specific strategies. In contrast, in non-cooperative games, such self-commitment is not possible.[1]

(2) As a natural solution concept for non-cooperative games, he introduced the concept of *equilibrium points* ([35], [38]), now usually described as *Nash equilibria.* He also established their existence in all finite games.[2]

(3) As a solution concept for two-person cooperative games, he proposed the *Nash bargaining solution,* first for games with *fixed threats* [37], and later also for games with *variable threats* [39]. He also showed that, in the latter case, the two players' optimal strategies will have *maximin* and *minimax* properties.

The best way to understand the importance of Nash's contributions is by comparing the state of game theory just after publication of von Neumann and Morgenstern's book in 1944 with its state after publication of Nash's four papers in 1953.

von Neumann and Morgenstern's book contains an excellent mathematical analysis of one class of *non-cooperative* games, viz. of *two-person zero-sum* games and of the *minimax* solution for such games. It contains also an excellent mathematical discussion of one *cooperative* solution concept, that of *stable sets,* for many specific games.

Yet, it so happens that the concept of two-person zero-sum games has *very few* real-life applications outside of the military field. The concept of stable sets has *even fewer* empirical applications

Had these two distinguished authors had Nash's notions of cooperative and non-cooperative games available to them, then presumably they would have asked the question of how to act rationally in a two-person *nonzero-sum* game or in a *more-than-two-person* game if this is played as a *non-cooperative* game, permitting no enforceable agreements and no irrevocable threats. Perhaps they would have asked also whether one could not find for *cooperative* games a more convincing solution concept than *stable sets* are. For instance, whether one could not find a solution concept yielding *sharper predictions* about the players' actual payoffs than the concept of stable sets does.

Of course, in actual fact, they did not have these two notions available to them and therefore *did not* ask these two questions. But I merely want to point out how much our ability to ask important game theoretic questions was enhanced by Nash's work.

Nash's contributions described above under (1), (2), and (3) had an almost immediate effect on game-theoretic research. At first their effect was to encourage game theorists to develop the theories of cooperative games and of non-cooperative games as virtually *separate* disciplines, and for some time to devote much more effort to devise alternative *cooperative* solution concepts than to further development on *non-cooperative* game theory.

Then, in about the decade 1970 – 80, the focus of game theoretic research shifted once more. Interest in cooperative solution concepts decreased whereas interest in non-cooperative games and in non-cooperative-game models of cooperative games substantially increased.

This shift was due to a number of different factors. But one of these factors was what came to be known as *Nash's program.* One of Nash's papers ([38], p. 295) contains the following interesting passage:

> "The writer has developed a "dynamical" approach to the study of cooperative games based on reduction to non-cooperative form. One proceeds by constructing a model of the pre-play negotiation so that the steps of [this] negotiation become moves in a larger non-cooperative game...describing the total situation.
>
> This larger game is then treated in terms of the theory of this paper[3]...and if values are obtained [then] they are taken as the values of the cooperative game. Thus, the problem of analyzing a cooperative game becomes the problem of obtaining a suitable, and convincing, non-cooperative model for the negotiation."

When game theorists speak of "Nash's program," it is this two-paragraph passage they have in mind. That is to say, they are talking about the program of trying to reduce *cooperative* games to *non-cooperative* games by means of suitable non-cooperative models of the bargaining process among the players.

It is an interesting fact of intellectual history (if I am right in my reading of this history) that Nash's papers in the early 1950's at first encouraged game theorists to cultivate *cooperative* and *non-cooperative* game theory as largely independent disciplines, with a concentration on *cooperative* theory. But twenty-five years later they encouraged a shift to *non-cooperative* game theory and to *non-cooperative* models of the negotiations among the players.

Both Reinhard Selten and I were very pleased indeed when we learned that we received our Nobel Memorial Prizes in Economics together with John Nash. Not only do we both have the highest regard for his work, but our own work in game theory has been to an important extent based on his.

One of Reinhard's important contributions was his distinction between *perfect* and *imperfect* Nash equilibria. It was based on his realization that even strategy combinations fully satisfying Nash's definition of Nash equilibria might very well contain some *irrational* strategies. To exclude such imperfect Nash equilibria containing such irrational strategies, at first he proposed what now are called *subgame-perfect* equilibria (Selten, [45]). Later he proposed the even more demanding concept of *trembling-hand perfect* equilibria (Selten[4] [46]).

Reinhard's work on *evolutionarily stable strategies* was likewise based on the concept of Nash equilibria.

In my own case, an important part of my own work was likewise based on Nash's results. Thus, in my first game-theoretic paper [17], my main point was to show the *mathematical equivalence* of Nash's and of Zeuthen's bargaining models.

In the same paper (pp. 152 – 53), I pointed out an interesting corollary to Nash's theory of optimal threats: Suppose we measure the costs of a conflict to either party in terms of von Neumann-Morgenstern utilities. Suppose also that one bargainer makes a threat against the other. Then this will *strengthen* his own bargaining position only if carrying out his threat would increase the costs of a conflict for his opponent in a *higher proportion* than it would increase the costs of a conflict for him.

In a later paper [18], I extended the Shapley value to games *without* transferable utility and showed that my new solution concept was not only a generalization of the Shapley value, but also a direct generalization of Nash's two-person bargaining solution with variable threats.

A Nash equilibrium is defined as a strategy combination with the property that every player's strategy is a *best reply* to the other players' strategies. This of course is true also for Nash equilibria in *mixed* strategies. But in the latter case, besides his mixed *equilibrium strategy*, each player will also have infinitely many *alternative* strategies that are his *best replies* to the other players' strategies. This will make such equilibria potentially unstable.

In view of this fact, I felt it was desirable to show [20], that "almost all" Nash equilibria can be interpreted as *strict* equilibria in *pure* strategies of a suitably chosen game with randomly fluctuating payoff functions.

KUHN

In the early sixties, I had the great good fortune to hire both John Harsanyi and our next speaker as consultants to a project that I initiated for a research company in Princeton, called MATHEMATICA. The project was funded by the Arms Control and Disarmament Agency and a major topic was games with incomplete information. Our speaker has written about this experience in his autobiographical note [47]: Reinhard Selten.

SELTEN

Let me first tell you that this intervention has been prepared by Peter Hammerstein and myself. When John Nash published his basic papers on 'equilibrium points in n-person games' [35], and 'non-cooperative games' [38], nobody would have foretold the great impact of Nash equilibrium on economics and social science in general. It was even less expected that Nash's equilibrium point concept would ever have any significance for biological theory. To most game theorists it came as a complete surprise that beginning with the pioneering paper by Maynard Smith and Price [31] non-cooperative game theory, as it was founded by Nash, became one of the central tools for understanding the evolutionary logic of animal and plant interaction.

EVOLUTIONARY STABILITY

Maynard Smith and Price [35] introduced the concept of an evolutionarily stable strategy (ESS). Initially they were not aware of the relationship between the concept of an ESS and that of a Nash equilibrium. Rational game theory looked at mixed strategies as produced by conscious randomization. Nash's interpretation of a mixed equilibrium as a mass action phenomenon was buried in his unpublished dissertation and not found in textbooks on game theory. In biology the mass action interpretation is very natural and guided the work on evolutionary stability already from its beginning.

In their original paper, Maynard Smith and Price [35] restricted their attention to two-person games in normal form. They defined an ESS as a strategy prescribed by a symmetric equilibrium point and imposed on this strategy an additional stability requirement. This requirement had its roots in the idea that a population in evolutionary equilibrium should be stable against the invasion of mutants. There is no problem of instability if the mutant does not play a best reply to the symmetric equilibrium. However, if it plays an alternative best reply, i.e., a best reply different from the equilibrium strategy, it may spread by genetic drift. Maynard Smith and Price argued that this is excluded if against the alternative best reply the equilibrium strategy achieves a higher payoff than the alternative best reply itself does. This is the additional stability requirement in the definition of an ESS.

Nowadays it almost seems to be obvious that the correct application of Darwinism to problems of social interaction among animals requires the use of non-cooperative game theory, but when this idea was first conceived it was a revolutionary great insight. Of course the strategies of animals and plants are not the result of conscious deliberation. They are thought of as behavioral programs transferred by genetical inheritance from generation to generation. Game equilibrium is achieved by the process of natural selection which drives organisms towards the maximization of fitness. Roughly speaking, Darwinian fitness is the expected number of surviving offspring.

The original restriction to symmetric two-person games was soon removed and much more general definitions of an ESS were elaborated. The fruitfulness of game-theoretic thinking in biology is revealed by a multitude of intriguing applications. References to the theoretical and empirical literature can be found in our review paper (Hammerstein and Selten [16]).

THE CRISIS OF DARWINIAN ADAPTATION THEORY

In the early forties, biological thought on evolution reached a consensus often referred to as the 'new synthesis'. The apparent contradiction between Mendelian inheritance and gradual adaptation had been resolved by the population genetic work of Fisher [11], Haldane [14], and Wright [55]. Fisher's famous 'fundamental theorem of natural selection' had shown that under appropriate assumptions about the genetical system, the mean fitness of a population rises until a maximum is reached. However, in the sixties a new generation of population geneticists became aware of the fact that plausible genetic systems are very unlikely to satisfy the assumptions of Fisher's theorem. In the framework of a standard selection model, Moran [32] found examples in which mean fitness decreases over time until an equilibrium is reached. He looked at a two-locus model in which an evolving trait is coded for by two genes. Later Karlin [26] showed that these examples are not just degenerate cases.

The curious phenomenon of decreasing mean fitness becomes understandable if one looks at the nature of the resulting equilibrium. In this equilibrium one finds genotypes of high and low fitness but the offsprings of high fitness genotypes can have the same mean fitness as those of low fitness genotypes. This is an effect of recombination which tears genes at different loci apart. The phenomenon of decreasing mean fitness is a serious challenge to the theory of Darwinian adaptation. Some population geneticists came to the conclusion that the whole idea of fitness maximization has to be discarded as the main explanatory principle of biological evolution. The difficulties arise in the context of what is called 'frequency-independent selection' or, in other words, when there is no game interaction. In the presence of game interaction, the situation is even less favorable for the maximization of fitness. Of course, mean fitness is not maximized by game theoretic equilibrium, but Moran's and Karlin's results mean that game equilibrium is not necessarily reached.

By these developments, Darwinian adaptation theory was thrown into a true crisis. However, very few empirically oriented biologists were really disturbed by this problem. To them the crisis seemed to be one of mathematical theory rather than a failure of Darwinism as an explanation of biological facts. They continued to be impressed by the overwhelming empirical evidence for adaptation by natural selection. Nevertheless, the problem posed a serious challenge to theory.

THE STREETCAR THEORY

The process which generates the phenomenon of decreasing mean fitness governs the adjustment of genotype frequencies in the absence of mutations. Eshel and Feldman [10] were the first to ask the question under what conditions a stable equilibrium reached by this process is also stable against the invasion of mutants. As has been shown by Moran [32] and Karlin [26], the 'internal stability' with respect to the process without mutation does not necessarily lead to fitness maximization of game equilibrium. However, they succeeded to show that for an internally stable state in a sufficiently small vicinity of an ESS, the inflow of a destablizing mutation has a tendency to initially move the system in the direction of the ESS.

This opens the possibility that the notion of an ESS has more significance for the analysis of genetic systems than one might think if one looks only at internal stability and not also at external stability against the invasion of mutants. Admittedly, the results of Eshel and Feldman do not yet go very far in this direction but they were an ingenious step towards a new genetic interpretation of Darwinian adaptation. In the process of writing our review paper for the handbook of game theory (Hammerstein and Selten [16]), we became intrigued by the possibility of providing a better foundation for the application of non-cooperative game theory in biology along the lines of Eshel and Feldman. We ended up in proving two theorems whose biological implications we like to describe by an analogy elaborated by one of us (Hammerstein [15]). The analogy involves a streetcar whose stops correspond to internally stable states. Only at the terminal stop the population state is phenotypically stable in the sense that the probabilities of pure strategies cannot be changed any more by the invasion of a mutant.

The first theorem shows that only a Nash equilibrium can be phenotypically stable in a standard two-locus model of population genetics with game interaction. This means that in the long run the process of natural selection and mutation if it converges at all, must converge to Nash equilibrium. It therefore turns out that Nash equilibrium is of central importance for evolutionary biology. Of course, the streetcar may often stay for a while at a temporary stop at which some passengers exit and others enter before, finally, the terminal stop is reached at which it stays much longer.

The second theorem shows that a phenotypically monomorphic population state can be a terminal stop if and only if it is an ESS in the sense of Maynard Smith and Price [31]. Wherever one has reason to suppose that a trait is phenotypically monomorphic, this result establishes a firm foundation for the concept of an ESS. However, polymorphism is often observed in nature and in this respect Nash equilibrium is of more far reaching significance.

CONCLUDING REMARK

Originally, von Neumann and Morgenstern [52] developed game theory as a mathematical method especially adapted to economics and social science in general. In the introduction of their book, they emphasized their view that methods taken over from the natural sciences are inadequate for their purpose. They succeeded in creating a new method of mathematical analysis not borrowed from physics. In the case of game theory the flow of methodological innovation did not go in the usual direction from the natural to the social sciences but rather in the opposite one. The basis for this extremely successful transfer is the concept of Nash equilibrium.

KUHN

About five years ago, the Economics Department at Princeton University was fortunate to have the next speaker as a visiting professor. He has been in the forefront of recognizing the importance of Nash's mass action interpretation: Jörgen Weibull.

WEIBULL

THE MASS ACTION INTERPRETATION

In his unpublished Ph.D. dissertation, John Nash provided two interpretations of his equilibrium concept for non-cooperative games, one rationalistic and one population-statistic. In the first, which became the standard interpretation, one imagines that the game in question is played only once, that the participants are "rational," and that they know the full structure of the game. However, Nash comments: "It is quite strongly a rationalistic and idealizing interpretation" ([36], p. 23). The second interpretation, which Nash calls the *mass-action* interpretation, was until recently largely unknown (Leonard [28], Weibull [53], Björnerstedt and Weibull [6]). Here Nash imagines that the game in question is played over and over again by participants who are not necessarily "rational" and who need not know the structure of the game:

> "It is unnecessary to assume that the participants have full knowledge of the total structure of the game, or the ability and inclination to go through any complex reasoning processes. But the participants are supposed to accumulate empirical information on the relative advantages of the various pure strategies at their disposal.
>
> To be more detailed, we assume that there is a population (in the sense of statistics) of participants for each position of the game. Let us also assume that the 'average playing' of the game involves n participants selected at random from the n populations, and that there is a stable average frequency with which each pure strategy is employed by the 'average member' of the appropriate population.
>
> Since there is to be no collaboration between individuals playing in different positions of the game, the probability that a particular n-tuple of pure strategies will be employed in a playing of the game should be the product of the probabilities indicating the chance of each of the n pure strategies to be employed in a random playing" ([36], pp. 21 – 22.)

Nash notes that if s_i is a population distribution over the pure strategies $\alpha \in A_i$ available to the i'th player position, then $s = (si)_{i \in I}$ is formally identical with a mixed strategy profile, and the expected payoff to any pure strategy α in a random matching between an n-tuple of individuals, one from each player population, is identical with the expected payoff $\pi_{i\alpha}(s)$ to this strategy when played against the mixed strategy profile s:

> "Now let us consider what effects the experience of the participants will produce. To assume, as we did, that they accumulate empirical evidence on the pure strategies at their disposal is to assume that those playing in position i learn the numbers $\pi_{i\alpha}(s)$. But if they know these they will employ only optimal pure strategies [...]. Consequently, since s_i expresses their behavior, s_i attaches positive coefficients only to optimal pure strategies, [...]. But this is simply a condition for s to be an equilibrium point.
>
> Thus the assumption we made in this 'mass-action' interpretation lead to the conclusion that the mixed strategies representing the average behavior in each of the populations form an equilibrium point." (op cit., p. 22)[5]

These remarks suggest that Nash equilibria could be identified as stationary, or perhaps dynamically stable, population states in dynamic models of boundedly rational strategy adaptation in large strategically interacting populations. In spirit, this interpretation is not far from Friedman's [13] subsequent "as if" defense of microeconomic axioms. For just as Nash argued that boundedly rational players will adapt toward strategic optimality, Friedman argued that only profit maximizing firms will survive in the long run under (non-strategic) market competition. Moreover, the view that games are played over and over again by individuals who are randomly drawn from large populations was later independently taken up by evolutionary biologists (Maynard Smith and Price [31], Taylor and Jonker [49]).

NOTATION AND PRELIMINARIES

Consider a finite n-player game G in normal (or strategic) form. Let A_i be the pure-strategy set of player position $i \in I = \{1,..., n\}$, S_i its mixed-strategy simplex, and $S = \Pi_{i \in I} S_i$ the polyhedron of mixed-strategy profiles. For any player position i, pure strategy $\alpha \in A_i$ and mixed strategy $s_i \in S_i$, let $s_{i\alpha}$ denote the probability assigned to α. A strategy profile s is called *interior* if *all* pure strategies are used with positive probability. The expected payoff to player position i when a profile $s \in S$ is played will be denoted $\pi_i(s)$, while $\pi_{i\alpha}(s)$ denotes the payoff to player i when he uses pure strategy $\alpha \in A_i$ against the profile

$s \in S$. A strategy profile $s \in S$ is a *Nash equilibrium* if and only if $s_{i\alpha} > 0$ implies $\pi_{i\alpha}(s) = \max_{\beta \in A_i} \pi_{i\beta}(s)$

In the spirit of the "mass-action" interpretation, imagine that the game is played over and over again by individuals who are randomly drawn from (infinitely) large populations, one population for each player position i in the game. A *population state* is then formally identical with a mixed-strategy profile $s \in S$, but now each component $s_i \in S_i$ represents the distribution of pure strategies in player population i, i.e., $s_{i\alpha}$ is the probability that a randomly selected individual in population i will use pure strategy $\alpha \in A_i$ when drawn to play the game. In this interpretation $\pi_{i\alpha}(s)$ is the (expected) payoff to an individual in player population i who uses pure strategy α – an "α-strategist" – and $\pi_i(s)$ $\Sigma_\beta s_{i\beta}\pi_{i\beta}(s)$ is the average (expected) payoff in player population i, both quantities being evaluated in population state s.

Suppose that every now and then, say, according to a statistically independent Poisson process, each individual reviews her strategy choice. By the law of large numbers the aggregate process of strategy adaptation may then be approximated by deterministic flows, and these may be described in terms of ordinary differential equations.

INNOVATIVE ADAPTATION

We first consider the case when strategy adaptation is memory-less in the sense that the time rate of strategy revision and the choice probabilities of strategy-reviewing individuals are functions of the current state s (only):

$$\dot{s}_{ia}(t) = f_{i\alpha}[s(t)] \tag{1}$$

for some functions $f_{ia} : S \to \mathbf{R}$. The quantity $f_{ia}(s)$ thus represents the net increase per time unit of the population share of α-strategists in player population i when the overall population state is s. The (composite) function f is assumed to be Lipschitz continuous and such that all solution trajectories starting in S remain forever in S. Such a function f will be called a *vector field* for (1).

The class of population dynamics (1) clearly allows for an innovative element; some individuals may begin using earlier unused strategies, either intentionally, by way of experimentation or calculation, or unintentionally, by way of mistakes or mutations. Indeed, a certain degree of inventiveness in this sense is easily seen to imply that only those population states that constitute Nash equilibria can be stationary.[6] The requirement is simple: if there is some (used or unused) pure strategy which results in a payoff above the current average payoff in the player population in question, then some such pure strategy will grow in population share. Formally, for any population state $s \in S$ and player position $i \in I$, let $B_i(s)$ denote the (possibly empty) subset of better-than-average pure strategies, $B_i(s) = \{\alpha \in A_i : \pi_{ia}(s) > \pi_i(s)\}$.

Inventiveness can then be formalized as

[IN]: *If* $B_i(s) \neq \emptyset$, then $f_{ia}(s) > 0$ for some $\alpha \in B_i(s)$.

This condition is, for instance, met if reviewing individuals move toward the best replies to the current population state. Note that [*IN*] requires no knowledge about payoffs to other player positions, nor is any detailed knowledge of the payoffs to one's own strategy set necessary. It is sufficient that individuals on average tend to twitch toward *some* of the better-than-average performing strategies.

Proposition 1 *Suppose f meets [IN]. If a population state s is stationary under the associated dynamics (1), then s constitutes a Nash equilibrium of G.*

An example of innovative adaptation is given by

$$f_{ia}^{+}(s) = \pi^{+}_{ia}(s) - s_{ia}\sum_{\beta\in A_i}\pi^{+}_{i\beta}(s) \tag{2}$$

where $\pi^{+}_{ia}(s) = \max\{\pi_{i\alpha}(s - \pi_i(s), 0\}$; the excess payoff to pure strategy α over the average payoff in its player population. It is not difficult to verify that f^{+} meets [*IN*]. The associated population dynamics (1) is nothing else than the continuous-time version of the iteration mapping introduced in Nash's [38] influential existence proof for equilibrium points – later adopted in general equilibrium theory, see Arrow and Debreu [1].[7]

In order to incorporate memory in the dynamic process of strategy adaptation, one may introduce real variables $P_{i\alpha}$, one for each player position i and pure strategy $\alpha \in A_i$, that represent the i'th population's recollection of earlier payoffs to pure strategy α. Assume that the recalled payoff to any pure strategy $\alpha \in A_i$ changes with time according to

$$P_{i\alpha}(t) = h_{i\alpha}(\pi_{i\alpha}[s(t)], p_{i\alpha}(t), t), \tag{3}$$

where $h_{i\alpha}$ is a Lipschitz continuous function such that the recalled payoff changes only if the current payoff differs from the recalled payoff $(h_{i\alpha}(\pi_{i\alpha}, p_{i\alpha}, t) = 0 \Rightarrow \pi_{i\alpha} = p_{i\alpha})$.

The full adaptation dynamics with memory is then a system of differential equations in the state vector $x = (s, p)$, where p moves according to (3) and s according to

$$\dot{s}_{i\alpha}(t) = f_{i\alpha}[s(t), p(t)] \tag{4}$$

A counterpart to the earlier requirement [*IN*] of inventiveness is: if there is some (used or unused) pure strategy which is *recalled* to result in a payoff above the average of the currently recalled payoffs in the player population in question, then some such pure strategy will increase its population share. Formally, for any state (s, p) and player position $i \in I$, let $B_i(s, p) = \{\alpha \in A_i : p_{i\alpha} > \Sigma_{\beta\in A_i} s_{i\beta} p_{i\beta}\}$. Inventiveness can then be formalized as

[**IN'**]: If $B_i(s, p), \neq \emptyset$ then $f_{i\alpha}(s, p) > 0$ for some $\alpha \in B_i(s, p)$.

The following extension of proposition 1 is straightforward:

Proposition 2 *Suppose f meets [IN']. If (s, p)* is stationary under (3) and (4), then *s* is a Nash equilibrium of *G*.[8]

A special case of memory processes of the above type is when the recalled payoff to a pure strategy is the *time average* of its earlier payoffs: $p_{i\alpha}(t) = \int^t_0 \pi_{i\alpha}[s(\tau)]d\tau$. This is the memory process in fictitious play (Robinson [40]), written in continuous time. (In that model players always use best replies against the time average of past play.) Differentiation of $p_{i\alpha}(t)$ with respect to t gives

$$h_{i\alpha}(\pi_{1\alpha}, p_{i\alpha}, t) = \frac{1}{t}(\pi_{i\alpha} - p_{i\alpha}), \tag{5}$$

a function which can be slightly modified so that it belongs to the above-discussed class (add an arbitrarily short time interval before $t = 0$).

IMITATIVE ADAPTATION

It may be argued that the above classes of population dynamics go somewhat beyond the spirit of the mass-action interpretation since they presume that individuals perform a certain amount of calculations. Therefore, now assume *no* memory and *no* inventiveness as defined above. Thus, individuals now switch only between strategies already in use, and they do so only on the basis of these strategies' current performance. Technically, this means that the population dynamics (1) has a vector field f of the form

$$f_{i\alpha}(s) = g_{i\alpha}(s)\, s_{i\alpha}. \tag{6}$$

The involved functions $g_{i\alpha}$ will be called *growth-rate functions* – $g_{i\alpha}(s)$ being the growth rate of the population share of pure strategy α in player population i when the population state is s. No vector field of the form (6) is innovative in the sense of condition [*IN*], because if all individuals in a player population initially use only one (or a few) pure strategy then they will continue doing so forever, irrespective of whether some unused strategy yields a high payoff or not. Consequently, stationarity does *not* imply Nash equilibrium for the present class of dynamics, which will be called *imitative.*

A prime example of such dynamics is the so-called replicator dynamics used in evolutionary biology (Taylor and Jonker [49], Taylor [48]). In this strand of literature, pure strategies represent genetically programmed behaviors, reproduction is asexual, each offspring inherits its parent's strategy, and payoffs represent reproductive fitness. Thus $\pi_{i\alpha}(s)$ is the number of (surviving) offspring to an α-strategist in population i, and $\pi_i(s)$ is the average number of (surviving) offspring per individual in the same population. In the standard version of this population model, each pure strategy's growth rate is proportional to its current payoff:[9]

$$g_{i\alpha}(s) = \pi_{i\alpha}(s) - \pi i(s). \tag{7}$$

We will here consider a broad class of vector fields which contains the replicator vector field as a special case. The defining requirement is close in spirit to that in the previous section: If there exists a pure strategy which results in a payoff above average in its player population (whether this pure strategy be currently used or not), then *some* such pure strategy has a positive *growth rate*. Hence, if all such strategies are present in the population, then some such population share will grow. Formally:

$$[\textbf{POS}]\text{: If } B_i(s) \neq \emptyset, \text{ then } g_{i\alpha}(s) > 0 \text{ for some } \alpha \in B_i(s).$$

The next proposition establishes the following implications under payoff positive imitation: (a) if all strategies are present in a stationary population state, then this constitutes a Nash equilibrium, (b) A dynamically stable population state constitutes a Nash equilibrium, (c) If a dynamic solution trajectory starts from a population state in which all pure strategies are present and the trajectory converges over time, then the limit state is a Nash equilibrium.[10] Claim (b) is a generalization of a result due to Bomze [7] for the single-population version of the replicator dynamics as applied to symmetric two-player games, and (c) generalizes a result due to Nachbar [34]. (See Weibull [54] for a proof.)

Proposition 3 *Suppose g meets [POS], and consider the associated population dynamics (1) where f is defined in (6).*

(a) *If s is interior and stationary, then s is a Nash equilibrium.*
(b) *If s is dynamically stable, then s is a Nash equilibrium.*
(c) *If s is the limit of some interior solution trajectory, then s is a Nash equilibrium.*

Note that claims (a) and (c) involve hypotheses that no pure strategies are extinct. Indeed, these claims are otherwise not generally valid. Implication (b), however, allows for the possibility that some pure strategy is extinct. This is permitted because dynamic stability by definition asks what happens when the population state is slightly perturbed – in particular, when currently extinct strategies enter the population in small population shares.

CONCLUSION

The mass-action interpretation of Nash equilibria is in stark contrast with the usual rationalistic interpretation, but is closely related to ideas in evolutionary game theory. It opens new avenues for equilibrium and stability analysis of social and economic processes, and suggests new ways to combine insights in the social and behavior sciences with economic theory.

KUHN

In Reinhard Selten's talk, he did not mention his major discovery of two refinements of the concept of Nash equilibria, the so-called subgame perfect equilibria [45] and trembling-hand perfect equilibria [46]. A large body of research followed these discoveries; it has been summarized in a magnificent manner in a book [50] by our next speaker: Eric van Damme.

VAN DAMME

Ideas, concepts and tools that were introduced by John Nash [36] have been extremely important in shaping modern economic theory. He introduced the fundamental solution concept for non-cooperative games, one of the main solution concepts for cooperative games and he proposed the Nash program for providing non-cooperative foundations of cooperative concepts. In his analysis he introduced seminal tools and techniques that served as essential building blocks in the later development of the theory and that contributed to its successful application. Below we provide a perspective on Nash's work and trace its influence on modern economic theory.

NASH EQUILIBRIUM: THE RATIONALISTIC INTERPRETATION

A non-cooperative game is given by a set of players, each having a set of strategies and a payoff function. A strategy vector is a *Nash equilibrium* if each player's strategy maximizes his pay-off if the strategies of the others are held fixed. In his Ph.D. thesis, Nash introduces this concept and he derives several properties of it, the most important one being existence of at least one equilibrium for every finite game. In published work ([35], [38]), Nash provides two alternative, elegant proofs, one based on Kakutani's fixed point theorem, the other based directly on Brouwer's theorem. These techniques have inspired many other existence proofs, for example, in the area of general equilibrium theory (see [9]).

In the section "Motivation and Interpretation" of his thesis, Nash discusses two interpretations of his equilibrium concept. The first, "mass-action" interpretation is discussed in Jörgen Weibull's contribution to this seminar. Here, we restrict ourselves to the "rationalistic and idealizing interpretation" which is applicable to a game played just once, but which requires that the players are rational and know the full structure of the game. Nash's motivation runs as follows:

> "We proceed by investigating the question: What would be a "rational" prediction of the behavior to be expected of rational playing the game in question? By using the principles that a rational prediction should be unique, that the players should be able to deduce and make use of it, and that such knowledge on the part of each player of what to expect the others to do should not lead him to act out of

> conformity with the prediction, one is led to the concept of a solution defined before." [36]

In other words, a theory of rational behavior has to prescribe the play of a Nash equilibrium since otherwise the theory is self-destroying. Note that the argument invokes three assumptions: (i) players actively randomize in choosing their actions, (ii) players know the game and the solution, and (iii) the solution is unique. Later work has scrutinized and clarified the role of each of these assumptions. Harsanyi ([20]) showed that a mixed strategy of one player can be interpreted as the beliefs (conjectures) of the other players concerning his behavior. This reinterpretation provides a "Bayesian" foundation for mixed strategy equilibria and eliminates the intuitive difficulties associated with them. Aumann developed the concepts of an interactive belief system, which provides a formal framework for addressing the epistemic conditions underlying Nash equilibrium, i.e., it allows one to formalize players' knowledge and to investigate how much knowledge is needed to justify Nash equilibrium. In 2-player games less stringent conditions are sufficient than in general n-player games. (Aumann and Brandenberger [4])

Since the rationalistic justification of equilibria relies on uniqueness, multiplicity of equilibria is problematic. Nash remarks that it sometimes happens that good heuristic reasons can be found for narrowing down the set of equilibria. One simple example that Nash provides (Ex. 5 [38]) is the game that is reproduced here in Figure 1. This game has equilibria at (a, α) and (b, β), as well as a mixed equilibrium. Nash writes that "empirical tests show a tendency toward (a, α) ," but he does not provide further details. One heuristic argument is that (a, α) is less risky than (b, β), an argument that is formalized by Harsanyi and Selten's [23] concept of risk dominance. It figures prominently both in the literature that builds on the "rationalistic interpretation" as well as in the literature that builds on the "mass-action" interpretation of Nash equilibrium. We will return to it in EQUILIBRIUM SELECTION.

	α	β
a	1,2	-1, -4
b	-4, -1	2,1

Fig. 1

THE NASH PROGRAM

It can be said that the "rationalistic argument" leading to Nash equilibrium was already discussed in von Neumann and Morgenstern [52] cf. their "indirect argument" (pp. 147 – 148). They advocate the (equilibrium) solution implied for the 2-person zero-sum case, however, they argue that this solution is not satisfactory for games outside this class, since in these one cannot neglect coalitions nor the possibility that players will want to make payments outside the formal rules of the game (p. 44). They argue that for these games "there seems no escape from the necessity of considering agreements concluded outside the game" (p. 223) and they see themselves forced to assume that coalitions and agreements concluded outside of the game are respected by the contracting parties (p. 224). Hence, they end up with having two distinct theories.

Nash proposes to distinguish between cooperative and non-cooperative games. In games of the latter type, players are unable to conclude enforceable agreements outside the formal rules of the game. Cooperative games allow such agreements. Nash suggests that non-cooperative games are more basic, that cooperative games may fruitfully be analyzed by reformulating them as non-cooperative ones and by solving for the Nash equilibria. This approach has come to be known as the *Nash program*. It allows unification of the theory and enables a better understanding of the different solution concepts that have been proposed in cooperative theory. (See Harsanyi [21] for an example dealing with the von Neumann and Morgenstern stable set concept; also see BARGAINING THEORY.) By following the Nash program, an abstract discussion about the "reasonableness" of certain outcomes or principles can be replaced by a more mundane discussion about the appropriateness of the rules of the game.

The non-cooperative approach also has its limitations. First, values can be obtained only if the game has a unique solution, i.e., one has to address the equilibrium selection problem. Secondly, the non-cooperative model must at the same time be relevant – similar to reality in its essential aspects, and mathematically tractable. Consequently, the axiomatic approach – which aims to derive the outcome directly from a set of 'convincing' principles, is not redundant. On the contrary, if a solution can be obtained from a convincing set of axioms, this indicates that the solution is appropriate for a wider variety of situations than those captured by the specific non-cooperative model. As Nash concludes "The two approaches to the problem, via the negotiation model or via the axioms, are complementary; each helps to justify and clarify the other." ([39], p. 129)

BARGAINING THEORY

According to orthodox economic theory, the bargaining problem is indeterminate: The division of the surplus will depend on the parties' bargaining skills. Nash breaks radically with this tradition. He assumes that bargaining between rational players leads to a unique outcome and he seeks to determine it. He solves the problem in the 2-person case and he derives his solution both by means of the axiomatic approach and as the outcome of a non-cooperative model.

In Nash [39] the axiomatic method is described in the following way:

> "One states as axioms several properties that it would seem natural for the solution to have and then one discovers that the axioms actually determine the solution uniquely." ([39], p. 129)

In the case of the fixed-threats, Nash's basic axioms are that rational players are characterized by von Neumann Morgenstern utility functions, and that the bargaining situation is fully represented by its representation, *B* in utility space. Three axioms specify the relation which should hold between the solution and the set *B*: (i) Pareto efficiency, (ii) symmetry and (iii) independence of irrelevant alternatives. These axioms determine the solution to be that point on the north-east boundary of *B* where the product of the utilities, $u_1 u_2$, is maximized.

Axion (iii) states that, if the set of feasible utility pairs shrinks but the solution remains available, then this should remain the solution. It is more difficult to defend than the others and there has been considerable discussion of it in the literature. Nash writes that it is equivalent to an axiom of "localization", specifically "Thinking in terms of bargaining, it is as if a proposed deal is to compete with small modifications of itself and that ultimately the negotiation will be understood to be restricted to a narrow range of alternative deals and to be unconcerned with more remote alternatives." ([39], p 139.) Recent developments in non-cooperative bargaining theory (which build on the seminal paper [42]) have confirmed this interpretation. Namely, assume players alternate in proposing points from *B* until agreement is reached. Assume that if an offer is rejected there is a small but positive probability that negotiations break down irrevocably. This game admits a unique subgame perfect Nash equilibrium (see EQUILIBRIUM REFINEMENT) and agreement is reached immediately. The equilibrium condition states that each time each responder is indifferent between accepting the current proposal and rejecting it. Consequently, the equilibrium proposals are close together when the stopping probability is small, hence, we obtain "localization" property. Indeed the equilibrium conditions imply that both equilibrium proposals have the same Nash product, hence, since they have the same limit, they converge to the Nash solution.

Of course, it is gratifying to find that this natural bargaining model implements Nash's bargaining solution. However, even more important is that this application of the Nash program may clarify some ambiguities concerning the choice of the threat point in applications of the Nash bargaining model. (See [5] for further discussion.)

In the variable threat case, each party has a choice how much pressure to put on the other. The theory now has to determine both the threats that the players will use in case they don't agree, as well as the agreement that will be concluded. Two additional axioms allow reduction of the problem to the case with fixed threats and, hence, determine the theory. The first is equivalent to assuming that each player has an optimal threat strategy, i.e., it is postulated that the problem admits a solution. The second says that a player cannot improve his payoff by eliminating some of his strategies. In the non-cooperative approach, Nash assumes that players first commit themselves to their threats. Players will be forced to execute their threats if they cannot come to an agreement in the second stage. Each pair of threats induces a (fixed-threat bargaining) subgame in which the distinguished equilibrium that maximizes the product of the utility gains is selected. Applying backwards induction and using this selection (i.e., by replacing each subgame with its unique solution), the choice of threat strategy in the first stage essentially reduces to a strictly competitive game, i.e., this reduced first stage game has an equilibrium with minmax properties. Consequently, the overall game has a value and optimal threat strategies. Needless to say, the solution obtained by the non-cooperative approach coincides with that obtained by means of the axioms.

EQUILIBRIUM REFINEMENT

Nash equilibrium expresses the requirement that a theory of rational behavior recommends to each player a strategy that is optimal in case all of the other players play in accordance with the theory. It imposes no conditions concerning behavior after a deviation from the theory has occurred. von Neumann and Morgenstern, however, already argued that a solution concept should also address the question of how to play when the others do not conform and that, in the presence of "non-conformists", a believer in the theory should still be willing to follow the theory's advice. It turns out that not all Nash equilibria have this desirable property: After a deviation from the equilibrium has occurred, a believer in this equilibrium may prefer to deviate from it as well. As an example, modify the game from Figure 1 such that player 1 (the "row player") makes his choice before player 2, with this choice being revealed before the latter makes his decision. The strategy pair in which player 1 chooses *a* and player 2 responds with α no matter what player 1 chooses, is a Nash equilibrium. However, the equilibrium action of player 2 is not optimal if player 1 deviates and chooses *b*: In that case player 2 prefers to deviate to ß. The equilibrium relies on a non-credible threat of player 2.

A clear discussion of the credibility issue can already be found in Nash's work on variable threat bargaining. Nash's paper is appropriately called "Two-person Cooperative Games" since it relies essentially on the existence of an umpire who enforces contracts and commitments, Nash writes "it is essential for the success of the threat that *A* be *compelled* to carry out his threat if *B* fails to comply. Otherwise it will have little meaning. For, in general, to execute the threat will not be something *A* would want to do, just of itself." (Nash [39], p. 130).

To eliminate equilibria that rely on non-credible threats, various refinements of the Nash equilibrium concept have been proposed, which will not be surveyed here see [50]. Let us just note that two papers of Reinhard Selten were fundamental. Selten [45] argues that a theory of rational behavior has to prescribe an equilibrium in every subgame since otherwise at least one player would have an incentive to deviate once the subgame is reached. He calls equilibria having this property subgame perfect. They can be found by a backwards induction procedure. Unfortunately, this procedure generally does not eliminate all "questionable" equilibria. Selten [46] suggests a further refinement that takes the possibility of irrational behavior explicitly into account, i.e., he suggests viewing perfect rationality as a limiting case of incomplete rationality. Formally, he considers slightly perturbed versions of the original game in which players with small probabilities make mistakes and he defines a (trembling hand) perfect equilibrium as one that is a limit of equilibrium points of perturbed games. It is interesting to note that Nash already discussed a game with an imperfect equilibrium (see Ex. 6 in [39]).

This suggestion to discriminate between equilibria by studying their relative stabilities had already been made in Nash's work on bargaining (see EQUILIBRIUM SELECTION). An important difference between Selten's approach and that of Nash, however, is that Selten requires stability only with respect to *some* perturbation, while Nash insisted on stability against *all* perturbations in a certain class. Consequently, a game typically allows multiple perfect equilibria. Kohlberg and Mertens [27] have argued that Selten's perfectness requirement is not restrictive enough and they have proposed various refinements that require stability, of sets of equilibria, with respect to *all* perturbations in a certain class. At present, the debate is still going on of whether these strong stability requirements indeed capture necessary requirements of rational behavior. What can be said, however, that Nash's ideas were fundamental in shaping this research program.

EQUILIBRIUM SELECTION

We have already argued that, since the rationalistic interpretation of Nash equilibrium relies essentially on the uniqueness assumption, the fact that a game frequently has multiple equilibria makes the equilibrium selection problem prominent. Nash already encountered this problem and in his study of the fixed-threat bargaining problem. In Nash's non-cooperative model both players simultaneously state their demands and if the pair of demands is feasible then each player gets his demand; otherwise disagreement results. Clearly, any pair of demands that is Pareto efficient constitutes a pure equilibrium of the game. The following quote describes the multiplicity problem as well as Nash's solution of it

> "Thus the equilibrium points do not lead us immediately to a solution of the game. But if we discriminate between them by studying their relative stabilities we can escape from this troublesome non-uniqueness. To do this we "smooth" the game to obtain a continuous pay-off function and then study the limiting behavior of the equilibrium points of the smoothed game as the amount of smoothing approaches zero." ([39], pp. 131 – 132)

The smoothed game is determined by a continuous, strictly positive, function h, where $h(d)$ can be interpreted as a probability that the demand vector d is compatible. (It is assumed that $h(d) = 1$ if d is feasible in the unperturbed problem, i.e., $d \in B$, and that h tapers off very rapidly towards zero as d moves away from B.) The smoothed game, in which players i's payoff function is $u_i^h(d) = dh_i(d)$ can be thought of as representing uncertainties in the information structure of the game, the utility scales, etc. ([39], p. 132). Any maximizer of the function $d_1 d_2 h(d)$ is an equilibrium of this perturbed game and all these maximizers converge to the unique maximizer of the function $u_1 u_2$ on B as the noise vanishes. Furthermore, if h varies regularly, the perturbed game will have the unique maximizer of $d_1 d_2 h(d)$ as its unique equilibrium. It follows that the Nash bargaining solution is the unique necessary limit of the equilibrium points of the smoothed games. Consequently, the original game has only one "robust" equilibrium, which may be taken as the solution of the game.

Building on Nash's ideas, and motivated by the attempt to generalize Nash's bargaining solution to games with incomplete information, Harsanyi and Selten [22] construct a coherent theory of equilibrium selection for general games. A crucial concept in this theory is that of risk dominance, and the influence of Nash's ideas on the theory is demonstrated by the following quote:

> "Our attempts to define risk dominance in a satisfactory way have been guided by the idea that it is desirable to reproduce the result of Nash's cooperative bargaining theory with fixed threats. The Nash-property is not an unintended by-product of our theory." ([22], p. 215)

The Nash-property that is referred to in this quote is the property that in certain classes of games (such as unanimity games and 2-person 2×2 games) the selected equilibrium is the one for which the product of the losses associated with deviating from the equilibrium is largest. For example, in the game of Figure 1, the equilibrium (a, α) has a Nash product of 30, while the Nash-product of (b, β) is 6. Hence, (a, α) risk-dominates (b, β). For the special case of 2×2 games, Harsanyi and Selten derive the risk-dominance relation from a convincing set of axioms that resembles those with which Nash justifies his bargaining solution. For more general games, risk dominance cannot be based on a simple comparison of Nash products and it is not clear that Harsanyi and Selten's definition (which is based on the tracing procedure and which will not be given here) is the most appropriate one. Carlsson and van Damme [8] compare several concepts that all derive their inspiration from Nash's work and that coincide with Nash's solution for 2×2 games, but that yield different outcomes outside of this class. In any case it is clear that Nash's ideas figure prominently in the theory of equilibrium selection.

EXPERIMENTAL GAMES

In the previous sections, we have documented the influence of Nash's ideas on the development of normative, rationalistic game theory. This paper would be incomplete if it would not also mention the pioneering work of Nash, together with Kalisch, Milnor and Nering [25] in experimental economics. That paper reports on a series of experiments concerning n-person games and aims to compare various theoretical solution concepts with the results of actual play, i.e., it deals with the behavioral relevance of the rationalistic theory. The authors find mixed support for various theoretical solution concepts and they discuss several reasons for the discrepancy between theoretical and empirical results. Among others, the role of personality differences, the fact that utility need not be linear in money and the importance of apparent fairness considerations are mentioned. In addition, several regularities are documented, such as framing effects, the influence of the number of players on the competitiveness of play, the fact that repetition of the game may lead to more cooperative play, and the possibility of inducing a more competitive environment by using stooges. As documented by the importance of the above mentioned concepts in current experimental economics, the paper is an important milestone in the development of descriptive game theory. (See [41]).

A second important contribution of Nash to the experimental economics literature is his discussion of the repeated prisoners' dilemma experiment conducted by Melvin Dresher and Merrill Flood. In this experiment, two players played 100 repetitions of a prisoners' dilemma. They did not constantly play the one-shot equilibrium, but they also did not succeed in reaching an efficient outcome either. The experimenters view their experiment as a test of the predictive relevance of the one-shot equilibrium and they interpret the evidence as refuting this hypothesis. Nash, however, argues that the experimental design is flawed, that the repeated game cannot be thought of as a sequence of independent games and he suggests that the results would have been very different if the interaction between the trials had been removed. He concedes that constant repetition of the static equilibrium is the unique equilibrium of the overall game, but he argues that a pair of trigger strategies ("Cooperate as long as the other Cooperates, Defect forever as soon as the other has Defected once") is nearly in equilibrium and that this pair is an exact equilibrium in the infinitely repeated game. Furthermore, he suggests that the situation might actually be better represented by the latter game "since 100 trials are so long that the Hangman's Paradox cannot possibly be well reasoned through on it". (Nash in [12]) Hence, he not only specifies an appropriate design for testing static equilibrium predictions; he also describes the essential insight in the theory of repeated games and he points to a specific form of bounded rationality as an explanation for observed discrepancies between theoretical predictions and empirical outcomes.

CONCLUSION

Aumann [2] has forcefully argued that a game theoretic solution concept should be judged primarily by the insights that it yields in applications, by "its success in establishing relationships and providing insights into the workings of the social processes to which it is applied" (pp. 28 – 29). On this score, "Nash equilibrium is without a doubt the most "successful" – i.e., widely used and applied – solution concept of game theory" (p. 48). Indeed, much of the modern literature in economics (and related disciplines) takes the following form: A social situation is modeled as a non-cooperative game, the Nash equilibria of the game are computed and its properties are translated into insights into the original problem.

The Nash bargaining solution can also be considered a very successful solution concept since it has also been applied frequently. Of course, its scope is much more limited than that of the equilibrium concepts. Furthermore, because of its more abstract nature, it is associated with ambiguities, which might inhibit successful applications. Such ambiguities may be resolved by application of the Nash program, i.e., by making explicit the bargaining process by means of which agreements are reached and by solving the resulting game for its equilibria.

The problems associated with multiplicity of equilibria and with the fact that not all equilibria need correspond to rational behavior, have hampered successful application of the Nash program. Nash resolved these difficulties for the special case of 2-person bargaining games. Inspired by his ideas and building on his techniques an important literature dealing with these issues has been developed, which enables the analysis and solution of more complicated, more realistic games. Hence, the domain of applicability of non-cooperative game theory has been extended considerably. It is to be expected that, as a result, our insights into the workings of society will be enhanced as well.

KUHN

I would now like to open the floor to questions for any of the participants including John Nash. I shall invoke a privilege of the chair to pose a question to him. Why did you not publish the interpretations which are in your thesis when it was made the basis of the article [38], in the Annals of Mathematics?

NASH
I am afraid I can't, simply can't answer that question. I really don't remember, but I do know that Tucker changed the form of what was to be my thesis and that the paper "Two person cooperative games", which might have been incorporated originally, if it had been allowed to, was not included. So that became a separate publication in Econometrica, differentiated from the rest of it, while that which could be presented more as a mathematical paper went into the Annals of Mathematics. So I don't know whether it was just pruned down in style for the Annals of Mathematics.

KUHN
It is certainly the case that the Annals of Mathematics has different standards than economics journals, and it may well have pruned down by an editor or a reviewer there, but I think it is a great shame, because the delay in recognizing these interpretations has been marked, I know that Jörgen Weibull was especially prominent in bringing forward the mass interpretation, and I think Eric has shown today that the reexamination, having the thesis available, has been very fruitful for a number of people. The meeting is now open to questions from anyone.

WERNER GÜTH (Humboldt University of Berlin)
I just want to ask one question, because I think John Nash proved a generic result by showing that for every finite game there exists a Nash equilibrium point. I found the assumptions that there are only finitely many strategies very intuitive, very natural, but of course to prove it you have to assume that you can vary the mixed strategies continuously. And if I now think that having only finitely many actions available is very natural. I also have to assume that only finitely many options in randomizing are available. Would you agree that this should be viewed as an assumption for the definition of rational players to justify that a player can continuously vary probabilities in choosing pure actions? How do you justify it? Otherwise I would have the conceptual philosophical problem. I think I can live with this finitely many actions, but the Nash theorem somehow has to rely on continuous variation of probabilities. Would you also see it as an assumption of rational players, so it is more philosophical. Thank you.

NASH
That's really a philosophical question. Mathematically of course it is clear that you must have the continuity. You can get quite odd numbers in fact. I think if you have two players and you have the mixed strategies, you have specific numbers that are rational, but if you have more players you get algebraic

numbers. So if there is some philosophical basis on which that type of number cannot be arrived at, describing a mixed strategy, then that's out.

There is something I just wanted to say. When I heard about the Nobel awards, and I heard that the persons were who they were, I wondered how they were connected. Of course I knew that Harsanyi and Selten made some use of the concept of equilibrium points or Nash equilibrium points, but I wondered what else there was of interrelation, and I started reviewing things, because I hadn't been following the field directly. And I discovered this book: "A General Theory of Equilibrium Selection in Games [23]", which I think was published in 1988 by joint authors Harsanyi and Selten, and then I discovered also that in relation to this book, from opinions expressed about it, that it is very controversial. It's very interesting, but also somewhat controversial. And talking to some persons I found that impression is sort of confirmed, that there may be specific aspects of it that are not immediately accepted. But something can be more interesting if it is not immediately accepted. So there is the problem; the possibility that all cooperative games could really be given a solution. This could be analogous to the Shapley value. If it were really valid you would be able to say, here is a game, here are the possibilities of cooperation, binding agreements, threats, everything, this is what it is worth to all the players. You have a management-labor situation, you have international politics, the question of membership in the common market; this is what it is worth. That is, if everything could be measured or given in terms of utilities. So the possibility that there could be something like that is very basic, but Shapley would have had that very early if the Shapley value were really the true value. But one example in this book I studied shows how the solution considered there in fact differs from the Shapley value, and so it is a very interesting comparison. In principle, experiments might distinguish between different theories, so I think that's a very interesting area. I think there will be further work. I had better not say too much, because of course Harsanyi and Selten will be speaking tomorrow and I don't exactly know that they, Harsanyi and Selten, what they will say.

NOTES

1 Actually, Nash also assumed that in a non-cooperative game, the players will be unable to *communicate* with each other. Yet, in my own view, this would be a needlesssly restrictive assumption. For if the players cannot enter into enforceable agreements, then their ability to communicate will be of no real help toward a cooperative outcome.

2 Note that Nash equilibria seem to be the only solution concept applying *both* to games in *normal* form and in *extensive* form.

3 Nash here refers to his theory of non-cooperative games based on the concept of Nash equilibria.

4 He does not use the term "trembling-hand perfect" equilibria. But this is the term used by many other game theorists to describe this class of Nash equilibria.

[5] Nash denotes payoffs with a Roman *p* instead of, as here, a Greek π.

[6] A population state $s \in S$ is *stationary* if no change over time takes place once the population is in state *s*, i.e., if $f_{i\alpha}(s) = \forall i, \alpha$.

[7] Nash [36] used the mapping $T : S \to S$ defined by $T_i(s) = s_i'$ for

$$s_{i\alpha}' = \frac{s_{i\alpha} + \pi_{i\alpha}^{+}(s)}{1 + \sum_{\beta \in A_i} \pi_{i\beta}^{+}(s)} \quad (\forall\ i \in I, \alpha \in A_i)$$

[8] In the present context, a state $x^* = (s^*, p^*)$ is *stationary* if $s(0) = s^*$ and $p(0) = p^*$ together imply $s(t) = s^*$ and $p(t) = p^*$ for all *t* in some open time interval containing 0.

[9] An alternative version (Maynard Smith [30], Hofbauer and Sigmund [24]) presumes $u_i(s) > 0$ and is given by $g_{i\alpha}(s) = u_{i\alpha}(s)/u_i(s) - 1$.

[10] A population state *s* is *dynamically stable* if small perturbations of the state do not lead the population away, i.e., if every neighborhood *V* of *s* contains a neighborhood *U* of *s* such that no solution curve starting in *U* leaves *V*.

REFERENCES

[1] Arrow, K., and G. Debreu. 1954. Existence of an equilibrium for a competitive economy. *Econometrica* 3: 265 – 290.

[2] Aumann, R. J. 1987. What is game theory trying to accomplish? In *Frontiers of Economics*, edited by K. Arrow and S. Honkapohja. Oxford: Basil Blackwell, 28 – 100.

[3] Aumann, R. J. 1987b. Game theory. In *The new Palgrave dictionary of economics*, edited by M. Milgate and P. Newman, 460 – 482.

[4] Aumann, R. and A. Brandenburger. 1991. *Epistemic conditions for Nash equilibrium*, working paper 91 – 042, Harvard Business School.

[5] Binmore, K., A. Rubinstein, and A. Wolinsky. 1986. The Nash bargaining solution in economic modelling. *Rand Journal of Economics* 17: 176 – 188.

[6] Björnerstedt, J., and J. Weibull. 1993. Nash equilibrium and evolution by imitation. In *The rational foundations of economic behavior*, edited by K. Arrow et al. New York: Macmillan, forthcoming.

[7] Bomze, I. 1986. Non-cooperative two-person games in biology: A classification. *International Journal of Game Theory* 15: 31 – 57.

[8] Carlsson, H., and E. Van Damme. 1993. Equilibrium selection in stag hunt games. In *Frontiers in game theory*, edited by K. Binmore and A. Kirman. Cambridge: MIT Press, 237 – 254.

[9] Debreu, G. 1984. Economic theory in the mathematical mode. In Les Prix Nobel 1983. (Reprinted in *American Economic Review* 74: 267 – 278.

[10] Eshel, I., and M. W. Feldman. 1984. Initial increase of new mutants and some continuity properties of ESS in two locus systems. *American Naturalist* 124: 631 – 640.

[11] Fisher, R. A. 1930. *The genetical theory of natural selection*. Oxford: Clarendon Press.

[12] Flood, M. M. 1959. Some experimental games. *Management Science* 5: 5 – 26.

[13] Friedman, M. 1953. *Essays in positive economics*. Chicago: University of Chicago Press.

[14] Haldane, J. B. S. 1932. *The causes of evolution*. London: Longman.

[15] Hammerstein, P. 1994. Darwinian adaptation, population genetics and the streetcar theory of evolution. *Journal of Mathematical Biology*, in press.

[16] Hammerstein, P., and R. Selten. 1994. Game theory and evolutionary biology. In *Handbook of game theory with economic applications*, vol. 2, edited by R. J. Aumann, and S. Hart, 929 – 993. Amsterdam: Elsevier.

[17] Harsanyi, John C. 1956. Approaches to the bargaining problem before and after the theory of games: A critical discussion of Zeuthen's, Hicks', and Nash's theories. *Econometrica* 24: 144 – 157.

[18] – – –. 1963. A simplified bargaining model for the n-person cooperative game. *International Economic Review* 4: 194 – 220.

[19] – – –. 1967 – 1968. Games with incomplete information played by Bayesian players. *Management Science* 14: 159 – 182, 320 – 334, 486 – 502.

[20] – – –. 1973. Games with randomly disturbed payoffs: A new rationale for mixed-strategy equilibrium points. *International Journal of Game Theory* 2: 1 – 23.

[21] – – –. 1974. An equilibrium-point interpretation of stable sets and a proposed alternative definition. *Management Science* 20: 1472 – 1495.

[22] Harsanyi, John C., and R. Selten. 1972. A generalized Nash solution for two-person bargaining games with incomplete information. *Management Science* 18: 80 – 106.

[23] – – –. 1988. *A general theory of equilibrium selection in games*. Cambridge: MIT Press.

[24] Hofbauer J., and K. Sigmund. 1988. *The theory of evolution and dynamical systems*. Cambridge: Cambridge University Press.

[25] Kalisch, G. K., J. W. Milnor, J. F. Nash, and E. D. Nering. 1954. Some experimental n-person games. In *Decision Processes* edited by R. M. Thrall, C. H. Coombs, and R. L. Davis. New York: Wiley, Chapter 21, 301 – 327.

[26] Karlin, S. 1975. General two-locus selection models: Some objectives, results and interpretations. *Theoretical Population Biology* 7: 364 – 398.

[27] Kohlberg, E., and J.-F. Mertens. 1986. On the strategic stability of equilibria. *Econometrica* 54: 1003 – 1037.

[28] Leonard, R. 1994. Reading Cournot, reading Nash: The creation and stabilization of the Nash equilibrium. *Economic Journal* 104: 492 – 511.

[29] Leonard, R. 1995. From parlor games to social science: von Neuman, Morgenstern, and the creation of game theory, 1928 – 1944. *Journal of Economic Literature*, in press.

[30] Maynard Smith, J. 1982 *Evolution and the theory of games*. Cambridge: Cambridge University Press.

[31] Maynard Smith, J., and G. R. Price. 1973. The logic of animal conflict. *Nature* 246: 15 – 18.

[32] Moran, P. A. P. 1964. On the nonexistence of adaptive topographies. *Annals of Human Genetics* 27: 338 – 343.

[33] Morgenstern, Oskar. 1976. The collaboration between Oskar Morgenstern and John von Neumann on the theory of games. *Journal of Economic Literature* 14: 805 – 816.

[34] Nachbar, J. 1990. 'Evolutionary' selection dynamics in games: Convergence and limit properties. *International Journal of Game Theory* 19: 58 – 89.

[35] Nash, Jr., John F. 1950a. Equilibrium points in n-person games. *Proceedings National Academy of Sciences* 36: 48 – 49.

[36] – – –. 1950b. *Non-cooperative games*, Ph.D. thesis, Mathematics Department, Princeton University.

[37] – – –. 1950c. The bargaining problem. *Econometrica* 18: 155 – 162.

[38] – – –. 1951. Non-cooperative games. *Annals of Mathematics* 54: 286 – 295.

[39] – – –. 1953. Two-person cooperative games. *Econometrica* 21: 128 – 140.

[40] Robinson, J. 1951. An iterative method of solving a game. *Annals of Mathematics* 54: 296 – 301.

[41] Roth, A. E. 1993. The early history of experimental economics. *Journal of the History of Economic Thought* 15: 184 – 209.

[42] Rubinstein, A. 1982. Perfect equilibrium in a bargaining model. *Econometrica* 50: 97 – 109.

[43] Rubinstein, A., Z. Safra, and W. Thomson. 1992. On the interpretation of the Nash bargaining solution and its extension to non-expected utility preferences. *Econometrica* 60: 1171 – 1186.

[44] Schelling, T. C. 1960. *The strategy of conflict*. Cambridge: Harvard University Press.

[45] Selten, Reinhard. 1965. Spieltheoretische behandlung eines oligopolmodells mit nachfrageträgheit. *Zeitschrift für die Gesamte Staatswissenschaft* 121: 301 – 324 and 667 – 689.

[46] – – –. 1975. Reexamination of the perfectness concept for equilibrium points in extensive games. *International Journal of Game Theory* 4: 25 – 55.

[47] – – –. 1993. In search of a better understanding of economic behavior. In *The makers of modern economics*, edited by A. Heertje. Hertforshire: Harvester Wheatscheaf, Vol. I: 115 – 139.

[48] Taylor, P. 1979. Evolutionarily stable strategies with two types of players. *Journal of Applied Probability* 16: 76 – 83.

[49] Taylor, P., and L. Jonker. 1978. Evolutionary stable strategies and game dynamics. *Mathematical Biosciences* 40: 145 – 156.

[50] van Damme, E. 1987. *Stability and perfection of Nash equilibria*. Berlin: Springer-Verlag.

[51] von Neumann, John. 1928. Zur theorie der gesellschaftsspiele. *Mathematische Annalen* 100: 295 – 320.

[52] von Neumann, John, and Oskar Morgenstern. 1944. *Theory of games and economic behavior.* Princeton: Princeton University Press.

[53] Weibull, J. 1994. The 'as if' approach to game-theory: Three positive results and four obstacles. *European Economic Review* 38: 868 – 882.

[54] Weibull, J. 1994. *Evolutionary Game Theory*. Cambridge: The MIT Press, forthcoming.

[55] Wright, S. 1931. Evolution in Mendelian populations. *Genetics* 16: 97 – 159.

Reinhard Selten

REINHARD SELTEN

I was born in Breslau on October 10th, 1930. At that time, Breslau, now called Wroclaw, belonged to Germany and only German was spoken there. After the second world war Breslau became Polish and the original German population was almost completely replaced by a Polish one. I have never visited Wroclaw after the war. Heavy fighting destroyed most of the town in which I grew up and most of the familiar places of my youth look different now.

When I was born my father owned a business called a "reading circle"; folders containing an assortment of magazines were lent to customers for one week, then recollected and lent out again. The older the folder, the lower was the fee. This was a florishing branch of industry. My father had built up his business in spite of the fact that he became blind at young years and had only three years of school education. Already in the mid-thirties he had to sell his firm because of his Jewish origin. Jews were forbidden to run a business connected to the press. My father did not belong to any religous community and my mother was a protestant. Originally my parents intended to let me grow up without any attachment to a particular religion in order to give me the opportunity to decide for myself later in my life. However, under the prevailing political circumstances it seemed to be better to have me baptized as a protestant. The ceremony is one of my early memories. Much later as a young man I left the protestant church and became unattached to any religion again. Unlike several other relatives my father did not become a victim of the holocaust, since he died after a serious illness already in 1942 before the worst of the terror began.

It was not easy for me to live as a half-Jewish boy under the Hitler regime. When I was 14 I had to leave high school and the opportunity to learn a trade was denied to me. The only career open to me was that of an unskilled worker. Fortunately it turned out that this did not matter much since after about half a year my mother, my brothers, my sister, and I left Breslau on one of the last trains before all outbound railway traffic stopped.

My situation as a member of an officially despised minority forced me to pay close attention to political matters very early in my life. Moreover I found myself in opposition to the political views shared by the vast majority of the population. I had to learn to trust my own judgment rather than official propaganda or public opinion. This was a strong influence on my intellectual development. My continuing interest in politics and public affairs was one of the reasons why I began to be interested in economics in my last high school years.

After we left Breslau we were refugees, first in Saxonia, then in Austria and finally in Hessia. Until schools opened again in 1946 I worked as a farm boy, first in Austria and later in the village in Hessia where we lived. In 1947, we moved to Melsungen, a small town in which I went to high school until 1951. In these years I developed a strong interest in mathematics. When we still lived in the village near Melsungen, I had to walk to school which took about three and a half hours there and back. During these walks I occupied my mind with problems of elementary geometry and algebra. I still like to hike in forested hills and to think while walking.

When I finished high school, it was clear to me that I would study mathematics, even if I also considered economics and psychology. It took me relatively long to reach my master's degree in mathematics. My studies were not sufficiently concentrated on this goal. One of the reasons was that I went to many lectures which had nothing to do with my study of mathematics. However, it later turned out that some of these extracurricular activities became important for my career. I studied mathematics at the university of Frankfurt from 1951 to 1957. Until I completed my "Vordiplom", the intermediate examination which roughly corresponds to the bachelor's degree, I also had to study physics. Originally I considered to take astronomy as a minor for my master's degree and I actually spent much time trying to get some knowledge of this field but now almost everything is forgotten. What finally turned me away from astronomy was that I became more and more involved in game theory and economics. I am grateful to the natural science faculty of Frankfurt university for the decision to permit mathematical economics as a minor for the master's degree in order to enable me to be the first one to take this choice.

My first contact with game theory was a popular article in Fortune magazine which I read in my last high school year. I was immediately attracted to the subject matter and when I studied mathematics I found the fundamental book by von Neumann and Morgenstern in the library and studied it. Somewhat later I saw the announcement of a student seminar for economists on game theory, headed by Professor Ewald Burger who taught advanced mathematical courses but also mathematics for economists. I participated in the seminar and Ewald Burger gave me the chance to write a master's thesis in cooperative game theory. He was a man of extraordinary mathematical erudition and an excellent teacher. I owe much to his guidance and to his patient advise.

My master's thesis and later my Ph.D. thesis had the aim of axiomatizing a value for n-person games in extensive form. This work made me familiar with the extensive form, in a time when very little work on extensive games was done. This enabled me to see the perfectness problem earlier than others and to write the contributions for which I am now honored by the prize in memory of Alfred Nobel.

After I had received my master's degree in 1957, I was hired by Professor Heinz Sauermann, an economist at the university of Frankfurt am Main, who employed me for ten years in various assistant positions. It was my task to do research funded by Deutsche Forschungsgemeinschaft, the German counterpart of the National Science Foundation. At first I was supposed to apply decision theory to the theory of the firm, but soon I became involved in economic laboratory experimentation. Fortunately the referees of Sauermann's research proposals approved of this new research direction. This made it possible to finance a small group of young people doing experimental research. Sauermann had about 15 assistants and only two to four of them were involved in experiments. I became something like a foreman of this small detachment. Reinhard Tietz, Volker Häselbarth, Otwin Becker, Klaus Schuster and others belonged to it for longer or shorter periods.

Heinz Sauermann was a remarkable man. He was one of the first to propagate Keynesianism in Germany. In spite of a lack of mathematical training he encouraged his students to do work based on formal models. He always had a good feeling for the trends of the field and therefore was very successful in suggesting the right problem areas to those who did research under his supervision. Moreover he was an excellent administrator and scientific organizer, who did much for the propagation of experimental economics. I owe much to him.

In 1959, I married Elisabeth Langreiner, who for all the years since then helped me to become the person I am now. We would have liked to have children but we do not have any. We both belong to the Esperanto movement and this is how we met. The international language Esperanto has still an important influence on our life.

My first publication was a journal article with the title "Ein Oligopolexperiment" (an oligopoly experiment) written together with Heinz Sauermann and published in 1959. When we began to do experimental economics at Frankfurt, such a field had not yet existed. My attempts to learn some psychology while I studied mathematics had made me acquainted to experimental techniques. I had listened to lectures of the gestalt psychologist Edwin Rausch, who was a careful experimenter, and I had participated in psychological experiments as a subject. Therefore it seemed natural to me to try an experimental approach to oligopoly.

In 1961, I received my Ph.D. in mathematics at the university of Frankfurt am Main. Shortly afterwards Oskar Morgenstern made it possible for me to participate in a game theory conference at Princeton. In the late 50's – I do not remember the year – he had given a talk at Frankfurt and my remarks in the subsequent discussion must have impressed him. In the following years he sometimes asked me to meet him when his travels brought him to Frankfurt. He also gave me financial support for staying several weeks longer at Princeton after the game theory conference. My short visit to Princeton was important for my life since it gave me the opportunity to interact with R. J. Aumann and M. Maschler who were members of Morgenstern's research group at that time.

Around 1958, I became aware of H. A. Simon's seminal papers on bounded rationality and was immediately convinced by his arguments. I tried to construct a theory of boundedly rational multigoal decision making. Together with Heinz Sauermann, I worked out an "aspiration adaptation theory of the firm" which was published as a journal article in 1962. After the Princeton conference in 1961, I visited Pittsburgh for two days in order to establish contacts with H. A. Simon and his associates. The problem of bounded rationality has occupied my mind for a long time but unfortunately with less success than I had hoped for. More and more I came to the conclusion that purely speculative approaches like that of our paper of 1962 are of limited value. The structure of boundedly rational economic behavior cannot be invented in the armchair, it must be explored experimentally.

In the early 60's I had run experiments on an oligopoly game with demand inertia. A game theoretical analysis of this model proved to be too difficult but I was able to solve a simplified version. I found a natural equilibrium but the game has many other equilibria. In order to describe the distinguishing features of my solution, I defined subgame perfectness. My paper "Ein Oligopolmodell mit Nachfrageträgheit" (an oligopoly model with demand inertia) was published in 1965. At that time I did not suspect that it often would be quoted, almost exlusively for the definition of subgame perfectness. Very soon it became clear to me that the perfectness problem is not completely solved by this concept. Therefore in a paper published in 1975, I defined a refined notion of perfectness, now often referred to as trembling hand perfectness.

In 1965, I was invited to a game theory workshop at Jerusalem which lasted for three weeks and had only 17 participants, but among them all the important researchers in game theory, with few exceptions. Game theory was still a small field. We had heated discussions about Harsanyi's new theory of games with incomplete information. This was the beginning of my long cooperation with John C. Harsanyi. Not long after the conference I became a member of a group of game theorists hired by the research firm MATHEMATICA to work on projects for the Arms Control and Disarmament Agency. The group often met for several days near Washington D.C.. I cooperated with John C. Harsanyi on bargaining under incomplete information, but I also did other work on models of nuclear deterrence. The group did not produce anything of practical value for the Arms Control and Disarmament Agency, but nevertheless it was very successful because important theoretical advances, e.g. in the analysis of repeated games of incomplete information by Aumann, Maschler, and Stearns were made there.

In Germany the Ph. D. is not yet the last formal requirement for a career as a university teacher. In addition to this, one is expected to work towards a "habilitation". For this purpose one presents a habilitation thesis, often a monography of an area of research. The habilitation is a permission to lecture independently. In my case the habilitation thesis was a monography on multiproduct pricing. In the academic year of 1967/68 I was visiting full professor at the business school of the University of California, Berkeley. I had completed my habilitation thesis shortly before I left to Berkeley and was habilitated when I came back. In 1970 my habilitation thesis was published as a book.

In 1969, I accepted an offer of the Free University of Berlin, where I was a full professor of economics until 1972. My wife and I liked to live in West Berlin. In these years Germany experienced a period of student unrest, which made teaching difficult and sometimes impossible. The student movement was especially strong at the Free University, but this was not the reason why I moved to the University of Bielefeld in 1972. I was attracted by plans to create a big institute of mathematical economics. However, these plans could not be realized since it finally turned out that the money was not available. Eventually a small institute with only three professors was established. I was not unhappy with this solution since I succeeded to convince the appointment committee that all positions should be held by game theorists. The positions were filled by Joachim Rosenmüller, Wulf Albers, and myself. The concentration on game theory gave us a chance to get some international reputation.

My years at the University of Bielefeld were a productive time. My experimental research continued but I mainly worked on game theory and its application to industrial organization and other areas. After John Harsanyi and I had completed our work on bargaining under incomplete information we decided to attack the problem of selecting a unique equilibrium for every game. He twice came to Bielefeld for a year and I often visited Berkeley for short periods of one or two months. It took us about 18 years to construct a reasonable general theory of equilibrium selection in games. In this time we considered many ideas and rejected two fairly well worked out approaches. Our book of 1988 only describes the theory we finally agreed upon.

On my frequent visits to Berkeley I also had a cooperation with Tom Marschak which resulted in a book on multiproduct pricing published in 1974. I also did experimental work on bargaining under incomplete information together with Austin Hoggatt and his younger associates. In the basement of Barrows Hall at the University of California, Berkeley, Austin Hoggatt had built up the first computerized laboratory for experimental economics. There our experiments were run.

In the twelve years I spent at Bielefeld, I began a close cooperation with Werner Güth, who in some sense is one of my students, even if we never held positions at the same university. We worked on applications of the equilibrium selection theory by John Harsanyi and myself, long before it had reached a final form, but we also did research on other problems like wage bargaining in the framework of a business cycle model. Also other people who later became university professors sometimes came to Bielefeld to seek my advise, namely Ulrike Leopold from Graz, Joël Moulen from Lyon, and Eric van Damme from Eindhoven. Ulrike Leopold also worked on the application of equilibrium selection theory and I wrote some papers together with her. Joël Moulen did Ph. D. work on cooperative game theory and became a professor of mathematics at Jaounde, Kameroun. Eric van Damme needed very little advise and is now a well known game theorist.

One of my students, Jon-ren-Chen, a Taiwanese who was my assistant for many years, has never worked on game theory. He does applied econometric research on international trade and development. He was habilitated at Bielefeld and is now a professor of economics at Innsbruck. A student of mine, Rolf Stoecker, who was a promising young experimentalist left me after his Ph. D., joined an insurance company and became its chief executive after 5 years. Later something similar happened to me again in Bonn. My assistant Gerald Uhlich who had done important experimental work on coalition bargaining left the university after his Ph. D. and became the second man in a furniture textile factory. Nevertheless I still nourish the hope that some of the students who now work on experimental economics under my guidance will become university teachers.

At the University of Bielefeld, cross fertilization between different fields is favored by the existence of a unique institution, the center for interdisciplinary research. Talks given there brought me into contact with biologists who made me aware of applications of game theory to biology. A young mathematician, Peter Hammerstein, who had a junior position as a statistical advisor in the biology department made me accquainted with the notion of evolutionary stability. From that time on I developed a strong interest in biological game theory. One of my contributions to this field is the investigation of evolutionary stability in extensive games. However, I also wrote other papers in this area, some with Peter Hammerstein and others with Avi Shmida, a botanist at the Hebrew University of Jerusalem, with whom I cooperate on theoretical models of pollination of flowers by bees. Peter Hammerstein is now a well established theoretical biologist. Another student of mine, Franz Weissing, also started a career as a university teacher of biology.

I find it very interesting to cooperate with scientists in different fields who have little mathematical training but much substantial knowledge. My first experience of this kind was my cooperation with the political scientist Amos Perlmutter with whom I developed the scenario bundle method, a systematic way of constructing simple game models of concrete international conflicts. Unfortunately the results of our research have never been formally published. It is the advantage of this kind of interaction that the judgement of the expert on the empirical facts is not yet contaminated by mathematical models. I had a similar experience with Avi Shmida, even if he as a natural scientist is not quite as unmathematical.

I am grateful to Avi Shmida, not only for his scientific cooperation but also for another reason. Before I came into contact with theoretical problems in botany I hardly could distinguish any flower from any other one. However, I felt that I could not really do work on pollination problems withour learning at least a little of the art of recognizing wild flowers. Since then I always carry a flower book on my hikes, except in the winter. I enjoy my often frustrated efforts to identify wild flowers. This activity has opened my eyes to the astonishing diversity and the marvelous beauty of flowering plants.

In 1984, I moved to the university of Bonn, where I am a professor of economics since then. I liked the interdisciplinary atmosphere at the University of Bielefeld, but I wanted to build up a computerized laboratory for experimental economics and Bonn was willing to offer me much better conditions in this respect. I came back to Bielefeld for the time from October 1, 1987, to September 30, 1988, in order to act as the organizer of a research year on "game theory in the behavioral sciences" at the center for interdisciplinary research. The cooperation of an international group of participants with backgrounds in economics, biology, mathematics, political science, psychology, and philosophy finally resulted in four volumes on "game equilibrium models" published in 1991.

At the university of Bonn my work and that of most of my assistants is concentrated on experimental economics. It is our goal to help to build up a descriptive branch of decision and game theory which takes the limited rationality of human behavior seriously. The financial support of the Deutsche Forschungsgemeinschaft in the framework of the Sonderforschungsbereich (special research unit) 303 enables us to work in this direction.

In 1991, it was discovered that both, I and my wife, suffer from diabetes. Probably we had this disease for some time without knowing it. As a consequence of diabetes my wife lost both legs up to the knee. Therefore she is now bound to the wheelchair. Moreover her eyesight has become very bad. Nevertheless she does many things in the house, even if everything takes much longer than it used to. She cooks and takes care of our three cats and, what is most important, she maintains a cheerful attitude towards life. We have learnt to adjust to our situation.

MULTISTAGE GAME MODELS AND DELAY SUPERGAMES

Nobel Lecture, December 9, 1994

by

REINHARD SELTEN, Bonn

Rheinische Friedrich-Wilhelms-Universität, Bonn, Germany

ABSTRACT

The order of stages in a multistage game is often interpreted by looking at earlier stages as involving more long term decisions. For the purpose of making this interpretation precise, the notion of a delay supergame of a bounded multistage game is introduced. A multistage game is bounded if the length of play has an upper bound. A delay supergame is played over many periods. Decisions on all stages are made simultaneously, but with different delays until they become effective. The earlier the stage the longer the delay.

A subgame perfect equilibrium of a bounded multistage game generates a subgame perfect equilibrium in every one of its delay supergames. This is the first main conclusion of the paper. A subgame perfect equilibrium set is a set of subgame perfect equilibria all of which yield the same payoffs, not only in the game as a whole, but also in each of its subgames. The second main conclusion concerns multistage games with a unique subgame perfect equilibrium set and their delay supergames which are bounded in the sense that the number of periods is finite. If a bounded multistage game has a unique subgame perfect equilibrium set, then the same is true for every one of its bounded delay supergames.

Finally the descriptive relevance of multistage game models and their subgame perfect equilibria is discussed in the light of the results obtained.

1. Introduction

In the economic literature one finds many game models, in which the players make simultaneous decisions on each of a number of successive stages, always fully informed about what has been done on previous stages. An early example can be found in my paper " a simple model of imperfect competition where 4 are few and six are many (Selten, 1973). In this oligopoly model the players first decide whether they want to take part in cartel bargaining. This participation stage is followed by a cartel bargaining in which quota cartels can be proposed and agreed upon. The third and last stage is a supply decision stage in which production quantities are fixed.

Another example is a two stage duopoly model with production capacity decisions on the first stage and Bertrand price competition on the second stage (Kreps and Scheinkman, 1983). Multistage game models can be analyzed on the basis of the subgame perfect equilibrium concept (Selten, 1965), the simplest refinement of ordinary game theoretic equilibrium (Nash, 1951). Sometimes additional selection criteria are combined with subgame perfect equilibria, like symmetry and local efficiency in the case of my above mentioned model. The analysis of my model yields the result that up to 4 competitors always form a cartel whereas in the presence of 6 or more competitors the probability of cartel formation is less than 2%. The model by Kreps and Scheinkman deepens our understanding of Cournot's (1838) oligopoly theory. In equilibrium Cournot quantity competition takes place on the first stage of their model. The examples show that the analysis of multistage game models can lead to interesting theoretical conclusions.

In some cases it may be justified to look at the stages of a multistage game model as decision points succeeding each other in time. However, often this direct temporal interpretation is not adequate. Many multistage game models do not really aim at the description of situations in which decisions must be made in a fixed time order. Thus the model of Kreps and Scheinkman places capacity choice before price choice, not because price choice cannot precede capacity choice, but rather because capacity decisions are considered to be more long term than price decisions. It seems to be natural to consider long term decisions as fixed, when short term decisions are made. "Term length" in the sense of a position on a short term-long term scale rather than time is the consideration underlying the order of stages. If decisions of greater term length are modelled as made on an earlier stage, this is intended to have the effect that in subgame perfect equilibrium more short term decisions are based on more long term decisions taken as fixed.

The term length interpretation looks at a multistage game model as a condensed description of an ongoing situation in which stage decisions are not made once and for all. Strategic variables may change over time, but more short term decisions are in some way subordinated to more long term ones. The reasons for this subordination are not explicitly spelled out.

Simple oligopoly models like the Cournot model which involve only one stage are usually also interpreted as condensed descriptions of ongoing situations. The literal interpretation as a one-shot game would leave little room for applied significance. One must think of such models as being played repeatedly in a supergame (Aumann, 1959, Friedman, 1977), but without making use of the potential for quasicooperation which may be present in such situations. The analysis of the one shot game instead of the supergame amounts to the assumption that any kind of collusion is excluded by effectively enforced cartel laws or for other reasons.

Similarly one could look at a multistage game model as representing the structure of a period in a supergame. However, this would mean that one sticks to the direct temporal interpretation of the order of stages. Obviously the term length interpretation requires a different picture of the underlying ongoing situation. It is the modest purpose of this lecture to provide an explicit model of the underlying situation which justifies the reduction to the multistage game with its subordination of the shorter term to the longer term.

What does it mean in the model by Kreps and Scheinkman that capacity decisions are long term and price decisions are short term? It could mean that due to exogenous institutional circumstances capacities can be adjusted only at certain points in time, say at the beginning of the year, whereas prices can be changed every day. Alternatively one could think of a difference of change costs, high for capacity adjustments and low for price changes. This would lead to a model in the spirit of the inertia supergame (Marschak and Selten, 1978). A third possibility is the answer given here. It focusses on the delay between the time a decision is made and the time at which it becomes effective. This delay may be two years for capacity adjustments and only one day for price adjustments. The longer the delay the more long term the decision is considered to be.

It seems to me that in many cases the difference between a more long term and a more short term decision is adequately explained as a difference of delay. Of course, in some multistage game models necessities of temporal order, exogenous institutional circumstances and differences of change costs may also be considerations in the interpretation of the order of stages. However, here we shall only be concerned with the term length interpretation elaborated by looking at differences of term length as differences of delay times needed until a decision becomes effective. The underlying ongoing situation will be modelled as a special kind of game, called a "delay supergame". In a delay supergame decisions on all strategic variables are made at the same time, period after period, but these decisions become effective with different delays. Thus, in period t decisions on the price in t+1 and capacity in t+10 may be made, on both variables at the same time and simultaneously by all players.

In a delay supergame the players have full information about previous history of play, but not about simultaneous decisions made by other players. All decisions made in a period become publicly known at the beginning of the next period.

It does not really matter exactly how long the delays are. For the analysis of delay supergames only the order of the decision variables with respect to delay length matters.

A delay supergame is not necessarily played for a fixed number of periods; the definition will involve a probability distribution over the number of periods played. We speak of a "bounded" delay supergame if the number of periods has a finite upper bound and of an "unbounded" one otherwise. The distinction between bounded and unbounded delay supergames is game theoretically important.

Every subgame perfect equilibrium of a bounded multistage game always generates a subgame perfect equilibrium for every one of its bounded or unbounded delay supergames. This is the first main conclusion of the paper (theorem 1 in 5.3). The generated equilibrium can roughly be described as the repeated application of the multistage game equilibrium strategies in every period played.

In general, a delay supergame and especially an unbounded one may have many additional subgame perfect equilibria. It is well known that this happens already in ordinary supergames (Rubinstein, 1976, 1980, Benoit and Krishna, 1985). Since normal form games are special multistage games with only one stage, supergames are special delay supergames.

A subgame perfect equilibrium set is a set of subgame perfect equilibria all of which yield the same payoffs not only in the game as a whole but also in each of its subgames. A multistage game or a delay supergame will be called "determinate" if the set of all of its subgame perfect equilibria is a subgame perfect equilibrium set. Every bounded delay supergame of a determinate bounded multistage game is determinate. This is the second main conclusion of this paper (theorem 2 in 5.5).

This lecture will not be concerned with the question which kind of "folk theorems" hold for which class of delay supergames. Such theorems are interesting from the point of view of normative game theory, but their applied significance is limited. Finite supergames of prisoners' dilemma games have only one subgame perfect equilibrium which prescribes the non-cooperative choice everywhere, but nevertheless experienced experimental subjects cooperate in such games until shortly before the end (Selten and Stoecker, 1986). On the other hand in some supergame-like oligopoly experiments cooperation is not observed (Sauermann and Selten, 1959, Hoggatt, 1959, Fouraker and Siegel, 1963, Stern, 1967). It is an empirical question under which conditions behavior in a delay supergame converges to a subgame perfect equilibrium of the underlying multistage game. At the end of the paper this problem will be discussed in more detail.

Instead of the usual framework of the extensive game (von Neumann and Morgenstern, 1944, Kuhn, 1953, Selten, 1975) a somewhat different one is used here, which is especially adapted to multistage games and their delay supergames. Simultaneous decisions are represented as being made at the same history of previous play and information is not explicitly modelled. A "choice set function" defined recursively together with a "path set" take over the role of the game tree. As in the usual extensive form a "probability assignment" describes the probability of random choices and a payoff function determines the payoffs at the end of a play. The framework could be made as general as that of an extensive game by the additional introduction of information partitions for the players but this will not be done here.

Even if our main conclusions are intuitively plausible and not surprising some formalism is necessary to make statements and their proofs precise.

2.4 *Definition of a multistage game*

A *multistage game*
$G = (s, A, p, h)$
is composed of four constituents, a start s, a choice set function A, a probability assignment p and a payoff function h, with the properties explained above (see 2.1, 2.2, and 2.3).

A multistage game $G = (s, A, p, h)$ is called *bounded,* if in G the length of a path is bounded from above. Obviously in such games a maximum length M of a path exists. It can be seen immediately that the existence of this maximum length M implies that the random stopping condition of 2.2 holds with $\mu = M$ simply because there are no preplays u with $|u| \geq M$.

2.5 *Strategies*

In sections 2.5 – 2.7 all definitions will refer to a fixed but arbitrary multistage game $G = (s, A, p, h)$. The set of all preplays at which player i is active is denoted by P_i. We call P_i *player i's preplay set.* A *local strategy* of a personal player i at a preplay $u \in P_i$ is a probability distribution b_{iu} over player i's choice set $A_i(u)$ which assigns positive probabilities to finitely many choices only. The probability assigned to a choice $a_i \in A_i(u)$ by b_{iu} is denoted by $b_{iu}(a_i)$.

A *behavior strategy* b_i of player i is a system of local strategies

$$b_i = (b_{iu})_{u \in Pi}$$

specifying a local strategy b_{iu} for every preplay u of player i. Player i's preplay set P_i may be empty. In this case the definition of a behavior strategy is to be understood in such a way that player i has exactly one behavior strategy, the *empty* strategy.

Comment: In multistage games every player is always fully informed about all choices on previous stages. This implies that such games have perfect recall. It is clear that the extensive games representing a multistage game have the formal property of perfect recall as it is usually expressed (Kuhn 1953, Selten 1975). Kuhn (1953) has proved a theorem which shows that without any essential loss the noncooperative analysis of finite extensive games with perfect recall can be restricted to behavior strategies. Aumann (1964) has generalized this theorem to extensive games in which a continuum of choices may be available in some choice sets. This is important in the context of multistage game models which usually involve continuously varying decision parameters.

In order to avoid tedious technical detail we shall restrict our attention to finite local strategies, i.e. local strategies with a finite carrier and finite behavior strategies which specify such local strategies only.

Further definitions: A local strategy is called *pure* if it assigns probability 1 to one of the choices. Pure local strategies can be identified with choices. The set of all finite local strategies of a player i at a preplay $u \in P_i$ is denoted by B_{iu}. The set of all behavior strategies of a personal player i is denoted by B_i. A *pure strategy* of a personal player i assigns a pure local strategy or, in other words, a choice at u to every $u \in P_i$.

A *strategy combination* $b = (b_1,..., b_n)$ is an n-tuple specifying a behavior strategy b_i for every personal player. A strategy combination is called *pure,* if all its components are pure. The set of all strategy combinations is denoted by B.

2.6 Realization probabilities

Consider a strategy combination $b = (b_1,..., b_n)$ and a preplay u. For every personal player i active at u let b_{iu} be the local strategy assigned to u by b_i. For every choice combination

$$a = (a_i)_{i\in N(u)} \text{ with } a_i \in A_i(u)$$

we define the *conditional realization probability* of a at u as the product of $p_0(a_0)$ and all $b_{iu}(a_i)$ with i active at u. This probability is denoted by $b_u(a)$:

$$b_u(a) = p_u(a_0) \prod_{i\in N(u)-\{0\}} b_{iu}(a_i)$$

In this way a probability distribution b_u over A(u) is associated to a strategy combination $b = (b_1,..., b_n)$ and a preplay u.

Now consider a path $v \in V$ with $v = sa^1...a^k$. We say that a path $u = sa^1...a^j$ is *on* v if we have $j \leq k$ and the first j choice combinations $a^1,...,a^j$ are the same in u and v. The *realization probability of v under* $b = (b_1,...,b_n)$ is the product of all $b_u(a)$ with ua on v: This probability is denoted by b(v).

$$b(v) = \prod_{ua \text{ on } v} b_u(a)$$

The realization probability of $v = sa^1...a^k$ is interpreted as the probability that in the course of playing the game with the strategies in b the play passes the choice combinations $a^1,...,a^k$ one after the other.

2.7 Expected payoffs

For every strategy combination $b = (b_1,...,b_n)$ we shall define *expected payoffs* $H_i(b)$ for every personal player $i = 1,...,n$. We shall focus on a fixed but arbitrary personal player i. In the case of a bounded multistage game G player i's expected payoffs are defined as follows:

$$H_i(b) = \sum_{z\in Z} b(z)h(z)$$

In the following we shall assume that G is an unbounded multistage game. In this case the definition of expected payoffs is essentially the same as in the bounded case, but it needs to be elaborated, since infinite sums do not necessarily converge. For k = 0,1,... let Z_k be the set of all plays z with $|z| = k$. Player i's expected payoff $H_i(b)$ is defined as

$$H_i(b) = \lim_{T\to\infty} \sum_{k=0}^{T} \sum_{z\in Z} b(z)h(z)$$

It has to be shown that the limit exists. For k = 0, 1,... let Q_k be the set of all preplays v with $|v| = k$. Define

$$b(Z_k) = \sum_{z\in Z_k} b(z)$$

$$b(Q_k) = \sum_{v\in Q_k} b(v)$$

$$Y_k = \sum_{z\in Z_k} b(z)h_i(z)$$

Since all local strategies assign positive probabilities to finitely many choices only, these sums are finite. Let μ and δ be numbers such that the random stopping condition holds with these numbers. The random stopping condition permits the conclusion that for $k = \mu, \mu+1,...$ we have

$$b(Q_{k+1}) \le (1-\delta)b(Q_k)$$

and therefore

$$b(Q_k) \le (1-\delta)^{k-\mu}b(Q_\mu)$$

Another conclusion from the second last inequality is the following one

$$b(Q_k) - b(Q_{k+1}) \le \delta\, b(Q_k)$$

for $k = \mu, \mu+1,...$ On the left hand side of the last inequality we find nothing else than $b(Z_{k+1})$ since after the next choice combination a preplay in Q_k becomes a preplay in Q_{k+1} or a play in Z_{k+1}. In view of $b(Q_\mu) \le 1$ the last two inequalities permit the following conclusion:

$$b(Z_{k+1}) \le \delta\,(1-\delta)^{k-\mu}$$

for $k = \mu, \mu+1,...$. The boundedness condition for payoffs can now be used to bound Y_k:

$$|Y_k| \le \delta(1-\delta)^{k-\mu-1}(C_0+C_1k) \quad \text{for } k = \mu, \mu+1, \mu+2,...$$

where C_0 and C_1 are numbers with the properties required by the boundedness condition on payoffs. It can be seen without difficulty that the infinite sum of the terms on the right-hand side converges. Therefore the same is true for the terms on the left-hand side. This has the consequence that the limit exists, by which $H_i(b)$ is defined. We call $H(b) = (H_1(b),...,H_n(b))$ the *expected payoff vector* of b. The function H which assigns H(b) to every $b \in B$ is referred to as the *expected payoff function.*

3. Equilibria

In this section we shall first define equilibrium in the framework of the multistage game. Then we look at subgames and subgame perfectness will be defined. As before, all definitions refer to a fixed but arbitrary multistage game G = (s, A, p, h).

3.1 Equilibrium

An *i-incomplete strategy combination* b_{-i} is an (n-1)-tupel of behavior strategies b_j with one strategy for all personal players except player i:

$$b_{-i} = (b_{i,}..., b_{i-1},-, b_{i+1},..., b_n)$$

We use the notation b_ib_{-i} for the strategy combination b which contains b_i and the components b_j of b_{-i}. We say that a behavior strategy $\tilde{b}_i$ is a *best reply* to b_{-i}, if we have

$$H_i(\tilde{b}_ib_{-i}) = \max_{b_i \in B_i} H_i(b_ib_{-i})$$

$\tilde{b}_i$ is a *best reply* to $b = (b_1,...,b_n)$, if it is a best reply to the i-incomplete strategy combination b_{-i} formed by the components of b except b_i. We say that $\tilde{b} = (\tilde{b}_i,...,\tilde{b}_n)$ is a *best reply* to $b = (b_1,... b_n)$, if for i = 1,...,n the behavior strategy $\tilde{b}_{i,}$ is a best reply to b.

A strategy combination $b = (b_1,... b_n)$ is an *equilibrium,* if it is a best reply to itself. An *equilibrium set* E is a set of equilibria with the property that the payoff vector H(b) is the same one for all $b \in B$.

3.2 Subgames

For every preplay u we define a *subgame* G^u at u of G. This subgame is the multistage game

$$G^u = (u, A^u, p^u, h^u)$$

whose constituents will be described in the following. The start is the preplay u and A^u is the restriction of A to the paths v such that u is on v. A path v of this kind permits a representation of the form:

$$v = ua^1...a^k$$

The set of all these paths is denoted by U^u. Paths in U^u are at the same time paths in G starting with s and paths in G^u starting with u. The probability assignment p^u is the restriction of p^u to U^u. The set of all plays in G^u is denoted by Z^u. The payoff function h^u is the restriction of h to Z^u. It can be seen immediately that u, A^u, p^u and h^u form a multistage game with all the properties required in 2.1, 2.2, and 2.3.

Comment: Even if we did not formally describe how a multistage game is mapped to an equivalent extensive game, it can be seen without difficulties that the subgames defined above correspond to the subgames of an equivalent extensive form.

3.3 Subgame perfectness

We continue to look at a subgame G^u of G. The set of all preplays in U^u at which player i is active is denoted by P_i^u. The restriction of a behavior strategy b_i for G to P_i^u is a behavior strategy b_i^u for the subgame G^u. We say that b_i^u is the strategy *induced by* b_i *on* G^u. Similarly a strategy combination $b^u = (b_1^u,..., b_n^u)$ is *induced* by $b = (b_1,...,b_n)$ if for $i = 1,...,n$ the behavior strategy b_i^u is induced by b_i on G^u. An i-incomplete strategy combination b^u_{-i} is *induced* by an i-incomplete strategy combination b_{-1} if every component of b^u_{-1} is induced by the corresponding component of b_{-1}. A set E^u of strategy combinations for G^u is *induced* by a set E of strategy combinations for G , if E^u is the set of all strategy combinations b^u induced by strategy combinations $b \in E$.

Let r_i be a best reply to a strategy combination $b = (b_1,...,b_n)$ of G. For every subgame G^u of G let r_i^u be the strategy induced by r_i on G^u and $b^u = (b_1^u,...,b_n^u)$ the strategy combination induced by b on G^u. We say that r_i is a *subgame perfect best reply* to b if for every subgame G^u of G the behavior strategy r_i^u is a best reply to b^u.

An equilibrium $\tilde{b} = (\tilde{b}_1,..., \tilde{b}_n)$ is *subgame perfect* if it induces an equilibrium on every subgame G^u of G or, in other words, if for $i = 1,...,n$ the behavior strategy $\tilde{b}_i$ is a subgame perfect best reply to $\tilde{b}$. Similarly an equilibrium set E of G is *subgame perfect* if it induces an equilibrium set E^u on every subgame G^u of G.

4. Delay supergames

In this section delay supergames will be formally defined. A game of this kind is associated with a bounded multistage game G. In addition to the underlying game G the description of a delay supergame involves further specifications. It is necessary to specify delays after which decisions made on different stages become effective, stopping probabilities as a function of time and initial conditions on what is carried over from the past.

The interpretation of a delay supergame will focus on the case that in the underlying bounded multistage game K decision variables are fixed one after the other by some or all players in K successive stages. The definition of a multistage game does not exclude the possibility that different kinds of decisions have to be made at different preplays of the same length. However, in such cases it may not be adequate to assume that the delay after which a decision becomes effective depends only on the length of the preplay at which it is made.

In section 4 all definitions refer to a fixed but arbitrary bounded multistage game G = (s, A, p, h) in which the maximum length of a play is K. A delay supergame of G is itself also a multistage game G* = (s*, A*, p*, h*) whose constituents are derived in a systematic manner from G and some additional specifications to be explained in 4.1 – 4.4.

4.1 *Delay vector*

In order to describe a delay supergame of G, it is necessary to specify a *delay vector*

$$m = (m_1,...,m_k)$$

whose components are non-negative integers with $m_j > m_k$ for $j < k$:

$$m_1 > m_2 > ... > m_K \geq 0$$

The number m_k is called the *delay of stage* k. It is interpreted as the number of periods after which a decision on stage k becomes effective.

4.2 *Stopping rule*

A delay supergame of G begins with an *initial period* t_o and is played either for at most finitely many periods t_o,..., T or for potentially infinitely many periods t_o, $t_o + 1$,... . In the first case the delay supergame is *bounded* and in the second case it is *unbounded*. In the bounded case a *reachable* period is one of the periods t_o,..., T. In the unbounded case all periods t_o, $t_o + 1$,... are reachable. The set of all *reachable* periods is denoted by R.

A *stopping rule* w assigns a *stopping probability* w_t with

$$0 \leq w_t < 1$$

to every reachable period $t \in R$. The stopping probability w_t is interpreted as the conditional probability with which the delay supergame stops in period t, if period t-1 has been reached. As will be explained later, no payoffs are obtained for period t if the game stops in period t. The players do not know whether the game stops in t when they make their choices at t. This depends on a random choice at t. All choices at t including this random choice are thought of as being made simultaneously. In the bounded case the game always stops after period T, if it is reached.

We think of w as a function together with the set R on which it is defined.

In the bounded case, T will always denote the *last reachable period.* In the unbounded case we shall always assume that w satisfies the following stopping requirement.

Stopping requirement: A real number δ with $0 < \delta < 1$ and a positive integer μ exist, such that the following is true:

$$w_t \geq \delta \text{ for all periods } t = t_o + \mu, t_o + \mu + 1, \ldots$$

As we shall see later, this stopping requirement secures the random stopping condition of 2.2 for unbounded delay supergames.

4.3 The initial status assignment

In the following m will always be a fixed but arbitrary delay vector, t_o will stand for the initial period, and w will be a fixed but arbitrary stopping rule.

As in 2.7 the set of all preplays u of G with $|u| = k$ is denoted by Q_k and Z_k stands for the set of plays z of G with $|z| = k$. For $k = 0,\ldots K$ a *k-prearrangement* is either a preplay of G of length k or a play z of G with $|z| \leq k$. The set of all k-prearrangements is denoted by S_k. We say that a choice at a preplay u of G is made on *stage* k or that it is a *stage* k *decision* if u belongs to Q_{k-1}.

Consider a delay m_k and a reachable period $t_o + \tau$ with $t < m_k$. The interpretation of m_k as the delay until a stage-k-decision becomes effective suggests that a stage k decision for period $t_o + \tau$ should not be modelled as being made within the delay supergame but rather as predetermined by the past. Accordingly the definition of a delay supergame associated with G requires the specification of all decisions of this kind in a way which will be explained below.

For $\tau = 0,1,\ldots$ we define a *predetermination span* $\delta(\tau)$ interpreted as the highest stage k for which decisions for a period $t_o + \tau$ are excluded by $\tau < m_k$. For $\tau = 0,\ldots, m_1 - 1$ the predetermination span $\delta(\tau)$ is the index k of the smallest delay m_k with $\tau < m_k$. For $\tau = m_1, m_1 + 1,\ldots$ we define $\delta(\tau) = 0$.

An *initial status assignment* assigns an *initial status*

$$x(t,s^*) \in S_\tau \text{ with } \tau = \delta(t-t_o)$$

to every reachable period t. The initial status $x(t,s^*)$ is interpreted as the description of what is predetermined at period t. What is predetermined must be a $\delta(t-t_o)$-prearrangement. Obviously we have:

$$x(t,s^*) = s \quad \text{for } t \geq t_o + m_1.$$

It is possible that $x(t,s^*)$ is a play of length K. This may happen for $t-t_o < m_K$. Later we shall also define $x(t, u^*)$ for every path u^* and for every period $t = t_o, t_o + 1,\ldots$ There, too, $x(t, u^*)$ will describe what is predetermined for period t, once u^* has been played in the delay supergame.

The notation $x(\cdot, s^*)$ will be used for the initial status assignment. In the following $x(\cdot, s^*)$ will always be a fixed but arbitrary initial status assignment fitting the delay vector m and the stopping rule w.

4.4 *Initial payoff vector*

As in an ordinary supergame in a delay supergame payoffs for the periods played are accumulated as the game goes on. However, it will be convenient to permit the possibility that some fixed payoffs will be earned in addition to this. One may think of these payoffs as carried over from the past in a similar fashion as the initial status assignment $x(\cdot,s^*)$. Such payoffs carried over from the past arise naturally in subgames of delay supergames.

An *initial payoff vector*

$$c = (c_1,..., c_n)$$

is an n-vector with real valued components. c_i is called *player i's initial payoff.* In the following c will always be a fixed but arbitrary initial payoff vector. The inclusion of an initial payoff vector among the specifications of a delay supergame has the purpose to define a delay supergame in such a way that the concept also covers the subgames of delay supergames.

4.5 *The choice set function of the delay supergame*

In 4.1 – 4.4 we have explained what has to be specified in order to describe a delay supergame associated to a bounded multistage game G: A delay vector m, an initial period t_o, a stopping rule w, an initial status assignment $x(\cdot,s^*)$, and an initial payoff vector c determine a delay supergame $G^* = \Gamma(G, m, w, x(\cdot,s^*), c)$. One may look at Γ as a function which assigns a multistage game G* to every bounded multistage game G augmented by the additional specifications shown as arguments of Γ. This will be made precise below.

The upper index * will be used wherever notation aims at details connected to G* which have a counterpart in G, e.g. preplays, plays, etc. . The star will not be used for symbols like m, w, x, and c which need not be distinguished from corresponding objects in G.

The start s* is a symbol which represents the situation before period t. We now recursively define the choice set function A*, the path set U*, and the status function $x(\cdot,\cdot)$ which assigns a path of G to every pair (t, u^*) of a reachable period t and a path $u^* \in U^*$. It is clear that s* is a path and that for all reachable t the status $x(t, s^*)$ is already given by the initial status assignment. The recursive definition rests on this basis.

For i = 0,...,n and for every path u* of G* let $D_i(u^*)$ be the set of all reachable periods of the form $t_o+|u^*|+ m_k$ with k = 1,..., K for which $A_i (x(t,u^*))$ is non-empty. $D_i(u^*)$ is interpreted as the set of all periods for which i has to make a decision at u*, if u* is a preplay. We refer to the elements of $D_i(u^*)$ as the *aim periods* and to $D_i(u^*)$ as the *aim period* set at u*. The union of all

$D_i(u^*)$ with $i = 0,\ldots,n$ is denoted by $D(u^*)$. This set is called the *joint aim period set* at u^*.

For $i = 0,\ldots n$ and every path u^* let $A^*\cdot_i(u^*)$ be the set of all systems of the form

$$a_i^* = (a_i^t)_{t \in D_i(u^*)} \text{ with } a_i^t \in A_i(x(t, u^*)) \text{ for all } t \in D_i(u^*)$$

If u^* is a preplay, then the elements a_i^* of $A\cdot_i^*$ are *choices* of player i and in the case of a personal player i, all choices of player i. The component a_i^t of a_i^* is called player i's *decision for* t *at* u^*. The random player has an additional choice ω, the *stopping choice*, at every preplay. If $A\cdot_o(u^*)$ is empty the random player also has a *continuation choice* $\tilde{\omega}$

$$A_o^*(u^*) = \omega \cup A\cdot_o(u^*) \text{ if } A\cdot_o(u^*) \neq \emptyset$$
$$A_o^*(u^*) = \{\omega,\tilde{\omega}\} \text{ if } A\cdot_o(u^*) = \emptyset$$

for every preplay u^*. The *choice sets* of the personal players are

$$A_i^*(u^*) = A\cdot_i(u^*) \text{ for } i = 1,\ldots,n$$

for every preplay u^*. For a play z^* we have:

$$A_i(z^*) = \emptyset \text{ for } i = 0,\ldots,n$$

It still needs to be explained what distinguishes a play z^* from a preplay u^*. A play z^* must be of the form

$$z^* = u^*a^* \quad \text{with } a^* \in A^*(u^*)$$

where u^* is a preplay. A path z^* of this form is a *play* if and only if one of the following conditions is satisfied.

(1) a^* has the random component $a_o^* = \omega$

(2) a^* does not have the random component $a_o^* = \omega$, the game G^* is bounded and $t_o + |z^*| = T+1$ is unreachable

In case (2) we speak of a *maximal* play and in case (1) of a *submaximal* play. In unbounded delay supergames plays cannot end in any other way than by a random choice $a_o^* = \omega$. However, in a bounded delay supergame a play can extend over all $T-t_o+1$ reachable periods $t_o,\ldots,T$. The length of a maximal play is $|z^*| = T-t_o+1$.

The periods of a play z^* in which the random choice was not ω are called *unstopped.* The last period $t_o + |z^*| -1$ of a submaximal play is called *stopped.* The set of all unstopped periods of a play z^* is denoted by $L(z^*)$. The set $L(z^*)$ can be empty. This happens if already t_o is stopped. In 4.7 it will be explained that in the course of a play payoffs are accumulated for unstopped periods only.

In order to complete the definition of the choice set function we still have to describe how the status of a reachable period t changes in the course of playing the game. For every path of the form u*a* the *status* x(t,u*a*) of t at u*a* is recursively defined as follows:

$$x(t,u^*a^*) = x(t,u^*)a^t \text{ with } a^t \text{ in } a^* \text{ for } t \in D(u^*)$$

$$x(t,u^*a^*) = x(t,u^*) \text{ for } t \notin D(u^*)$$

for every preplay u* and every $a^* \in A^*(u^*)$. This means that the status of t at u* is changed by the decisions for t in a* but, of course, only if t is an aim period of u*. It is clear how the choice set function A*, the preplay set U*, the preplay set Z*, and the *status function* $x(\cdot,\cdot)$ are determined by the joint recursive definition given above.

4.6 *The probability assignment of the delay supergame*

The probability of a random choice a_o^* at a preplay u* according to the probability assignment p* of G* may be thought of as the result of independent random draws according to p for all aim periods in $D_o(u^*)$ combined with an independent decision on whether to stop with probability $w_{|u^*|}$ or to continue. In order to make this more precise consider a random choice a_o^* at a preplay u* of G*. For every $t \in D_o(u^*)$ let π^t be the probability

$$\pi^t = p_u(a_o^t) \quad \text{with } u = x(t,u^*) \text{ and } a_o^t \text{ in } a_o^*$$

Moreover let π be the product of all π^t with $t \in D_o(u^*)$. Then we have:

$$p_u^*(\omega) = w_{|u^*|}$$
$$p_u^*(\varpi) = 1-w_{|u^*|} \text{ for } A\cdot_o(u^*) = \varnothing$$
$$p_u^*(a_o^*) = (1-w_{|u^*|})\pi \text{ for } a_o^* \in A\cdot_o(u^*)$$

It can be seen without difficulty that the random stopping requirement imposed on w in 4.2 secures the random stopping condition of 2.2 for p*.

4.7 *The payoff function of the delay supergame*

A path u* of G* has the form of a sequence starting with s* and continuing with |u*| choice combinations at the periods $t_o,\ldots,t_o+|u^*|-1$. Accordingly we say that periods t with $t_o \le t < t_o+|u^*|$ are *in the past* of u*. The other reachable periods from $t_o+|u^*|$ on are *in the future* of u*. All decisions for a period t in the past of u* which may have to be made as long as the status of t is a preplay, must be made before t or at t. Therefore the status x(t,u*) of a period in the past of u* must be a play of G.

$$b_i^* = (b_{iu^*})_{u^* \in P_i^*}$$

with

$$b_{iu^*}(a_i^*) = \prod_{t \in D_i(u^*)} b_i(a_i^t) \text{ with } a_i^t \text{ in } a_i^*$$

for every $a_i^* \in A_i(u^*)$. This means that at u^* decisions for the aim periods are chosen by independent draws with the appropriate probabilities specified by b_i. It is clear that b_i^* has the properties of a behavior strategy for G^*.

We say that $b^* = (b_1^*,...,b_n^*)$ is *generated* by $b = (b_1,...,b_n)$ if for $i = 1,...,n$ the behavior strategy b_i^* is generated by b_i. Similarly an i-incomplete strategy combination b_{-i}^* is *generated* by b_{-i} if the components of b_{-i}^* are generated by the corresponding components of b_{-i}.

The set of all preplays v^* of G^+ with $|v^*| = t-t_o$ is denoted by Q_t^*. (This definition is not exactly analogous to that of Q_t in 2.7.) The preplays in Q_t^* are those which are followed by choices at period t. We shall have to look at the probability that one of these preplays is reached and that then the game is not stopped in period t. This probability, denoted by W_t is the product of the $t-t_o+1$ terms $1-w_\tau$ with $\tau = t_o,...,t$. Obviously a payoff for period t is obtained with probability W_t. Therefore we call W_t the *payoff probability* of t.

For every reachable period $t \in R$ the subgame of G at the initial status x (t, s*) will be denoted by $G^t = (s^t, A^t, p^t, h^t)$. Of course, s^t is just another name for x (t, s*). Let $b = (b_1,...,b_n)$ be a strategy combination for G and for every $t \in R$ let $b^t = (b_1^t,...,b_n^t)$ be the strategy combination induced by b on G^t. Moreover let b^* be the strategy combination generated by b in G^*. Then we have:

$$b^*(t, z) = W_t b^t(z)$$

for every play z of G^t. Therefore for every $t \in R$ the period payoff vector of t for b^* is as follows:

$$F^t(b^*) = W_t H^t(b^t)$$

where H^t is the expected payoff function for G_t. This yields

$$H^*(b^*) = \sum_{t \in R} W_t H^t(b^t)$$

In this way expected payoffs for strategy combinations generated in delay supergames can be expressed as payoffs in subgames of the underlying bounded multistage game.

5.2 *Generated subgame perfect best replies*

In this section we prove a lemma which leads to the conclusion that a subgame perfect equilibrium generates a subgame perfect equilibrium.

Lemma 1: Let $b = (b_1,...,b_n)$ be a strategy combination for G and let $b^* = (b_1^*,...,b_n^*)$ be the strategy combination generated by b in G^*. Moreover let r_i be a subgame perfect best reply to b and let r_i^* be generated by r_i in G^*. Then r_i^* is a subgame perfect best reply to b^*.

Proof: Let b_{-i} and b_{-i}^* be the i-incomplete strategy combinations whose components are in b and b^* respectively. Let f_i^* be any behavior strategy for G^*. We are interested in player i's period payoffs $F_i^t\ (f_i^*\ b_{-i}^*)$. As before, Q_t^* is the set of all preplays v^* with $|v^*| = t-t_o$. For every period $t \in R$, every preplay $v^* \in Q_t^*$, every preplay u of G^t and every choice $a_i \in A_i(u)$ let

$$f_{iu}^{v^*}\ (a_i)$$

be the probability with which a_i is chosen as player i's decision for t at the appropriate place on the path v^*. Obviously $f_{iu}^{v^*}$ is a local strategy at u. Let $f_i^{v^*}$ be the behavior strategy for G^t which assigns these local strategies to the preplays of G^t. For every preplay $v^* \in Q_t^*$ let $\varphi\ (v^*)$ be the conditional probability that v^* is realized by $f_i^{v^*}b_{-i}^*$ under the condition that a preplay in Q_t^* is reached. This conditional probability is well defined, since every reachable period is reached with positive probability. We have:

$$F_i^t\ (f_i^*\ b_{-i}^*) = W_t \sum_{v^* \in Q_t^*} \varphi\ (v^*)\ H_i^t\ (f_i^{v^*}\ b_{-i})$$

Since r_i is a subgame perfect best reply to b_{-i} we have:

$$H_i^t\ (f_i^{v^*}\ b_{-i}) \le H_i^t\ (r_i\ b_{-i})$$

In view of the fact that $\varphi\ (\cdot)$ is a probability distribution over Q_t^* this yields

$$F_i^t\ (f_i^*\ b_{-i}^*) \le W_t\ H_i^t\ (r_i\ b_{-i}) = F^t\ (r_i^*\ b_{-i})$$

This is true for every reachable period t. Therefore we can conclude that

$$H^*\ (f_i^*\ b_{-i}^*) \le H^*\ (r_i^*\ b_{-i}^*)$$

holds for every strategy f_i^* for G^*. Consequently r_i^* is a best reply to b^*. Since the subgames of G^* are delay supergames, the same argument can be applied to all subgames of G^*. This shows that r^* is a subgame perfect best reply to b^*.

5.3 Subgame perfect equilibria generate subgame perfect equilibria

The first main conclusion of this paper is the following theorem.

Theorem 1: Let b be a subgame perfect equilibrium of a bounded multistage game G and let b^* be the strategy combination generated by b in a delay supergame G^* of G. Then b^* is a subgame perfect equilibrium of G^*.

Proof: The assertion is an immediate consequence of the lemma of 5.2

5.4 Determinate multistage games

A multistage game is called *determinate,* if it has at least one subgame perfect equilibrium and if, in addition to this, the set of all its subgame perfect equilibria is a subgame perfect equilibrium set. In the following we shall introduce some definitions and notations connected to determinate bounded multistage games.

Let G be a determinate multistage game. Let E be the set of all subgame perfect equilibria of G. Since G is determinate, E is a subgame perfect equilibrium set of G. For every subgame G^u of G at a preplay u of G let E^u be the set induced by E on G^u. Since E is a subgame perfect equilibrium set, E^u is a subgame perfect equilibrum set, too. Moreover E^u is the set of all subgame perfect equilibria of G^u. For every preplay u of G let

$$e(u) = (e_1(u),...,e_u(u))$$

be the common expected payoff vector $H^u(b^u)$ for all $b_u \in E_u$. The game G itself is a subgame of G at the start s of G. Accordingly e(s) is the common payoff vector H(b) for all $b \in E$. For the case that u is a play define e(u) = h(u). We call e(u) the *replacement payoff vector* at u and refer to $e_i(u)$ as the *replacement payoff of* player i.

The name "replacement payoff" suggests itself by the use of which we are going to make of e(u). For every preplay v of G we construct a *truncated subgame* G_v. This game G_v results from the subgame G^v as follows: Every subgame G^u of G^v with u = va and $a \in A(v)$ is replaced by the payoff vector e(u). This means that all preplays u = va are plays of G_v with the payoff vector

$$h_v(a) = (h_{v1}(a),..., h_{vn}(a)) = e(va)$$

It can be seen without difficulty that a subgame perfect equilibrium b^v of G^v induces an equilibrium on G_v. We shall make use of a simple fact expressed by the following lemma.

Lemma 2: Let $r_v = (r_{v1},..., r_{vn})$ be an equilibrium of a truncated subgame G_v of a determinate multistage game G. Then we have

$$H_v(r_v) = e(v)$$

where Hv is the expected payoff function of G_v and e(v) is the replacement payoff vector at v in G.

Proof: Let $b^v = (b_1{}^v,..., b_n{}^v)$ be a subgame perfect equilibrium of the subgame G^v. Let r^v be the strategy combination whose components $r_i{}^v$ assign the local strategy r_{iv} to v and agree with $b_i{}^v$ everywhere else. It can be seen immediately that r^v is a subgame perfect equilibrium of G^v. It is also clear that the payoff vector for r^v in G^v is nothing else than the payoff vector for r_v in G_v. In view of the determinateness of G we have

$$H_v(r_v) = H^v(r^v) = e(v)$$

for every preplay v of G.

5.5 *Determinateness of bounded delay supergames of determinate bounded multistage games*

The following theorem is the second main conclusion of this paper.

Theorem 2: Every bounded delay supergame of a determinate bounded multistage game is determinate.

Proof: Let G be a determinate bounded multistage game and let G* be one of its bounded delay supergames. Since G is determinate, G has at least one subgame perfect equilibrium. Let r be a subgame perfect equilibrium of G and let r* be the strategy combination generated by r in G*. In view of theorem 1, this strategy combination r* is a subgame perfect equilibrium of G*. It remains to show that all subgame perfect equilibria of G* form a subgame perfect equilibrium set. We shall prove this by induction on the number $T-t_o+1$ of the reachable periods $t_o, \ldots T$ of G*.

Consider first the case $T-t_o+1 = 1$ in which $t_o = T$ is the only reachable period. The game ends after the choice combination at t_o. All plays have the form s*a with $a \in A(s^*)$. A strategy combination for G* is a strategy combination for G_v with $v = x(t_o, s^*)$. It follows by lemma 2 that the same expected payoff vector is obtained for all equilibria of G*. Consequently G* is determinate.

From now on assume that the number of reachable periods in G* is greater than 1 and that the assertion holds for all delay supergames with a smaller number of reachable periods.

As above let r be a subgame perfect equilibrium of G and let r* be generated by r in G*. All subgames of G* at preplays of the form s*a* with $a^* \in A^*(s^*)$ are determinate since they have a smaller number of reachable periods. A strategy b_i^* of a personal player i for G* is called *semigenerated* by r if for all preplays v* of G* with $|v^*| > 0$ the local strategy assigned to v* is the local strategy assigned by r*. In view of the determinateness of the subgames of G* starting with period t_o+1 the payoffs in these subgames and their subgames do not depend on the particular subgame perfect equilibrium played. Therefore it is sufficient to show that the set of all equilibria in strategies semigenerated by r is an equilibrium set.

It follows by lemma 1 that it is always possible to find a semigenerated subgame perfect best reply to a combination of semigenerated strategies for G*.

It can be seen easily that in the case of a combination of strategies semigenerated by r, a subgame perfect best reply can be found among the strategies semigenerated by r.

In order to show that the set of all equilibria in strategies semigenerated by r is an equilibrium set it is sufficient to look at the following *truncated game* G^+ of G^*. This game G^+ results from G^* by the replacement of all subgames at preplays of the form s^*a^* with $a^* \in A^*(s^*)$ by their subgame perfect equilibrium payoff vectors. This game G^+ is a multistage game with only one stage. The pure strategies of the personal players in G^+ are their choice sets $A_i^*(s^*)$. For the sake of shortness we write A_i^+ instead of $A_i^*(s^*)$ for $i = 0,\ldots, n$ and A^+ instead of $A^*(s^*)$.

It can be seen immediately that the subgame perfect equilibria in strategies semigenerated by r form an equilibrium set if the set of all equilibria of the truncated game G^+ is an equilibrium set. It remains to show that this is the case. For this purpose we shall look at the expected payoff $H^+(a^*)$ for a choice combination $a^* \in A^+$. Let N^+ be the set of players active at s^* in G^*. For $i = 0,\ldots, n$ let D_i^+ be the aim period set $D_i(s^*)$ and let D^+ be the aim period set $D(s^*)$.

Let $a^* \in A^*$ be a choice combination. For every $i \in N^+$ let a_i^* be the choice of i in a^* and for every $t \in D_i^+$ let ait be the decision for t specified by a_i^* and at the decision combination specified by a^* for t. After the choice of a^* every reachable period has the status x (t,s^*a^*). Later decisions for t are made with the probabilities required by r. Therefore the expected period payoff vector of t for a^* is $e(x(t,s^*a^*))$ multiplied by W_t. This yields

$$H^+(a^*) = c + \sum_{t=t_o}^{T} W_t\, e(x(t,s^*a^*))$$

We have

$$\begin{aligned} x(t,s^*a^*) &= x(t,s^*)a^t \text{ for } t \in D^+ \\ x(t,s^*a^*) &= (t,s^*) \text{ for } t \in R \setminus D^+ \end{aligned}$$

The period payoff vectors for $t \in R \setminus D^+$ do not depend on a^*. Let J be the sum of all these period payoff vectors and c. We obtain

$$H^+(a^*) = J + \sum_{t \in D^+} W_t e(x(t,s^*)a^t)$$

Let $f = (f_1,\ldots, f_n)$ be a strategy combination for G^+. For every $i \in N^+$, every $t \in D^+$, and every $a_i^t \in A_i(x(t,s^*))$ let $f_i^t(a_i^t)$ be the probability that a choice a_i^* is taken by f_i which specifies a_i^t as the decision for t. The function f_i^t defined in this way is a behavior strategy for the truncated subgame of G at $x(t,s^*)$. The symbol G_t is used for this game. Let $f^t = (f_1^t,\ldots,f_n^t)$ be the strategy combination containing these behavior strategies and the empty strategies of the players not active at $x(t,s^*)$. The conditional realization probability $f^t(a^t)$ of a^t at $x(t,s^*)$ is the probability that a choice combination a^* results from the use of the strategies in f, such that a^* specifies the decision combination a^t for period t. We can now express the expected payoff vector for f in G^+ as follows:

$$H^+(f) = J + \sum_{t \in D^+} W_t \sum_{a^t \in A(x(t,s^*))} f^t(a^t)e(x(t,s^*)a^t)$$

Let $f = (f_1,..., f_n)$ be a strategy combination for G^+. It will now be shown that the following is true: if f is an equilibrium of G^+, then for every $t \in D^+$ the strategy combination f^t must be an equilibrium of G^t. In order to see this, suppose that for one $t \in D^+$ this is not the case. Then in G_t one personal player i has a pure best reply $\tilde{a}_i^t$ which yields a better payoff against the strategies of the others in f^t than f_i^t does. If this is the case, player i can improve its payoff by the following change of behavior: If f_i selects a choice a_i^* which does not specify $\tilde{a}_i$ for t, then the choice specified by a_i^* for t is replaced by $\tilde{a}_i^t$ and the changed choice resulting from a_i^* in this way is taken. Otherwise the behavior prescribed by f_i remains unchanged. The behavior strategy g_i thereby obtained improves player i's period payoff for t and lets other period payoffs of player i unchanged.

It is a consequence of the determinateness of G that for every $t \in D^+$ the set of all equilibria of G_t is an equilibrium set. Otherwise it would be possible to construct two subgame perfect equilibria of the subgame G^t at $x(t,s^*)$ of G with different payoff vectors. We can conclude that the set of all equilibria of G^+ is an equilibrium set. This completes the proof of the theorem.

6. *Discussion*

After the concepts and conclusions of this paper have been made precise their significance for economic theory will be discussed in this section.

6.1 *The relationship between multistage games and their delay supergames*

Multistage game models often do not really aim at one shot strategic interactions in which stage decisions are made once and for all in a strict temporal order, but rather ongoing situations, in which decisions represented as made at earlier stages are thought of as more long term than those made on later stages. What is the essential difference between more long term and more short term decisions? It has been argued in the introduction that in many cases the dislinguishing feature seems to be the length of the delay until a decision becomes effective. The formal elaboration of this idea leads to the notion of a delay supergame of a multistage game.

Of course, other differences between more long term and more short term decisions may also enter the picture in specific applications. It is not clear to what extent additional dislinguishing features like greater change costs for more long run decisions would force us to modify our conclusions. This is a question which needs to be explored with the help of more general dynamic game models associated to multistage games. No attempt in this direction can be made here. The conclusions drawn in this paper cannot claim to achieve more than a precise interpretation of subgame perfect equilibria in multistage game models which do not permit a direct temporal interpretation of the order of stages. In this way the gap between model and reality is not closed, but maybe diminished or at least illuminated.

6.2 Consequences of the assumption of full rationality

In the remainder of the paper we shall always look at a bounded multistage game and one of its delay supergames. We first discuss the consequences of the assumption that the delay supergame is played by fully rational players with commom knowledge about its rules. In the case of a unique subgame perfect equilibrium set of the multistage game and a bounded delay supergame, theorem 2 yields the conclusion that the behavior to be expected in the delay supergame is essentially correctly described by the perfect equilibrium set of the multistage game. In this case not all subgame perfect equilibria of the delay supergame are generated by those of the multistage game, but this does not matter as far as payoffs in the whole game and all its subgames are concerned.

In all other cases we cannot say more than what has been shown by theorem 1. Every subgame perfect equilibrium of the multistage game generates a subgame perfect equilibrium of the delay supergame. In addition to this the delay supergame may have many other equilibria some of which may yield higher payoffs for all players. In such cases the non-cooperative analysis of the multistage game fails to reveal the potential for quasicooperative subgame perfect equilibrium behavior in the delay supergame. This raises a problem with respect to the interpretation of subgame perfect equilibria of the multistage game.

6.3 The finiteness argument

An upper bound, say a million years, can be named for the survival of any economic situation. Therefore unbounded delay supergames should be looked upon as simplified descriptions of long lasting ongoing situations of finite duration. Conclusions which rest on the feature of unboundedness cannot be taken seriously. In this way the non-cooperative analysis of a multistage game with a unique subgame perfect equilibrium set can be defended as a satisfactory substitute for the full treatment of the delay supergame.

However, is this argument really valid? Experimental results clearly show, that experienced players cooperate in 10-period supergames of the prisoner's dilemma game until shortly before the end (Selten and Stoecker 1986) in spite of the fact that this is excluded by subgame perfect equilibrium.

6.4 Slightly imcomplete information

In order to deal with the phenomenon of cooperation in finite prisoner's dilemma supergames without an essential relaxation of rationality assumptions one can take the point of view that the supergame is not the game really played, and that instead of this the players are involved in an similar, but different game. Kreps, Wilson, Milgrom and Roberts (1982) assume that with a small probability a player may be of a different type, with preferences which make it profitable to take the cooperative choice as long as the opponent has been observed to do this. The introduction of such types transforms the supergame to a game with slightly incomplete information, and thereby opens quasicooperative opportunities similar to those in the case of infinite repetition.

The approach of Kreps, Wilson, Milgrom and Roberts (1982) is not a convincing explanation of the experimental evidence. If cooperation in the finitely repeated prisoner's dilemma were the result of sophisticated rational deliberation, then it should be observed already in the first supergame played and not only after a considerable amount of experience as it happens in our experiments (Selten and Stoecker 1986). Kreps and Wilson (1982) have applied the same incomplete information approach to the chain store paradox (Selten 1978). Here, too, the experimental evidence points in a different direction (Jung, Kagel, and Levin 1994). The bounded rationality approach of my (1978) paper seems to be in better agreement with the data.

6.5 Institutional reasons for the absence of cooperation

From what has been said up to now, it is clear that, even if the assumptions of theorem 2 are satisfied, we cannot rely on the desciptive validity of the non-cooperative analysis of the multistage game as a substitute for the full treatment of the delay supergame. However there may be institutional reasons for the exclusion of cooperation or subgame perfect quasicoope-ration in the supergame.

Consider the case of an oligopoly in an economy with strictly enforced cartel laws and assume that the oligopolistic market is adequately modelled as a delay supergame of a bounded multistage game. Presumably the cartel laws forbid collusion, but what does this mean? Obviously the cartel laws cannot simply demand that a subgame perfect equilibrium of the delay supergame is played. This may fail to exclude subgame perfect quasicooperation.

It seems to be natual to define the absence of collusion as a state of affairs, in which a subgame perfect equilibrium of the delay supergame is played which is generated by a subgame perfect equilibrium of the underlying multistage game. If the absence of collusion in this sense is effectively enforced, then the non-cooperative analysis of the multistage game is a satisfactory substitute for that of the delay supergame.

However, against this argument the objection can be raised, that it remains unclear, how the cartel laws are enforced. Presumably the enforcement agency does not have the same knowledge of the market which is avaialble to the oligopolists. The same may be true for the court to whom the oligopolists can appeal in the case of a disagreement with the cartel authority. It would be desirable to model the cartel authority explicitly as a player in order to throw light on its strategic interaction with the oligopolists.

In an open oligopoly collusion may have the disadvantage that new entrants are attracted by high profits. This may have the effect that after the entry of new competitors the profits of the incumbents achieved by collusion are lower then they would have been without entry in the absence of collusion. In a paper with the title "Are cartel laws bad for business" (Selten 1984) I have presented a multistage game model which yields the conclusion that under plausible conditions about the distribution of the market parameters total profits of all firms in the economy are increased by effectively enforced cartel laws compared with a situation in which cartels can be legally formed. This effect is due to excessice entry in the absence of cartel laws. Thus the task of the cartel authority may be facilitated by an economy wide advantage for industrial enterprises, even if the firms on some markets would gain by the possibility of legal cartel formation.

6.6 An adaptive interpretation

Experimentally observed behavior is only boundedly rational and the same must be expected of the bahavior of firms in real markets. Research on the behavioral theory of the firm (Cyert and March, 1963; Earl, 1988) provides ample evidence for this. In the following I shall try to present some tentative ideas on the consequences of bounded rationality for the interpretation of subgame perfect equilibria of multistage game models and those generated in their delay supergames. Admittedly my remarks in the remainder of the paper will be sketchy and speculative. No attempt is made to support them by a thorough examination of the relevant experimental literature.

Experimental subjects do not compute the solutions of complex optimization tasks in order to make their decisions. Apart from very simple cases it cannot be expected that subgame perfect equilibria are found by rational deliberation. However this does not mean that such equilibria are irrelevant for the prediction of behavior. In repetitive experimental settings equilibria can be learned by adaptation to past experience.

The experimental literature on double auction markets initiated by Vernon Smith (1962, 1964) provides a well known example. Usually competitive equilibrium is reached after a relatively small number of identical repetitions of the same market. The traders do not compute the equilibrium price. Convergence to competitve equilibrium is the result of an adaptive process which adjusts bids and asks to observed imbalances of supply and demand.

The double auction is a very complex game with imcomplete information. Behavior does not converge to an equilibrium of this game, but rather to an equilibrium of a fictitious associated game with complete information, in which reservation prices and resale values of all traders are publicly known. Something similar can be observed in Cournot oligopoly experiments in which the producers are not informed about the costs of their competitors (e.g. Sauermann and Selten 1959). It is my impression that convergence to an equilibrium of the fictitious complete information game, which would be played if all private information were public, is favored by the incomplete knowledge about the other players' payoffs. This lack of knowledge hides the quasicooperative opportunities of the complete information game.

In a bounded multistage game played just once, with stages following each other in temporal succession, adaptive adjustment processes cannot work. This is different in sufficiently long delay supergames. Here players repeatedly face the necessity to adapt their decisions on all stages. There is a good chance that, under favorable conditions, subgame perfect equilibria generated by those of the underlying bounded multistage game, are learnt by experience. Conditions are favorable, if the game which is played is not really the delay supergame but a modified version with reduced payoff information in the following sense: The players have little knowledge about the other players' payoff functions and do not observe their payoffs. However as in the unmodified delay supergame they do observe the other players' past choices and they know their own payoff functions.

My thoughts about the descriptive relevance of the non-cooperative analysis of multistage game models can be summarized by the following hypothesis: *Learning in a modified delay supergame with reduced payoff information converges to behavior in agreement with the predictions derived from a subgame perfect equilibrium of the underlying multistge game, the more so, the less the players know about other players' payoffs.*

It is necessary to run experiments specifically designed to test this hypothesis. If the hypothesis succeeds to survive the tests, it will provide descriptive content to the non-cooperative analysis of multistage game models.

6.7 Non-monetary motivation

The hypothesis stated above may have to be weakened in several directions. One difficulty which may arise is the influence of non-monetary motivation. The monetary payoffs offered in an experimental game are often not the only motivational factors present. The ultimatum game has an obvious subgame perfect equilibrium, if only monetary payoffs are considered, but nonmonetary motivational forces make it unacceptable for the recipient of the ultimatum (Güth, Schmittberger and Schwarze, 1982; Güth and Tietz 1990). In the case of the ultimatum game the motivational force is resistance to unfairness.

Another motivational factor is clearly visible in an experimental labor market (Fehr, Kirchberger and Riedl 1993). A reciprocity norm induces employees to supply more effort than they have to as a voluntary reward for high wages, in a situation which excludes reputation effects by the experimental set up. This results in considerable deviations from competitive equilibrium.

Much more could be said about the experimental evidence for non-monetary motivations, but this will not be done here. Interestingly resistance to unfairnessö and reciprocity both depend on at least some knowledge of the other player's payoff. A lack of such knowledge does not only hide quasi-cooperative opportunities but also weakens the force of social norms which facilitate non-equilibrum cooperation. However, one cannot expect that it will always be poosible to ignore the influence of non-monetary motivational forces on behavior in modified delay supergames with reduced payoff information.

REFERENCES

Aumann, R.J., 1959, Acceptable Points in General Cooperative n-Person Games, in: R.D. Luce and A.W. Tucker (eds.) *Contributions to the Theory of Games IV*, Ann. Math. Study 40, Princeton, N.J., 287 – 324

Benoit, J.P., and V. Krishna 1985, Finitely Repeated Games, *Econometrica* 53, 905 – 922

Cournot, A., 1838, *Recherches de la théorie des richesses*, Paris

Fehr, E., G. Kirchsteiger, and A. Riedl, 1993, Does Fairness Prevent Market Clearing?. An Experimental Investigation, *Quarterly Journal of Economics*, 108, 2, 437 – 460

Fouraker, L.E., and S. Siegel 1963, *Bargaining Behavior*, New York

Friedman, J., 1977, Oligopoly and the *Theory of Games*, North-Holland Publishing Company, Amsterdam-New York-Oxford

Güth W., R. Schmittberger, and B. Schwarze, 1982, An Experimental Analysis of Ultimatum Bargaining, *Journal of Economic Behavior and Organization*, 3, 3, 367 – 88

Güth, W., and R. Tietz, 1990, Ultimatum Bargaining Behavior – A Survey and Comparison of Experimental Results, *Journal of Economic Psychology* 11, 417 – 449

Hoggatt, A.C., 1959, An Experimental Business Game, *Behavioral Science*, 4, 192 – 203

Jung, Y.J., J.H. Kagel, and D. Levin, 1994, On the Existence of Predatory Pricing: An Experimental Study of Reputation and Entry Deterrence in the Chain Store Game, *Rand Journal of Economics* 25, 1, 72 – 93

Kreps, D.M., and J.A. Scheinkman, 1983, Quantity Precommitment and Bertrand Competition Yield Cournot Outcomes, *Bell Journal of Economics*, 14, 326 – 337

Marschak, Th., and R. Selten, 1978, Restabilizing Responses, Inertia Supergames and Oligopolistic Equilibria, *Quarterly Journal of Economics*, 92, 71 – 93

Nash, J.F., 1951, Non-Cooperative Games, *Annals of Mathematics* 54, 286 – 295

Rubinstein, A., 1978, Equilibrium in Supergames with the Overtaking Criterion, *Journal of Economic Theory* 21, 1 – 9

Rubinstein, A., 1980, Strong Perfect Equilibrium in Supergames, *International Journal of Game Theory* 9, 1 – 12

Sauermann, H., and R. Selten, 1959, Ein Oligopolexperiment, *Zeitschrift für die gesamte Staatswissenschaft*, 115, 427 – 471, 9 – 59

Selten, R., 1965, Spieltheoretische Behandlung eines Oligopolmodells mit Nachfrageträgheit, *Zeitschrift für die gesamte Staatswissenschaft*, 121, 301 – 24, 667 – 89

Selten, R., 1973, A Simple Model of Imperfect Competition where 4 are Few and 6 are Many, *International Journal of Game Theory* 2, 141 – 201. (Reprinted in Selten, R., 1988, *Models of Strategic Rationality*, Dordrecht: Kluwer)

Selten, R., 1978, The Chain Store Paradox, *Theory and Decision*, 9, 127 – 159 (Reprinted in Selten, R., 1988, *Models of Strategic Rationality*, Dordrecht: Kluwer)

Selten, R., 1984, Are Cartel Laws Bad for Business? in H. Hauptmann, W. Krelle and K.C. Mosler (eds.) *Operations Research and Economic Theory*, Berlin: Springer Verlag (Reprinted in Selten, R., 1988, *Models of Strategic Rationality*, Dordrecht: Kluwer)

Selten, R., and R. Stoecker, 1986, End Behavior in Finite Prisoner's Dilemma Supergames, Journal of Economic Behavior and Organization, I, 47 – 70

Smith, V., 1962, An Experimental Study of Competitive Market Behavior, *Journal of Political Economy*, 70, 111 – 137

Smith, V., 1964, Effect of Market Organization on Competitve Equilibrium, Quarterly *Journal of Economics* 78, 181 – 201

Stern, D.H., 1967, Some Notes on Oligopoly Theory and Experiments, in M. Shubik (ed.) *Essays in Mathematical Economics*, Princeton, N.J., 255 – 281

von Neumann, J., and O. Morgenstern, 1944, *Theory of Games and Econimc Behavior*, Princeton University Press, Princeton, N.J.

ECONOMIC SCIENCES 1995

ROBERT E. LUCAS, JR.

for having developed and applied the hypothesis of rational expectations, and thereby having transformed macroeconomic analysis and deepened our understanding of economic policy

THE SVERIGES RIKSBANK (BANK OF SWEDEN) PRIZE IN ECONOMIC SCIENCES IN MEMORY OF ALFRED NOBEL

Speech by Professor Lars E.O. Svensson of the Royal Swedish Academy of Sciences.
Translation of the Swedish text.

Your Majesties, Your Royal Highnesses, Ladies and Gentlemen,

Robert Lucas is the social scientist who has had the greatest influence on macroconomic research since 1970. The main objective of macroeconomic research is to study fluctuations in total production, employment and inflation. Lucas's contributions have transformed macroeconomic analysis and deepened our understanding of economic policy. They have led to a more realistic appreciation of what economic policy can, and cannot, achieve. Lucas has also given us more reliable methods to evaluate the effects of changing economic policy.

A recurrent theme in Lucas's work is the importance of expectations. Lucas postulated that households, firms and organizations use available information in an efficient way. This hypothesis of rational expectations has had far-reaching consequences for macroeconomic analysis.

The change in our understanding of the Phillips curve is an excellent example of Lucas's contributions. The Phillips curve, named after its discoverer, a British economist, displays a positive relation between inflation and employment. In the late 1960s, there was considerable empirical support for the Phillips curve; it was regarded as one of the more stable relationships in economics. It was generally interpreted as an option for governments and central banks to bring about a permanent increase in employment by pursuing an expansionary policy that results in more inflation.

However, in an analysis carried out around 1970, Lucas used the concept of rational expectations to demonstrate that employment could definitely not be permanently increased by allowing inflation to rise. Although Lucas was able to explain why the Phillips curve appeared to have so much empirical support, he could also show that any attempt to exploit the Phillips curve and permanently increase employment by systematically creating higher inflation would be futile. According to Lucas's analysis, the Phillips curve would not remain stable; it would shift when expectations adjusted to higher rates of inflation.

This was not merely an academic subtlety, as was soon demonstrated in practice. During the 1970s governments and central banks in many countries allowed inflation to soar, in order to achieve high employment. In accordance with the theory, there was no sustained increase in employment; the Phillips curve shifted, as Lucas had predicted.

This gives rise to two important policy conclusions. The first is that there are no permanent gains to society from high inflation. On the contrary, high inflation has sustained drawbacks. By now, this conclusion is generally accepted and has become the foundation for the monetary policy pursued in several countries, including Sweden, which aim at achieving low and stable inflation.

The second conclusion is that high unemployment and low employment can be successfully remedied only by other means than inflationary monetary and fiscal policy, for instance by structural measures to make the labor market and wage formation function more efficiently.

The fate of the Phillips curve demonstrates the dangers in uncritically using a statistical relationship to draw economic-policy conclusions. The insights into these dangers were developed further in the so-called Lucas Critique. Lucas showed that not only the Phillips curve, but several other significant relationships that had previously been considered stable (for instance, the dependence of consumption and investments on wages, interest rates and taxes) on closer examination are likely to change due to shifts in economic policy. Hence, economic-policy conclusions based on these relationships are not reliable.

But Lucas was not content with these negative implications. Instead, he proposed new theoretical and statistical methods that avoid these pitfalls and can serve as the foundation for more reliable evaluation of the consequences of altering economic policy. Nowadays, these are commonly accepted methods which are used regularly in analysis of economic policy.

In addition to his work in macroeconomics, Lucas has made outstanding contributions to several other research fields than macroeconomics, such as monetary theory, financial economics, public economics and economic growth. In each of these fields, Lucas's work has given research a new direction and generated an extensive new literature.

Dear Professor Lucas,
Your development and application of the theory of rational expectations has fundamentally transformed macroeconomic analysis. It has deepened our understanding of economic policy. Your work has also had a profound impact on research in several other fields of economics. It is a privilege and an honor to convey to you my warmest congratulations, on behalf of the Royal Swedish Academy of Sciences. Please step forward to receive the Prize from His Majesty the King.

ROBERT E. LUCAS, Jr.

I was born in 1937, in Yakima, Washington, the oldest child of Robert Emerson Lucas and Jane Templeton Lucas. My sister Jenepher was born in 1939 and my brother Peter in 1940. My parents had moved to Yakima from Seattle, to open a small restaurant, The Lucas Ice Creamery. The restaurant was a casualty of the 1937–38 downturn, and during World War II our family moved to Seattle, where my father found work as a steamfitter in the shipyards and my mother resumed her earlier career as a fashion artist. My brother Daniel was born in Seattle in 1948.

My parents were admirers of President Roosevelt and the New Deal. Their parents and most of our relatives and neighbors were Republicans, so they were self conscious in their liberalism and took it as emblematic of their ability to think for themselves. The idea that one could decide for oneself what kind of person to be, and that one ought to think about these decisions, was not limited to politics. I remember discussions, with my mother especially, of religion (she was a liberal protestant), of decor (she favored hardwood floors and oriental rugs), even on how to choose what kind of cigarette to smoke.

After the war, my father found a job as a welder at a commercial refrigeration company, Lewis Refrigeration. He became a draftsman, then a sales-engineer, then sales manager, and eventually president of the company. He had no college degree and no engineering training, and learned the engineering he needed from the people he worked with and from handbooks. I remember many technical and managerial discussions with him, as well as our ongoing political arguments. When I took calculus in high school, he enlisted my help on a refrigeration design problem he was working on–and actually used my calculations! It was my first taste of real applied mathematics, and an exciting one.

I attended Seattle Public Schools, graduating from Roosevelt High School (where my parents had graduated in 1927) in 1955. I was good at math and science, and it was expected that I would attend the University of Washington in Seattle and become an engineer. But by the time I was seventeen I was ready to leave home, a decision my parents agreed to support if I could obtain a scholarship. MIT did not grant me one but the University of Chicago did. Since Chicago did not have an engineering school, this ended my engineering career. But when I began the 44 hour train trip "back east" to Chicago, I was pretty sure something interesting would turn up.

What to do instead? I took some mathematics at Chicago, but lost interest soon after my courses got past the material I had half learned in high school. I did not have the nerve to major in Physics, which is what you did at Chicago in those days if you thought you could make it. The real excitement for me was in the liberal arts core of the Chicago College, courses from the Hutchins era with names like History of Western Civilization, and Organization, Methods, and Principles of Knowledge. Everything in these courses was new to me. All of them began with readings from Plato and Aristotle, and I wanted to learn all I could about the Greeks. I took a sequence in Ancient History, and became a history major. Though I had no real idea what a professional historian does, I had learned that one can make a living by pursuing one's intellectual interests and writing about them. I began to think about an academic career.

I obtained a Woodrow Wilson Doctoral Fellowship, and entered the graduate program in History at the University of California. With no Greek or French and minimal Latin and German, I was in no position to pursue my classical interests, so I began work at Berkeley with little more than an open mind. The most exciting modern historian I had read at Chicago had been the Belgian historian Henri Pirenne, whose account of the end of the Roman era stressed the continuity of economic life in the face of major political disruptions. For me, Pirenne's shift of focus away from emperors and dreary Merovingian kings and on to the daily lives of private citizens was novel and exciting, and fit my sense of what was important. At Berkeley, I took courses in Economic History and audited an economic theory course. I liked economics at once, but it was obvious that to apply it with any confidence I would need to know much more than I could pick up on the side as a history student. I decided to move into economics and, since there appeared to be no hope of financial support from Berkeley's Economics Department, I returned to Chicago. During the rest of that academic year I took some undergraduate economics at Chicago and one or two graduate courses, to prepare for my real start as a graduate student the next fall.

It was lucky for me that one of my undergraduate texts referred to Paul Samuelson's *Foundations of Economic Analysis* as "the most important book in economics since the war." Both the mathematics and the economics in *Foundations* were way over my head, but I was too ambitious to spend my summer on the second most important book in economics, and Samuelson's confident and engaging style kept me going. All my spare time that summer went in to working through the first four chapters, line by line, going back to my calculus books when I needed to. By the beginning of fall quarter I was as good an economic technician as anyone on the Chicago faculty. Even more important, I had internalized Samuelson's standards for when an economic question had been properly posed and when it had been answered, and was in a position to take charge of my own economic education.

In the fall of 1960, I began Milton Friedman's price theory sequence. I had been looking forward to this famous course all summer, but it was far more exciting than anything I had imagined. What made it so? Many Chicago students have tried to answer this question. Certainly Friedman's brilliance and intensity, and his willingness to follow his economic logic wherever it led all played a role. After every class, I tried to translate what Friedman had done into the mathematics I had learned from Samuelson. I knew I would never be able to think as fast as Friedman, but I also knew that if I developed a reliable, systematic way for approaching economic problems I would end up at the right place.

Friedman's course ended my long career as a conscientious, near-straight-A student. Now if a course did not promise to be a life-changing experience, I lost interest and attended only sporadically. I accumulated many C's, but also a lot of time to pursue what I found interesting. I took my first rigorous analysis courses, and a statistics course using Volume I of Willam Feller's *An Introduction to Probability Theory and Its Applications.* I still pick up Feller's book from time to time, as I do Samuelson's, just for the pleasure of the author's company.

There was also plenty of interesting economics going on at Chicago. My interest in probability and statistics stemmed from an interest in econometrics, stimulated by courses of Zvi Griliches and Gregg Lewis. Donald Bear, a new Assistant Professor from Stanford, taught a valuable mathematical economics course, and gave valuable encouragement to technically inclined students. Arnold Harberger's sequence in public finance was a lasting influence on me too. My thesis, which used data from U.S. manufacturing to estimate elasticities of substitution between capital and labor, was written under Harberger and Lewis, and was part of a larger project of Harberger's analyzing the effects of various changes in the U.S. tax structure.

There was a terrific collection of students at Chicago in the early 1960s. My closest friends were Glen Cain, Neil Wallace, Sherwin Rosen, and G.S. Maddala, and there were many others who now have international reputations. For many of us, the shock wave of Friedman's libertarian-conservative ideas forced a rethinking of our whole social philosophy. Intense student discussions ranged far beyond technical economics. I tried to hold on to the New Deal politics I had grown up with, and remember voting for Kennedy in 1960. "Nixon? Bob, you couldn't," my sister had said, and she was right (for then!). But however we voted, Friedman's students came away with the sense that we had acquired a powerful apparatus for thinking about economic and political questions.

In 1963 Richard Cyert, the new Dean of the Graduate School of Industrial Administration at Carnegie Institute of Technology (now Carnegie-Mellon University), offered me a faculty position. I had met Allan Meltzer and Leonard Rapping at my job seminar there, and I knew GSIA would be a stimulating and congenial place for me. GSIA's leading intellectual figure was Herbert Simon. Although Simon was no longer working in economics when I came to Carnegie, he was always ready to talk about economics (or any other area of social or management science) at lunch or coffee. He gave all of us at GSIA the feeling of being in the major leagues, and helped us to outgrow the sense that all the important work was going on at Chicago or Cambridge.

Once my thesis was finished, I began theoretical work on the decisions of business firms to invest in physical capital and in improved technology. Dale Jorgenson had served on my Chicago thesis committee, and his work on investment had stimulated me. I spent a lot of time in my first years at Carnegie Tech learning the mathematics of dynamical systems and optimization over time, and trying to see how these methods could best be applied to economic questions. Economists of my cohort all over the world were engaged in this enterprise in the 1960s, and I remember exciting conferences on this theme at Chicago and Yale, led by Hirofumi Uzawa.

During my years there, Carnegie-Mellon had a remarkable group of economists interested in dynamics and the formation of expectations. Foremost, of course, was John Muth, my colleague in my first three years there. Morton Kamien and Nancy Schwartz had come from Purdue about the time I came from Chicago. Dick Roll, a student of Eugene Fama's at Chicago, brought the ideas of efficient market theory to GSIA. Thomas Sargent came to Carnegie-Mellon from Harvard in the middle of writing his thesis, and I remember the discussions he and Roll had about interest rates (that none of the rest of us could follow). Morris DeGroot taught a course in statistical decision theory that influenced Edward Prescott, and through Ed, me. John Bossons and later Michael Lovell studied direct evidence on expectations. It would be hard to think of a better group of colleagues, given my interests in economic dynamlcs.

At Carnegie I became involved in two collaborations, both of which bore immediate fruit and also influenced my thinking for years afterward. One of these was a project with Leonard Rapping, my closest friend and colleague at that time, in which we undertook to provide a neoclassical account of the behavior of U.S. wages and employment from 1929 to 1958. The paper was a bolder step into new territory then I would have taken then on my own, and the project never would have been undertaken or completed without Leonard's confidence and his expertise in labor economics.

Edward Prescott had come to GSIA as a doctoral student in the same year I joined the faculty, and we were immediate friends. A few years later, when Ed had become a faculty member at Penn, I enlisted his help on a theoretical project I had begun on the dynamics of an imperfectly competitive industry. That problem defeated us, but in the course of failing to solve it we found ourselves talking and corresponding about everything in economic dynamics. In a couple of years we learned large chunks of modern general equilibrium theory, functional analysis, and probability theory, and wrote a paper, "Investment under Uncertainty," that reformulated John Muth's idea of rational expectations in a useful way . During this brief period my whole point of view of economic dynamics took form (along with Ed's), in a way that has served me well ever since.

David Cass, who came to Carnegie-Mellon in 1971, had earlier aroused my interest in Samuelson's overlapping generations model of a monetary economy. At about the same time, Edmund Phelps convinced me that Rapping's and my model of labor supply needed to be situated in a general equilibrium context. These influences, combined with much that I had learned working with Prescott, came together in my paper, "Expectations and the Neutrality of Money," which was completed in 1970 and published in 1972. The role of this paper, certainly the most influential of my writings, is one of the subjects of my Nobel lecture. In May, 1995, Rao Aiyagari organized a 25th Anniversary Conference for this paper, sponsored by the Federal Reserve Bank of Minneapolis. This occasion ranks high among the professional pleasures and honors I have received.

In 1974 I returned to Chicago as a faculty member. In 1980 I became the John Dewey Distinguished Service Professor at Chicago, the position I hold today. Chicago has been a marvellous place for me, as I knew it would be from my student experiences, and I have been stimulated by colleagues and graduate teaching into research on monetary theory, international trade, fiscal policy, and economic growth: all the basic topics in macroeconomics. But the main features of one's approach to science, like the main features of one's personality more generally, are set early on. For me, the influences of my parents, my undergraduate and graduate years at Chicago, and my years at Carnegie Mellon were critical, so it is these influences I have focused on here.

I have had a rewarding personal life, intertwined with the intellectual life that I have described in these notes. Rita Cohen, also an undergraduate at Chicago, and I were married in New York in August, 1959, just before I began graduate studies at Berkeley. Our son Stephen was born in Chicago in September, 1960. Our son Joseph was born in Pittsburgh in January, 1966. Steve is now a securities trader at the Chemical Bank in New York. Joe is a graduate student in History at Boston University, and his wife Tanya is a resident at Beth Israel Hospital in Boston. Rita and I were separated in 1982, and divorced several years later.

Since 1982 I have lived with Nancy Stokey, who is now a colleague of mine at Chicago. We have collaborated in papers on growth theory, public finance, and monetary theory. Our monograph, *Recursive Methods in Economic Dynamics*, was published in 1989. Since then, our collaboration has been a domestic one only . We have an apartment on Chicago's north side, and a summer house on Lake Michigan, in Door County, Wisconsin.

CURRICULUM VITAE

PERSONAL
Birth Date: September 15, 1937; Yakima, WA
Social Security: 531-34-0962
Home Address: 460 West Barry Avenue, Chicago IL 60657

EDUCATION

1959 University of Chicago, B.A., History
1964 University of Chicago, Ph.D., Economics

FELLOWSHIPS AND HONORS

1955–59	Proctor and Gamble Scholarship
1959–60	Woodrow Wilson Fellowship
1961–62	Brookings Fellowship
1963	Woodrow Wilson Dissertation Fellowship
1966–67	Ford Foundation Faculty Fellowship
1981–82	Guggenheim Fellow
1959	Phi Beta Kappa
1976	Fellow, Econometric Society
1980	Fellow, American Academy of Arts and Sciences
1981	Member, National Academy of Sciences
1992	Doctorat Honoris Causa, Universite Paris-Dauphine
1994	Doctorat Honoris Causa, Athens University of Economics and Business
1995	Nobel Prize in Economic Sciences

EMPLOYMENT

1962–63	Lecturer, Department of Economics, University of Chicago
1963–67	Assistant Professor of Economics, Carnegie Institute of Technology
1967–70	Associate Professor of Economics, Carnegie-Mellon University
1970–74	Professor of Economics, Carnegie-Mellon University
1974–75	Ford Foundation Visiting Research Professor of Economics, University of Chicago
1975–80	Professor of Economics, University of Chicago
1981–82	Visiting Professor of Economics, Northwestern
1980–	John Dewey Distinguished Service Professor of Economics, Present University of Chicago

PROFESSIONAL SERVICE

1975–83	Vice-Chairman, Department of Economics, University of Chicago
1986–88	Chairman, Department of Economics, University of Chicago
1972–78	Associate Editor, *Journal of Economic Theory*
1977–	Associate Editor, *Journal of Monetary Economics*
1978–81, 1988–	Editor, *Journal of Political Economy*
1979–82	Member, Executive Committee, American Economic Association
1982–84	Member, Council, Econometric Society
1987–	Vice-President, American Economic Association
1991–95	Member, Council, American Academy of Arts and Science
1995	Second Vice-President, Econometric Society

INVITED LECTURES

1980 Marion O'Kellie McKay Lecture, University of Pittsburgh
1980 Journal of Money, Credit and Banking Lecture, Ohio State University
1985 Marshall Lectures, Cambridge, England
1985 David Horowitz Lectures, Jerusalem and Tel-Aviv, Israel
1985 Yrjo Jahnsson Lectures, Helsinki, Finland
1985 W.A. Mackintosh Lecture, Queens University, Canada
1986 Carl Snyder Memorial Lecture, University of California at Santa Barbara
1986 Chung-Hua Lecture, Taipei, Republic of China
1987 Lionel McKenzie Lecture, University of Rochester
1989 Hicks Lecture, Oxford University
1991 Harry Johnson Lecturer, Royal Economic Society
1991 Fisher-Schultz Lecture, Econometric Society, Cambridge, England

BOOKS

"Substitution Between Labor and Capital in U.S. Manufacturing; 1929–1958," unpublished University of Chicago doctoral dissertation.
"Capital-Labor Substitution in U.S. Manufacturing," in A.C. Harberger and M.J. Bailey, eds., *The Taxation of income from Capital*, Washington: The Brookings Institution, 1969.
"Real Wages, Employment and Inflation" (with L.A. Rapping), in E.S. Phelps, et al., *The New Microeconomics in Employment and Inflation Theory*, New York: W.W. Norton, 1970.
Rational Expectations and Econometric Practice, co-editor with Thomas J. Sargent, Minneapolis: University of Minnesota Press, 1981.
Studies in Business-Cycle Theory. Cambridge: MIT Press, 1981.
Models of Business Cycles, 1985 Yrjo Jahnsson Lectures, Oxford, England: Basil Blackwell.
Recursive Methods in Economic Dynamics (with Nancy L. Stokey and Edward C. Prescott). Cambridge: Harvard University Press, 1989.

ARTICLES

"Notes on Estimated Aggregate Quarterly Consumption Functions" (with Z. Griliches, G.S. Maddala, and N. Wallace), *Econometrica*, 1962.
"Optimal Investment Policy and the Flexible Accelerator," *International Economic Review*, 1967.
"Tests of a Capital-Theoretic Model of Technological Change," *Review of Economic Studies*, 1967.
"Adjustment Costs and the Theory of Supply," *Journal of Political Economy*, 1967.
"Estimation and Inference for Linear Models in which Subsets of the Dependent Variable are Constrained" (with T. McGuire, J. Farley and W. Ring), *Journal of the American Statistical Association*, 1968.
"Real Wages, Employment, and Inflation" (with L. Rapping), *Journal of Political Economy*, 1969.
"Price Expectations and the Phillips Curve" (with L. Rapping), *American Economic Review*, 1969.
"Capacity, Overtime and Empirical Production Functions, *American Economic Review*, 1970
"Investment under Uncertainty" (with Edward C. Prescott), *Econometrica*, 1971.
"Optimal Management of a research and Development Project," *Management Science*, 1971.
"A Note on Price Systems in Infinite Dimensional Space" (with Edward C. Prescott), *International Economic Review*, 1972.
"Expectations and the Neutrality of Money, *Journal of Economic Theory*, 1972.
"Unemployment in the Great Depression: Is There a Full Explanation?" (with L. Rapping), *Journal of Political Economy*, 1972.
"Some International Evidence on Output-Inflation Trade-Offs," *American Economic Review*, 1973

"Econometric Testing of the Natural Rate Hypothesis," in Otto Eckstein, ed., *The Econometrics of Price Determination Conference*, Washington, 1972.

"Equilibrium Search and Unemployment" (with Edward C. Prescott), *Journal of Economic Theory*, 1974; reprinted in Diamond and Rothschild, eds., *Uncertainty in Economics: A Book of Readings*, 1974.

"Econometric Policy Evaluation: A Critique," in K. Brunner and A. Meltzer, eds., *The Phillips Curve and Labor Markets*, North Holland, 1975.

"An Equilibrium Model of the Business Cycle," *Journal of Political Economy*, 1975.

"Understanding Business Cycles," in K. Brunner and A. Meltzer, eds., *Stabilization of the Domestic and International Economy*, North Holland, 1977. Carnegie-Rochester Conference Serieson Public Policy, Vol 5, a supplementary series to the *Journal of Monetary Economics.*

"Asset Prices in an Exchange Economy," *Econometrica* 46 (1978): 1429–45.

"On the Size Distribution of Business Firms," *Bell Journal of Economics* (1978): 508–23.

"Unemployment Policy," *American Economic Review* 68 (1978): 353–57.

"After Keynesian Macroeconometrics" (with T.J. Sargent), in *After the Phillips Curve*, Federal Reserve Bank of Boston, Conference Series No. 19: 49–72; reprinted in the Federal Reserve Bank of Minneapolis *Quarterly Review* 3 (1979): 1–6.

"Rules, Discretion and the Role of the Economic Advisor," in Stanley Fischer, ed., *Rational Expectations and Economic Policy*, Chicago: University of Chicago Press for the NBER, 1980

"Equilibrium in a Pure Currency Economy," in John H. Karaken and Neil Wallace, eds., *Models of Monetary Economics*, Minneapolis: Federal Reserve Bank of Minneapolis, 1980 and in *Economic Inquiry*, 1980.

"Two Illustrations of the Quantity Theory of Money," *American Economic Review*, 1970 (1980): 1005–14.

"Methods and Problems in Business Cycle Theory," *Journal of Money, Credit and Banking* 12 (1980): 696–717.

"Tobin and Monetarism: A Review Article," *Journal of Economic Literature*, 19 (1981): 558–67.

"Interest Rates and Currency Prices In A Two-Country World," *Journal of Monetary Economics* 10 (1982): 335–60.

"Distributed Lags and Optimal Investment Policy," in Lucas and Sargent, *op. cit.*

"Optimal Investment with Rational Expectations," in Lucas and Sargent, *op. cit.*

"Optimal Growth with Many Consumers" (with Nancy L. Stokey), *Journal of Economic Theory* 32 (1984).

"Optimal Fiscal and Monetary Policy in an Economy Without Capital," (with Nancy L. Stokey), *Journal of Monetary Economics* 12 (1983): 55–94.

"Money in a Theory of Finance." in K. Brunner and A. Meltzer, eds., *Essays on Macroeconomic Implications of Financial and Labor Markets and Political Processes*, North-Holland, 1984. Carnegie Rochester Series on Public Policy, Vol. 21, a supplementary series to the *Journal of Monetary Economics.*

"Principles of Fiscal and Monetary Policy," *Journal of Monetary Economics* 17 (1986).

"Adaptive Behavior and Economic Theory," *Journal of Business* 59 (1986): S401–S426.

"Money and Interest in a Cash-In-Advance Economy," (with Nancy L. Stokey), *Econometrica* 55 (1987): 491–514

"On the Mechanics of Economic Development," *Journal of Monetary Economics* 22 (1988): 3–42.

"Money Demand in the United States: A Quantitative Review," *Carnegie-Rochester Conference Series on Public Policy* 29 (1988).

"Liquidity and Interest Rates," *Journal of Economic Theory* 50 (1990): 237–264.

"Why Doesn't Capital Flow from Rich to Poor Countries?" *American Economic Review* 80 (1990): 92–96.

"Supply Side Economics: An Analytical Review," *Oxford Economic Papers* 42 (1990): 293–316.

"On Efficient Distribution with Private Information," (with Andrew G. Atkeson), *Review of Economic Studies*, 59 (1992): 427–453.

"On Efficiency and Distribution," *Economic Journal* 102 (1992): 233–247.
"Making a Miracle," *Econometrica* 61 (1993): 251–272.
"Review of Milton Friedman and Anna J. Schwartz's 'A Monetary History of the United States, 1867–1960'," *Journal of Monetary Economics* 34 (1994): 5–16.
"Efficiency and Equality in a Simple Model of Efficient Unemployment Insurance," (with Andrew G. Atkeson) *Journal of Economic Theory* 66 (1995): 64–88.
"Review of Robert Skidelsky, 'John Maynard Keynes: Hopes Betrayed, 1883–1920' and 'John Maynard Keynes: The Economist as Savior'," *Journal of Modern History* 67 (1995): 914–17.

WORKING PAPERS
"Constant Returns to Scale and the Measurement of Technological Change," presented at the Conference on Technological Change, Philadelphia, 1966.
"Real Effects of Monetary Shocks in an Economy with Sequential Purchases." (with Michael Woodford), 1992.
"On the Welfare Cost of Inflation," 1994.

MONETARY NEUTRALITY

Prize Lecture, December 7, 1995

by

ROBERT E. LUCAS, JR *

University of Chicago, USA

INTRODUCTION

The work for which I have received this prize was part of an effort to understand how changes in the conduct of monetary policy can influence inflation, employment, and production. So much thought has been devoted to this question and so much evidence is available that one might reasonably assume that it had been solved long ago. But this is not the case: It had not been solved in the 1970s when I began my work on it, and even now this question has not been given anything like a fully satisfactory answer. In this lecture I will try to clarify what it is about the problem of bringing available evidence to bear on the assessment of different monetary policies that makes it so difficult, and to review the progress that has been made toward solving it in the last two decades.

From the beginnings of modern monetary theory, in David Hume's marvelous essays of 1752, *Of Money* and *Of Interest*, conclusions about the effect of changes in money have seemed to depend critically on the way in which the change is effected. In formulating the doctrine that we now call the quantity theory of money, Hume stressed the units-change aspect of changes in the money stock, and the irrelevance of such changes to the behavior of rational people. "It is indeed evident," he wrote in *Of Money*, "that money is nothing but the representation of labour and commodities, and serves only as a method of rating or estimating them. Where coin is in greater plenty, as a greater quantity of it is required to represent the same quantity of goods, it can have no effect, either good or bad...any more than it would make an alteration on a merchant's books, if, instead of the Arabian method of notation, which requires few characters, he should make use of the Roman, which requires a great many." (p.28)[1]

He returns to this idea that changes in the quantity of money are just units

* I thank Nancy Stokey for invaluable discussion and criticism. I am also very grateful for comments from William Brock, John Cochrane, Milton Friedman, Anil Kashyap, Randall Kroszner, Casey Mulligan, Sherwin Rosen, Allen Sanderson, Thomas Sargent, John Taylor, Neil Wallace, Warren Weber, and Jörgen Weibull.

[1] All page references to Hume's essays are to Hume (1970). I have left the spelling as in the original and modernized the punctuation.

changes in *Of Interest:* "Were all the gold in England annihilated at once, and one and twenty shillings substituted in the place of every guinea, would money be more plentiful or interest lower? No surely: We should only use silver instead of gold. Were gold rendered as common as silver, and silver as common as copper, would money be more plentiful or interest lower? We may assuredly give the same answer. Our shillings would then be yellow, and our halfpence white, and we should have no guineas. No other difference would ever be observed, no alteration on commerce, manufactures, navigation, or interest, unless we imagine that the color of money is of any consquence." (p. 47)

These are two of Hume's statements of what we now call the quantity theory of money: the doctrine that changes in the number of units of money in circulation will have proportional effects on all prices that are stated in money terms, and no effect at all on anything real, on how much people work or on the goods they produce or consume. Notice, though, that there is something a little magical about the way that changes in money come about in Hume's examples. All the gold in England gets "annihilated." Elsewhere he asks us to "suppose that, by miracle, every man in Great Britain should have five pounds slipt into his pocket in one night." (p. 51) Money changes in reality do not occur by such means. Is this just a matter of exposition, or should we be concerned about it? This turns out to be a crucial question. In fact, Hume writes: "When any quantity of money is imported into a nation, it is not at first dispersed into many hands but is confined to the coffers of a few persons, who immediately seek to employ it to advantage. Here are a set of manufacturers or merchants, we shall suppose, who have received returns of gold and silver for goods which they have sent to Cadiz. They are thereby enabled to employ more workmen than formerly, who never dream of demanding higher wages, but are glad of employment from such good paymasters. [The artisan]...carries his money to the market, where he finds every thing at the same price as formerly, but returns with greater quantity and of better kinds for the use of his family. The farmer and gardener, finding that all their commodities are taken off, apply themselves with alacrity to raising more...It is easy to trace the money in its progress through the whole commonwealth, where we shall find that it must first quicken the diligence of every individual before it encrease the price of labour." (p. 38)

Symmetrically, Hume believes that a monetary contraction could induce depression. "There is always an interval before matters be adjusted to their new situation, and this interval is as pernicious to industry when gold and silver are diminishing as it is advantageous when these metals are increasing. The workman has not the same employment from the manufacturer or merchant though he pays the same price for everything in the market. The farmer cannot dispose of his corn and cattle, though he must pay the same rent to his landlord. The poverty, and beggary, and sloth which must ensue are easily foreseen." (p. 40)

Hume makes it clear that he does not view his opinions about the initial effects of monetary expansions as major qualifications to the quantity theory, to his view that "it is of no manner of consequence, with regard to the domestic happiness of a state, whether money be in a greater or less quantity." Perhaps he simply did not see that the irrelevance of units changes from which he deduces the long run neutrality of money has similar implications for the initial reaction to money changes as well. Why, for example, does an early recipient of the new money "find every thing at the same price as formerly." If everyone understands that prices will ultimately increase in proportion to the increase in money, what force stops this from happening right away? Are people committed, perhaps even contractually, to continue to offer goods at the old prices for a time? If so, Hume does not mention it. Are sellers ignorant of the fact that money has increased and a general inflation is inevitable? But Hume claims that the real consequences of money changes are "easy to trace" and "easily foreseen." If so, why do these consequences occur at all?

These questions do not involve mere matters of detail. Hume has deduced the quantity theory of money by purely theoretical reasoning from "that principle of reason" that people act rationally and that this fact is reflected in market-determined quantities and prices. Consistency surely requires at least an attempt to apply these same principles to the analysis of the *initial* effects of a monetary expansion or contraction. I think the fact is that this is just too difficult a problem for an economist equipped with only verbal methods, even someone of Hume's remarkable powers.

This tension between two incompatible ideas: that changes in money are neutral units changes, and that they induce movements in employment and production in the same direction, has been at the center of monetary theory at least since Hume wrote. Though it has not, in my opinion, been fully resolved, important progress has been made on at least two dimensions. The first is a purely theoretical question: Under what assumptions and for what kinds of changes can we expect monetary changes to be *neutral?* (I take this terminology from Don Patinkin's *Money, Interest, and Prices* (1965), the book that introduced so many economists of my cohort to these theoretical issues.) The theoretical equipment we have for sharpening and addressing such questions has been vastly improved since Hume's day, and I will draw on these improvements below. Of at least equal importance, an enormous amount of evidence on money, prices, and production has been accumulated over the past two centuries, and much fruitful thought has been applied to issues of measurement. In the next section, I will examine some of this evidence.

EVIDENCE

It is hard to tell from the essays what evidence Hume actually had in front of him. Certainly he wrote before systematic data on money supplies were collected anywhere in the world, before the invention of price indexes, and long before the invention of national income and product accounting. His development of the quantity theory was based largely on purely theoretical reasoning, though tested informally against his vast historical knowledge, and his belief in short run correlations between changes in money and changes in production was apparently based mainly on his everyday knowledge. (He cites one Mons. du Tot for the assertion that "in the last year of Louis XIV, money was raised three sevenths but prices augmented only one." In a footnote he characterizes his source as "an author of reputation," but feels obliged to "confess that the facts which he advances on other occasions are often so suspicious as to make his authority less in this matter." Even in the eighteenth century, it seems, there were tensions between theorists and econometricians!)

The central predictions of the quantity theory are that, in the long run, money growth should be neutral in its effects on the growth rate of production and should affect the inflation rate on a one-for-one basis. The modifier "long run" is not free of ambiguity, but by any definition the use of data that are heavily averaged over time should isolate only long run effects. Figure 1, taken from McCandless and Weber (1995), plots 30 year (1960-1990) average annual inflation rates against average annual growth rates of M2 over the same 30 year period, for a total of 110 countries. One can see that the points lie roughly on the 45-degree line, as predicted by the quantity theory. The simple correlation between inflation and money growth is .95. The monetary aggregate used in constructing Figure 1 is M2, but nothing important depends on this choice. McCandless and Weber report a simple correlation of .96 if M1 is used, and .92 with M0 (the monetary base). They also report correlations for subsets of their 110 country data set: .96 (with M2) with only OECD countries; .99 with 14 Latin American countries.

It is clear from these data (and from the many other studies that have reached similar conclusions) that the applicability of the quantity theory of money is not limited to currency reforms and magical thought experiments. It applies, with remarkable success, to co-movements in money and prices generated in complicated, real-world circumstances. Indeed, how many specific economic theories can claim empirical success at the level exhibited in Figure 1? Central bankers and even some monetary economists talk knowledgeably of using high interest rates to control inflation, but I know of no evidence from even one economy linking these variables in a useful way, let alone evidence as sharp as that displayed in Figure 1. The kind of monetary neutrality shown in this figure needs to be a central feature of any monetary or macroeconomic theory that claims empirical seriousness.

McCandless and Weber also provide evidence on correlations between money growth and growth in real output, averaged over the 1960–1990 period Figure 2 is their plot for the full 100 country IMF data set. Evidently, there is no relation between these 30-year averages.[2] For examining short term trade-offs, of course, one does not want to use such time-averaged data.

[2] It must be said that the evidence of long run links between money growth and output growth is more mixed than one would infer from Figure 2. McCandless and Weber find a weak positive relation for the OECD economies. Both positive and negative correlations have been found, by other investigators on other data sets.

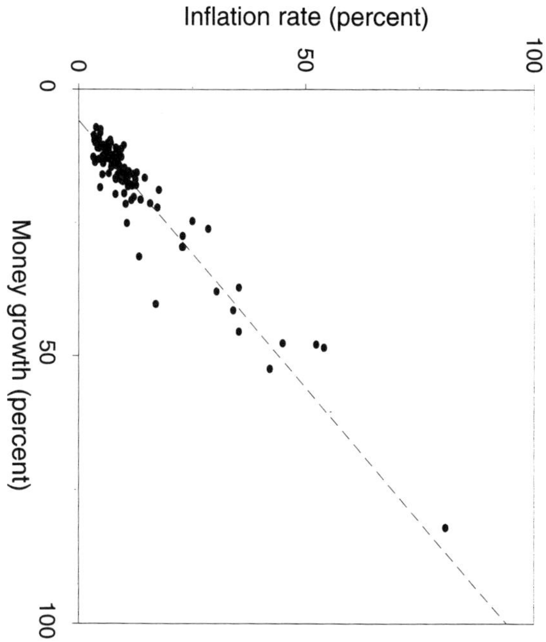

FIGURE 1

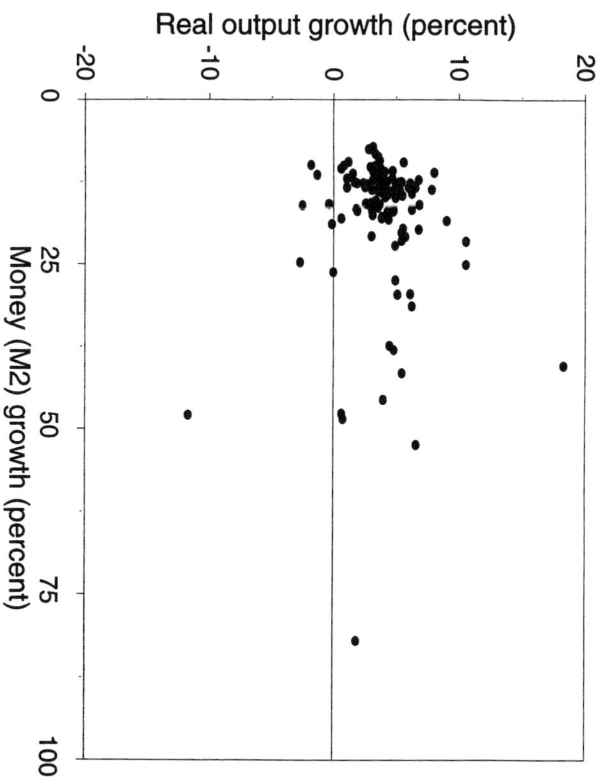

FIGURE 2

Figure 3, taken from Stockman (1996), provides six plots of annual inflation rates against unemployment rates for various sub-periods of the years 1950–1994, for the United States. Panel (f), in the lower right, plots the Phillips curve[3] for the entire period. In this panel, the two variables appear to be completely unrelated. On the other hand, the five panels for subperiods (or at least, for the subperiods since 1960) seem to show a clear, negative relation. But then look at the axes in these six panels! In order to see inflation and unemployment as lying on a negatively sloped curve, one needs to keep shifting the curve.

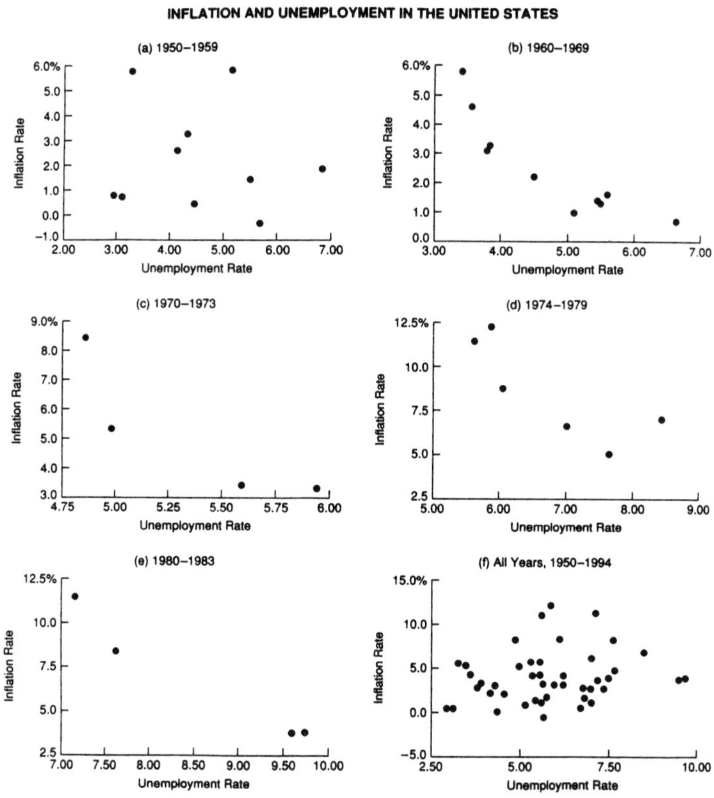

FIGURE 3

Evidence on trade-offs is also marshalled, though in a very different way, in Friedman and Schwartz's (1963) monograph *A Monetary History of the United States*. These authors show that every major depression in the United States over the period 1867–1960 was associated with a large contraction in the money supply, and that every large contraction was associated with a depression. These observations are correlations of a sort, too, but they gain force from the size of the largest contractions. In a period like the post-World

[3] After A.W. Phillips (1958).

War II years in the United States, real output fluctuations are modest enough to be attributable, possibly, to real sources. There is no need to appeal to money shocks to account for these movements. But an event like the Great Depression of 1929–1933 is far beyond anything that can be attributed to shocks to tastes and technology. One needs some other possibilities. Monetary contractions are attractive as the key shocks in the 1929–1933 years, and in other severe depressions, because there do not seem to be any other candidates.

Sargent (1986) also examines large, sudden reductions in rates of money growth (though not reductions in the *levels* of money stocks). In his case, these are the monetary and fiscal reforms that ended four of the post-World War I European hyperinflations. These dramatic reductions in growth rates of the money supply dwarf anything in Friedman and Schwartz or in the post-war data used by McCandless and Weber. Yet as Sargent shows they were not associated with output reductions that were large by historical standards, or possibly by any depressions at all. Sargent goes on to demonstrate the likelihood that these reductions in money growth rates were well anticipated by the people they affected and, because of visible and suitable fiscal reforms, were expected by them to be sustained.

In summary, the prediction that prices respond proportionally to changes in money in the long run, deduced by Hume in 1752 (and by many other theorists, by many different routes, since), has received ample–I would say, decisive–confirmation, in data from many times and places. The observation that money changes induce output changes in the same direction receives confirmation in some data sets, but is hard to see in others. Large scale reductions in money growth can be associated with large scale depressions or, if carried out in the form of a credible reform, with no depression at all.

THEORETICAL RESPONSES

Hume was able to theorize rigorously and, as we have seen, with great empirical success, about comparisons of long run average behavior across economies with different average rates of money growth. For short run purposes, on the other hand, he was obliged to rely on much looser reasoning and rough empirical generalizations. As economic theory evolved in the last century and most of this one, the double standard that characterized Hume's argument was perpetuated. The quantity theoretic "neutrality theorems" were stated with increasing precision and worked through rigorously, using the latest equipment of static general equilibrium theory. The dynamics had a kind of patched-in quality, fitting the facts, but only in a manner that suggests they could equally well fit *any* facts. Patinkin interprets all of monetary theory from Wicksell's *Interest and Prices* (1898) through his own *Money, Interest and Prices* as concerned with processes of adjustment between one quantity-theoretic equilibrium position and another, conceived as outside the framework of general equilibrium theory in a way that seems to me very much at the level of Hume's analysis. The passages on dynamics that I cited from Hume in Section 1 could be slipped into Keynes's *Treatise on Money (1930)* or Hayek's *Monetary Theory and the Trade Cycle (1933)* without inducing any sense of anachronism.

Yet all of these theorists *want* to think in general equilibrium terms, to think of people as maximizing over time, as substituting intertemporally. They resort to disequilibrium dynamics only because the analytical equipment available to them offers no alternative. Even in Hume's scenario, the motives and expectations of economic actors during the transition are described, even rationalized: The adjustment to a new equilibrium is not seen as a purely mechanical *tâtonnement* process, the character of which is determined by forces apart from the producers and consumers of the system. Certainly Wicksell, and I would say Patinkin, too, are trying to think through the way the dynamic adjustment process appears to people as it occurs, to see the actions people take as rational responses to their situations. Though the theoretical formalism on which they draw involves a static equilibrium combined with a mechanical process to describe dynamic adjustments, their verbal descriptions of periods of transition, like Hume's before them, show that they are in fact thinking of people solving intertemporal decision problems.

The intelligence of these attempts to deal theoretically with the real effects of changes in money is still impressive to the modern reader, but only serves to underscore the futility of attempting to talk through hard dynamic problems without any of the equipment of modern mathematical economics. Hayek and Keynes and their contemporaries were willing to make assumptions and to set out something like a model, but they were simply not able to work out the predictions of their own theories.

The depression of the 1930s shifted attention away from the subtle problems of monetary neutrality, and toward the potential of monetary policy for short run stimulus. Keynes's *General Theory (1936)* was one product of this change of focus. Another was Tinbergen's (1939) development of an explicit statistical model of the U.S. economy. Tinbergen's model and its immediate successors made little or no contact with earlier traditions in monetary theory, but in the atmosphere of the 1930s and 40s this was perhaps an advantage, and it fit well with the revolutionary rhetoric of Keynes's book. Economic theory aside, the macroeconometric models that evolved from Tinbergen's work had two important advantages over all earlier macroeconomic theory. They were mathematically explicit and so could be estimated from and tested against data in a much more disciplined way than could earlier theories. Moreover, they could be simulated to yield quantitative answers to policy questions. It was these features that excited younger researchers and had such a dramatic influence on future developments in the field.

By the 1960s, then, two very different styles of macroeconomic theory, both claiming the title of Keynesian economics, co-existed. There were attempts at a unified monetary and value theory, like Patinkin's, based on extensions of static general equilibrium theory to accommodate money, combined with some kind of *tâtonnement* process to provide some dynamics. These theories were developed with great attention to earlier monetary theory and to developments in economic theory more generally, but they lacked the operational character of the macroeconometric models: No one could tell exactly what their predictions were, or what normative implications they carried. On the other hand, there were macroeconometric models that could be fit to data and simulated to yield quantitative answers to policy questions, but whose relation to microeconomic theory and classical monetary theory was unclear.

Virtually no one at the time regarded this situation as healthy. Everyone paid lip service to the idea of unification of micro- and macroeconomics, or of discovering the microeconomic "foundations" of macroeconomic theories, and a vast amount of creative and valuable economics, focused on intertemporal decision problems, was inspired by this goal. The work of Friedman (1957) and Modigliani and Brumberg (1954) on consumption, Eisner and Strotz (1963) and Jorgenson (1963) on investment in physical capital, Becker (1962) and Ben Porath (1967) on investment in human capital, Baumol (1952), Tobin (1956), Meltzer (1963), and Brunner and Meltzer (1963) on money demand, all contributed. Mathematically inclined economists who entered the profession in the 1960s were drawn to methods for studying intertemporal decision problems, the calculus of variations, the theory of optimal control, and Bellman's (1957) dynamic programming. Work on optimal growth by Cass (1965), and Uzawa (1964) was followed by applications of similar methods to a variety of problems in all subfields of economics. In these applications, the dynamics were an integral part of the theory, not tacked-on *tâtonnement* processes. When Leonard Rapping and I began our collaboration on the study of labor markets over the business cycle, (Lucas and Rapping (1969)), we thought of these studies of individual intertemporal decision problems as models of what we wanted to do.[4]

The prevailing strategy for macroeconomic modeling in the early 1960s held that the individual or sectoral models arising out of this intertemporal theorizing could then simply be combined in a single model, the way Keynes and Tinbergen and their successors assembled a consumption function, an investment function, and so on into a model of an entire economy. But models of individual decisions over time necessarily involve expected, future prices. Some microeconomic analyses treated these prices as known; others imputed adaptive forecasting rules to maximizing firms and households. However it was done, though, the "church supper" models assembled from such individual components implied behavior of *actual* equilibrium prices and incomes that bore no relation to, and were in general grossly inconsistent with, the price expectations that the theory imputed to individual agents.

As intertemporal elements and expectations came to play an increasingly

[4] See Phelps *et al.* (1970) for several similarly motivated studies.

explicit and important role, this modeling inconsistency became more and more glaring. John Muth's (1961) "Rational Expectations and the Theory of Price Movements" focused on this inconsistency, and showed how it could be removed by taking into account the influences of prices, including *future* prices, on quantities and *simultaneously* the effects of quantities on equilibrium prices.[5] The principle of rational expectations he proposed thus forces the modeler toward a market equilibrium point of view, although it took some time before a style of thinking that recognized this fact had a major effect on macroeconomic modeling.

Other considerations reinforced a move in the same direction. In the late 1960s, Friedman (1968) and Phelps (1968) saw, by thinking through the issue at a general equilibrium level, that there could be no long run Phillips curve tradeoff between inflation and real output. But such long run tradeoffs were implicit in all of the macroeconometric models of the day, and the econometric methods that were in standard use at that time seemed to reject the Friedman-Phelps natural rate hypothesis. This conflict led to a re-thinking of the theoretical basis of these statistical tests, and the discovery of serious difficulties with them. Sargent (1971) and Lucas (1972), (1976) showed that the conventional rejections of the natural rate hypothesis depended critically on *irrational* expectations, or to put the same point backward, that if one assumed rational expectations these tests settled nothing. It seemed clear that it was necessary to put macroeconomics on a general equilibrium basis that incorporated rational expectations.

GENERAL EQUILIBRIUM MACROECONOMICS

By the 1960s, two closely related general equilibrium frameworks were in fact already available for thinking about economic dynamics. One was the mathematical model of general equilibrium, developed by Hicks (1939), Arrow (1951), Debreu (1954), and McKenzie (1954), in which the commodity vector is defined to include dated claims to goods, possibly made contingent on random events. Prescott and I (1971) adopted this framework for the construction of a rational expectations model of investment in a competitive industry, taking a stochastically shifting demand curve (rather than prices) as given. And, in a paper that was to set the research agenda for the next decade, Kydland and Prescott (1982) utilized a version of the stochastic growth optimal growth model of Brock and Mirman (1972) as an operational model of a competitive economy undergoing recurrent business cycles, induced by shifts in the technology. This turned out to be a tremendously fruitful idea, whose potential is still being realized. But such a model without money is obviously not suited to the study of Hume's problem. Economists

[5] Eugene Fama's (1965) theory of efficient markets was another application of economic reasoning directly to the behavior of *equilibrium* prices, in a setting in which stochastic shocks were an intrinsic part of the economic model.

who believed that monetary forces were at the center of the business cycle needed to look elsewhere.

A second general equilibrium framework, due to Samuelson (1958), was also available, and seemed better suited to the study of monetary questions. That paper introduced a deceptively simple example of an economy in which money with no direct use in either consumption or production nonetheless plays an essential role in economic life. I used this model in my (1972) paper in an attempt to show how monetary neutrality might be reconciled with the appearance of a short-term stimulus from a monetary expansion. The model is so simple and flexible that it can be used to illustrate many issues. I will introduce a version of it here, along with enough notation to permit discussion of some interesting details.

In Samuelson's model, people live for two periods only, so that the on-going economy is always populated by two age cohorts, one young and the other old. Here I assume a constant population, so that per capita and economy-wide magnitudes can be used interchangeably. At each year's end, the old die, the young become old, and a new young group arrives. It is important for my purposes (as it was for Samuelson's) to assume that there is no family structure in this economy: no inheritances and no financial support by one cohort for another. Suppose that a young person in this economy can work and produce goods, while an old person likes to consume goods but has no ability to produce them. Denote a person's two objects of choice by the pair (c, n), where n is units of labor supplied when young and c is units of the good consumed when old. Assume that everyone's preferences over these two goods are given by

$$U(c) - n.$$

Assume a labor-only technology in which one unit of labor yields one unit of goods.

If the good were storable, everyone would produce in his youth and carry the production over for his own later consumption, solving the problem

$$\max_n \,[U(n) - n]. \tag{1}$$

Call the solution to this problem n^*. But I will assume that the good cannot be stored, so that any individual acting purely on his own *cannot* produce for his own pleasure.[6] Acting alone, the best one can do is to enjoy leisure when young and never consume anything. Clearly society as a whole should be able to do *much* better than that, by somehow inducing the young to produce for the consumption of their *contemporary* old. Some institution is needed to achieve this.

[6] In fact, Cass and Yaari (1966) show that even if storage is possible the autarchic allocation can be improved upon, as it ties up goods in inventory permanently and unnecessarily.

A social security system may be one real world instance of such an institution. (Or it may not: Everything hinges on the realism of the assumption of no family structure.) As Samuelson noted, a monetary system may be another such institution, for one can view the failure of the autarchic allocation as arising from the absence of the double coincidence of wants that barter exchange requires. Those who wish to consume goods, the old, have nothing to offer in return to those who are able to produce, the young. But suppose there were some paper money in circulation, initially in the hands of the old. The old would offer this cash to the young, in exchange for goods, establishing a market price of some kind. Would the young accept these tokens–intrinsically useless, in Wallace's (1980) terms–and hence keep the value of tokens in terms of goods at any level above zero? Maybe not: This possibility can certainly not be ruled out. If the young were willing to produce goods in exchange for fiat money, it would have to be because they hoped to be able to trade the money they received for goods in their own old age.

The interesting thing about Samuelson's example is that this second scenario cannot be ruled out. It is possible, though by no means necessary, that the money in this economy will circulate forever, being exchanged over and over again for goods. If this exchange takes place in a single competitive spot market and the price p is established, then a young person who begins with no money and works n units will acquire pn units of cash. If he spends it all on goods next period, this yields $(pn)/p = n$ units of consumption. Thus everyone solves the problem (1). If the money supply is constant and evenly distributed over the old in the amount m per person, the equilibrium price will also be constant, at the level $p = m/n^*$. Evidently, this equilibrium is quantity-theoretic in Hume's sense: if m is (somehow) increased, the equilibrium price level will be increased in the same proportion, and quantities of labor and production will not be affected at all.

When we consider monetary changes that differ from once-and-for-all changes in the money *stock,* however, the issue of neutrality becomes more complicated. To see this, suppose that we replace the assumption of a constant money supply with the assumption that the quantity of money grows at a constant percentage rate. We need to be explicit (another point in favor of Samuelson's model) about the way the new money gets into the system, and it matters how this is done. Assume, to begin with, that each young person receives an equal share of the newly created money, in between his youth and old age, and that the size of this addition to his cash is independent of the amount he has earned by working. Then if the money supply is m and is to be augmented by the lump sum transfer $m(x-1)$, each young person now solves

$$\max_n \left[U\left(\frac{pn + (x-1)m}{p'}\right) - n \right], \tag{2}$$

where p is the price at which he sells goods, today, and p' is the price at which he buys goods, tomorrow. The first order condition for this problem is

$$U'(\frac{pn+(x-1)m}{p'})\frac{p}{p'}=1. \tag{3}$$

In order to work out a rational expectations equilibrium for this model, we exploit the observation that the only thing that changes over time in this situation is the money supply, which is simply multiplied by the known factor x in every period. It seems natural, then, to seek an equilibrium in which the price level is proportional to the money stock, $p = km$ for some constant k, and in which labor is constant at some value $\hat{n}$. In such an equilibrium, the constant k will evidently be $1/\hat{n}$. Tomorrow's price is then $p' = kmx = mx/\hat{n}$. Inserting all this information into the first order condition (3), one obtains

$$U'(\hat{n}) = x. \tag{4}$$

In this circumstance, then, the price level will increase between periods at exactly the rate of growth of the money supply. The equilibrium level of employment $\hat{n}$ will, from (4), be a decreasing function of the rate of money growth.[7]

The quantity-theoretic predictions we saw confirmed in Figures 1 and 2 would also be confirmed in this hypothetical world. But note that this does *not* mean that the rate of money growth (and the equal rate of price inflation) are merely units changes, of no consequence to anyone. The faster money grows, the more important is the overnight transfer, relative to the cash accumulated through working. The monetary transfers dilute the return from working. Goods production declines as the inflation rate rises, and everyone is made worse off. This is a non-neutrality of money, a real effect of a money change (some would prefer to call it a real effect of the fiscal transfer that is used to bring the money change about) but this effect is obviously not the stimulating effect of a monetary expansion that Hume discusses. In this example, inflation does not "quicken the diligence of every individual." It is a kind of tax that deadens diligence by reducing its real return.

This inflation tax is an issue of the first importance, I think, and its effects are captured in a useful way by the theoretical example I have just worked through. But further study of the inflation tax is not going to bring us any closer to an understanding of the tradeoff that Hume thought he observed, and that so many others have seen since. Let us then get the inflation tax out of the picture by assuming that the fiscal transfers via which the money supply expands are made in proportion to the balances one has earned through working. That is, if one works n units, one receives the transfer $pn\,(x-1)$, not $m\,(x-1)$, and thus has pnx to spend next period. In this situation, the first order condition (4) becomes

[7] Jörgen Weibull points out to me that one could obtain a version of this example in which equilibrium employment is an *increasing* function of the money shock x by assuming that only some of the young receive the entire transfer, and by making the right assumptions about the curvature of the function U.

$$U'(\hat{n}) = 1$$

independent of x, and $\hat{n}$ is always at its efficient level n^*: there is no inflation tax. These proportional transfers are just an assumption of convenience, but one that will simplify the discussion of some hard questions.

Now how might this overlapping generations economy be modified so that a monetary expansion will act as a stimulus to production? One might think this could be achieved by replacing the assumption that the transfer variable x is constant with the assumption that it is drawn independently each period from some fixed probability distribution. Evidently, if the current period realization is known to everyone, this won't change anything. What is perhaps less obvious, but equally true, is that even if the transfer realization is known directly only to the old, it will be revealed perfectly to the young by the equilibrium price that it induces. As in the constant money growth example we worked through above, prices are determined by m and x. What else is there in this context? If m is known and p is observed, as of course it must be in competitive trading, then one can infer the value of x.

In order to get an output effect from a monetary shock, then, it is not enough simply to introduce uncertainty. We need to imagine that the exchange of money for goods takes place in some manner other than in a centralized Walrasian market. In my (1972) paper, I assumed that exchange occurs in two markets, each with a different number of goods suppliers. In this circumstance, a given price increase can signal a supplier that the money transfer x is large, in which case he wants to treat it like a units change and not respond, or it can mean that there are only a few suppliers in his market, in which case he wants to treat it like a real shift in his favor and respond by producing more. The best the individual can do, given his limited information, is to hedge. On average, then, labor supply and production are an increasing function $f(x)$ of the monetary transfer. Equilibrium prices, $mx/f(x)$, move in proportion to m which is known to all traders, but increase less than proportionally with the transfer x. By next period, the transfer x is known, and prices complete their proportional increase, but not without a transition during which production is increased.

The resemblance of this scenario to the one I quoted from Hume in my introduction seems clear. In an important sense the new scenario is an improvement, since in place of the unexplained errors of judgment or ignorance that lie at the center of Hume's account, this one rests on an assumption that people lack complete information. But perhaps this only pushes the question back one step: *Why is it* that people cannot obtain that last bit of information that would enable them to diagnose price movements accurately? In reality, up-to-date information on the money supply does not seem all that hard to come by.

Let us step back from the specifics of this particular, information-based version of Hume's scenario, and consider the possibilities more abstractly. Assume simply that old and young engage in some kind of trading game, to which the old bring the cash m obtained in the previous period's trading.[8] Either before, or perhaps during, the play of this game, the old receive a proportional transfer that totals x. Let each young person and each old person select a trading strategy. Notice that the strategy of a young person can depend on m, and the strategy of an old person can depend on m and x. On the basis of these choices, suppose a Nash equilibrium is reached under which each young person supplies some amount of labor and ends up with some amount of cash. I will restrict attention to symmetric equilibria, so that in equilibrium each young person ends up with mx dollars. Each young person also ends up supplying $f(m, x)$ units of labor, and this quantity is also the equilibrium consumption of each old person, where the notation is chosen to emphasize that m and x are the only state variables in this model. Different specifications of the trading game will have different implications for this *outcome function* f.

Now assume that before the play of such a game begins, the money stock m is evenly distributed over the old; that everyone, young and old, knows what it is; and that everyone knows how transfers occur — the rules of this trading game. In these circumstances, changes in m must be neutral units changes, so that f is constant with respect to m and can be written $f(m, x) = f(x)$ for some function f. Given this function f, the average price of goods is just the money stock divided by production, or $p = mx/f(x)$. In competitive trading, f is a constant function, so price is proportional to mx, where x is known, but in many other trading games the function f will vary with the value x. In this notation, rationalizing a trade-off of the type described by Hume translates into constructing a game that rationalizes an increasing function $f(x)$.

One such game (though that equilibrium was not quite symmetric) was described in Lucas (1972). There, the response in output was based on suppliers' imperfect information about the transfer x. But at this level of abstraction there are many other non-competitive trading games that have outcomes with these same features. Some of these achieve this end by assuming that some nominal prices are set in advance, as in Fischer (1977), Phelps and Taylor (1977), Taylor (1979), or Svensson (1986). Others postulate games in which the transfer is only gradually revealed, as in Eden (1994), Williamson (1995), or Lucas and Woodford (1994). All of these papers offer rationalizations of a short-run monetary non-neutrality in the sense of an increasing function $f(x)$, though of course in quite different ways. In an important sense, then, Hume's paradox has been resolved: We have a wide variety of theories that reconcile long-run monetary neutrality with a short-run trade-off. All of them (and any other game that fits into the formalism above) carry the implication that anticipated money changes will not stimulate production and that at least some unanticipated changes can do so.[9]

Does it matter which of these rationales is appealed to? The answer to this

[8] This point of departure has long been advocated by Shubik. See, for example, Shubik (1980).

[9] Of course, this conclusion requires the usual *caveat* about the inflation tax.

harder question must depend on what our purposes are. Any of these models leads to the distinction between anticipated and unanticipated changes in money, the distinction that seems to me the central lesson of the theoretical work of the 1970s. On the other hand, none of these models deduces the function f from assumptions on technology and preferences alone. Of course f depends on such factors, but it also depends on the specific assumptions one makes about the strategies available to the players, the timing of moves, how information is revealed, and so on. Moreover, these specifics are all, for the sake of tractability, highly unrealistic and stylized: We cannot choose among them on the basis of descriptive realism. Consequently, we have no reason to believe that the function f is invariant under changes in monetary policy–it is just a kind of Phillips curve, after all–and no reliable way to break it down into well understood components.

Theories that emphasized the distinction between anticipated and unanticipated money shocks led to a variety of statistical tests. Sargent (1976) interpreted the prediction that anticipated money would have no real effects as the hypothesis that money would not "cause," in the sense of Granger (1969) and Sims (1972), changes in unemployment rates, and he found that this prediction was confirmed for U.S. time series. Barro (1977) used residuals from regressions of M1 on its own lagged values as measures of unanticipated money shocks, and concluded that the unemployment rate responded to these shocks but did not respond to current and lagged M1.[10] The signal processing feature of the model of Lucas (1972) implied that the magnitude of a money multiplier should decline as the variance of money changes increased. This prediction was confirmed in the cross-country comparisons reported in Lucas (1973) and Alberro (1981), and by the much more extensive results reported in Kormendi and Meguire (1984).

In the models in Lucas (1972) and (1973), trade takes place in competitive markets, though these markets are incomplete, so any real effects of monetary policy need to work through movements in prices. The tests described in the last paragraph do not use data on prices and so do not test this prediction. Other econometric work that did require money shocks to be transmitted through price movements was much less favorable. Estimates in Sargent (1976) and in Leiderman (1979) indicated that only small fractions of output variability can be accounted for by unexpected price movements. Though the evidence seems to show that monetary surprises have real effects, they do not seem to be transmitted through price surprises, as in Lucas (1972).[11]

[10] Whether this work in fact tests implications of the model in Lucas (1972) is questioned in King (1981).

[11] Wallace (1992) develops a variation of the Lucas (1972) model in which real shocks need not be perfectly negatively correlated across markets (so that real shocks can be positive in the aggregate). In this more general model, money shocks can induce output movements in the same direction (but not perfectly correlated) and the inflation-output correlation can have either sign. The evidence in Sargent (1976) and Leiderman (1979) is not decisive against such a variation.

CONCLUSIONS

The main finding that emerged from the research of the 1970s is that anticipated changes in money growth have very different effects from unanticipated changes. Anticipated monetary expansions have inflation tax effects and induce an inflation premium on nominal interest rates, but they are not associated with the kind of stimulus to employment and production that Hume described. Unanticipated monetary expansions, on the other hand, can stimulate production as, symmetrically, unanticipated contractions can induce depression. The importance of this distinction between anticipated and unanticipated monetary changes is an implication of every one of the many different models, all using rational expectations, that were developed during the 1970s to account for short-term trade-offs. This distinction is consistent with the long-run evidence displayed in Figures 1 and 2, with the year-to-year changes displayed in Figure 3, with Friedman and Schwartz's account of depressions in the United States, and with Sargent's account of the ending of the European hyperinflations.

The discovery of the central role of the distinction between anticipated and unanticipated money shocks resulted from the attempts, on the part of many researchers, to formulate mathematically explicit models that were capable of addressing the issues raised by Hume. But I think it is clear that none of the specific models that captured this distinction in the 1970s can now be viewed as a satisfactory theory of business cycles. Perhaps in part as a response to the difficulties with the monetary-based business cycle models of the 1970s, much recent research has followed the lead of Kydland and Prescott (1982) and emphasized the effects of purely real forces on employment and production.[12] This research has shown how general equilibrium reasoning can add discipline to the study of an economy's distributed lag response to shocks, as well as to the study of the nature of the shocks themselves. More recently, many have tried to re-introduce monetary features into these models, and I expect much future work in this direction.

But who can say how the macroeconomic theory of the future will develop, any more than anyone in 1960 could have foreseen the developments I have described in this lecture? All one can be sure of is that progress will result from the continued effort to formulate explicit theories that fit the facts, and that the best and most practical macroeconomics will make use of developments in basic economic theory.

REFERENCES

1. Alberro, José 1981. "The Lucas Hypothesis on the Phillips Curve: Further International Evidence." *Journal of Monetary Economics*, 7: 239–250.
2. Arrow, Kenneth J. 1951. "An Extension of the Basic Theorems of Classical Welfare Economics," in *Proceedings of the Second Berkeley Symposium on Mathematical Statistics and Probability*. J. Neyman, ed. (Berkeley: University of California Press): 507–532.

[12] The approach of directly testing the implications of Euler equations, initiated in Hall (1978) and advanced by methods described in Hansen (1982), has also been productively pursued.

3. Barro, Robert J. 1977. "Unanticipated Money Growth and Unemployment in the United States." *American Economic Review*, 67: 101–115.
4. Baumol, William J. 1952. "The Transactions Demand for Cash: An Inventory-Theoretic Aproach." *Quarterly Journal of Economics*, 66: 545–556.
5. Becker, Gary S. 1962. "Investment in Human Capital: a Theoretical Analysis." *Journal of Political Economy,*, 70: 9–49.
6. Bellman, Richard X. 1957. *Dynamic Programming* (Princeton: Princeton University Press).
7. Ben-Porath, Yoram. 1967. "The Production of Human Capital and the Life Cycle of Earnings." *Journal of Political Economy*, 75:352–365.
8. Brock, William A., and Leonard J. Mirman. 1972. "Optimal Economic Growth and Uncertainty: the Discounted Case." *Journal of Economic Theory*, 4: 479–513.
9. Brunner, Karl, and Allan H. Meltzer. 1963. "Predicting Velocity: Implications for Theory and Policy." *Journal of Finance*, 18.
10. Cass, David. 1965. "Optimum Growth in an Aggregative Model of Capital Accumulation." *Review of Economic Studies*, 32: 233–240.
11. Cass, David, and Menahem E. Yaari. 1966. "A Re-examination of the Pure Consumption Loans Model." *Journal of Political Economy*, 74: 353–367.
12. Debreu, Gerard. 1959. *The Theory of Value* (New Haven: Yale University Press).
13. Eden, Benjamin. 1994. "The Adjustment of Prices to Monetary Shocks When Trade is Uncertain and Sequential." *Journal of Political Economy*, 102: 493–509.
14. Eisner, Robert, and Robert Strotz. 1963. "Determinants of Business Investment," in Commission on Money and Credit. *Impacts of Monetary Policy*. (Englewood Cliffs: Prentice-Hall).
15. Fama, Eugene F. 1965. "The Behavior of Stock-Market Prices." *Journal of Business*, 38:34–105.
16. Fischer, Stanley. 1977. "Long-term Contracts, Rational Expectations, and the Optimal Money Supply Rule." *Journal of Political Economy*, 85:191–206.
17. Friedman, Milton. 1957. *A Theory of the Consumption Function* (Princeton: Princeton University Press, for the National Bureau of Econ. Res.)
18 Friedman, Milton, and Anna J. Schwartz. 1963. *A Monetary History of the United States, 1867–1960*. Princeton: Princeton University Press, for the National Bureau of Economic Research).
19. Friedman, Milton. 1968. "The Role of Monetary Policy." *American Economic Review*, 58:1–17.
20. Granger, Clive W.J. 1969. "Investigating Causal Relations by Econometric Models and Cross-spectral Methods." *Econometrica*, 37: 424–438.
21. Hall, Robert E. 1978. "Stochastic Implications of the Life Cycle-Permanent Income Hypothesis: Theory and Evidence." *Journal of Political Economy*, 86:971–988.
22. Hansen, Lars P. 1982. "Large Sample Properties of Generalized Method of Moments Estimators." *Econometrica*, 50: 1029–1054.
23. Hayek, Friedrich A. von. 1933. *Monetary Theory and the Trade Cycle* (London: Jonathan Cape).
24. Hume, David. 1970. *Writings on Economics*. Eugene Rotwein, ed. (Madison: University of Wisconsin Press).
25. Jorgenson, Dale W. 1963. "Capital Theory and Investment Behavior." *American Economic Review, 53: 247–259.*
26. Keynes, John Maynard. 1930. *A Treatise on Money* (London: Macmillan).
27. Keynes, John Maynard. 1936. *The General Theory of Employment, Interest, and Money* (London: Macmillan).
28. King, Robert G. 1981. "Monetary Information and Monetary Neutrality." *Journal of Monetary Economics*, 7: 195–206.
29. Kormendi, Roger C., and Philip G. Meguire. 1984. "Cross-Regime Evidence of Macroeconomic Rationality." *Journal of Political Economy*, 92: 875–908.
30. Kydland, Finn E., and Edward C. Prescott. 1982. "Time to Build and Aggregate Fluctuations." *Econometrica*, 50: 1345–1370.

31. Leiderman, Leonardo. 1979. "Expectations and Output-Inflation Tradeoffs in a Fixed Exchange Rate Economy." *Journal of Political Economy*, 87: 1285–1306.
32. Lucas, Robert E., Jr. and Leonard A. Rapping. 1969. "Real Wages, Employment, and Inflation." *Journal of Political Economy*, 77: 721–754.
33. Lucas, Robert E., Jr. and Edward C. Prescott. 1971. "Investment under Uncertainty." *Econometrica*, 39: 659–681.
34. Lucas, Robert E., Jr. 1972. "Expectations and the Neutrality of Money." *Journal of Economic Theory*, 4: 103–124.
35. Lucas, Robert E., Jr. 1972. "Econometric Testing of the Natural Rate Hypothesis," in *The Econometrics of Price Determination Conference.* Otto Eckstein, ed. (Washington: Board of Governors of the Federal Reserve System).
36. Lucas, Robert E., Jr. 1973. "Some International Evidence on Output-Inflation Tradeoffs." *American Economic Review*, 63: 326–334.
37. Lucas, Robert E., Jr. 1976. "Econometric Policy Evaluation: A Critique." *Carnegie-Rochester Conference Series*, 1: 19–46.
38. Lucas, Robert E., Jr., and Michael Woodford. 1994. "Real Effects of Monetary Shocks in an Economy with Sequential Purchases." University of Chicago working paper.
39. McCandless, George T., Jr. and Warren E. Weber. 1995. "Some Monetary Facts." *Federal Reserve Bank of Minneapolis Quarterly Review*, 19,3: 1–11.
40. McKenzie, Lionel W. 1954. "On Equilibrium in Graham's Model of World Trade and Other Competitive Systems." *Econometrica*, 21:147–161.
41. Meltzer, Allan H. 1963. "The Demand for Money: The Evidence from Time Series." *Journal of Political Economy*, 71: .
42. Modigliani, Franco, and Richard Brumberg. 1954. "Utility Analysis and the Consumption Function: An Interpretation of Cross-Section Data," in K.K. Kurihara, ed., *Post-Keynesian Economics* (New Brunswick: Rutgers University Press).
43. Muth, John F. 1961. "Rational Expectations and the Theory of Price Movements." *Econometrica*, 29: 315–335.
44. Patinkin, Don. 1965. *Money, Interest, and Prices.* 2nd Ed. (New York: Harper and Row).
45. Phelps, Edmund S. 1968. "Money Wage Dynamics and Labor Market Equilibrium." *Journal of Political Economy*, 76: 687–711.
46. Phelps, Edmund S. *et al.* 1970. *Microeconomic Foundations of Employment and Inflation Theory* (New York: Norton).
47. Phelps, Edmund S., and John B. Taylor. 1977. "Stabilizing Powers of Monetary Policy under Rational Expectations." *Journal of Political Economy*, 85: 163–190.
48. Phillips, A.W. 1958. "The Relation Between Unemployment and the Rate of Change of Money Wage Rates in the United Kingdom, 1861–1957." *Economica* 25: 283–299.
49. Samuelson, Paul A. 1958. "An Exact Consumption-Loan Model of Interest with or without thre Contrivance of Money." *Journal of Political Economy*, 66: 467–482.
50. Sargent, Thomas J. 1971. "A Note on the Accelerationist Controversy." *Journal of Money, Credit, and Banking*, 3: 721–725.
51. Sargent, Thomas J. 1976. "A Classical Macroeconometric Model for the United States." *Journal of Political Economy*, 84: 207–238.
52. Sargent, Thomas J. 1986. "The Ends of Four Big Inflations." Ch. 3 in *Rational Expectations and Inflation* (New York: Harper and Row).
53. Shubik, Martin. 1980. "The Capital Stock Modified Competitive Equilibrium," in John H. Karaken and Neil Wallace, eds. *Models of Monetary Economies* (Minneapolis: Federal Reserve Bank of Minneapolis).
54. Sims, Christopher A. 1972. "Money, Income, and Causality." *American Economic Review*, 62: 540–552.
55. Stockman, Alan C. 1996. *Introduction to Economics* (Fort Worth:The Dryden Press).
56. Svensson, Lars E.O. 1986. "Sticky Goods Prices, Flexible Asset Prices, Monopolistic Competition, and Monetary Policy." *Review of Economic Studies*, 53:385–405.
57. Taylor, John B. 1979. "Estimation and Control of a Macroeconomic Model with Rational Expectations." *Econometrica*, 47: 1267–1284.
58. Tinbergen, Jan. 1939. *Business Cycles in the United States of America, 1919–32* (Geneva: League of Nations).

59. Tobin, James. 1956. "The Interest-Elasticity of Transactions Demand for Cash." *Review of Economics and Statistics*, 38: 241–247.
60. Uzawa, Hirofumi. 1964. "Optimal Growth in a Two-Sector Model of Capital Accumulation." *Review of Economic Studies*, 31: 1–24.
61. Wallace, Neil. 1980. "The Overlapping Generations Model of Fiat Money," in John H. Karaken and Neil Wallace, eds. *Models of Monetary Economies* (Minneapolis: Federal Reserve Bank of Minneapolis)
62. Wallace, Neil. 1992. "Lucas's Signal-Extraction Model: A Finite State Exposition with Aggregate Real Shocks." *Journal of Monetary Economics*, 30:433–448.
63. Wicksell, Knut. 1898. *Interest and Prices*, R.F. Kahn, trans. (London: Macmillan), 1936.
64. Williamson, Stephen D. 1995. "Optimal Monetary Policy in an Economy with Sequential Service." University of Iowa working paper.